Online
Marketing
Handbook

Other VNR Business Technology/Communications books. . . .

Online Marketing Handbook

How to Sell, Advertise, Publicize, and Promote

Your Products and Services on the Internet

and Commercial Online Systems

Daniel S. Janal

VAN NOSTRAND REINHOLD

I(T)P™ A Division of International Thomson Publishing Inc.

New York • Albany • Bonn • Boston • Detroit • London • Madrid • Melbourne
Mexico City • Paris • San Francisco • Singapore • Tokyo • Toronto

TRADEMARKS
The words contained in this text which are believed to be trademarked, service marked, or otherwise to hold proprietary rights have been designated as such by use of intial capitalization. No attempt has been made to designate as trademarked or service marked any personal computer words or terms in which proprietary rights might exist. Inclusion, exclusion, or definition of a word or term is not intended to affect, or to express judgment upon, the validity of legal status of any proprietary right which may be claimed for a specific word or term.

For more information, contact:

Van Nostrand Reinhold
115 Fifth Avenue
New York, NY 10003

International Thomson Publishing GmBH
Königswinterer Strasse 418
53227 Bonn
Germany

International Thomson Publishing Europe
Berkshire House 168-173
High Holborn
London WCIV 7AA
England

International Thomson Publishing Asia
221 Henderson Road #05-10
Henderson Building
Singapore 0315

Thomas Nelson Australia
102 Dodds Street
South Melbourne, 3205
Victoria, Australia

International Thomson Publishing Japan
Hirakawacho Kyowa Building, 3F
2-2-1 Hirakawacho
Chiyoda-ku, 102 Tokyo
Japan

Nelson Canada
1120 Birchmount Road
Scarborough, Ontario
Canada M1K 5G4

International Thomson Editores
Campos Eliseos 385, Piso 7
Col. Polanco
11560 Mexico D.F. Mexico

2 3 4 5 6 7 8 9 10 QEBFF 01 00 99 98 97 96 95

Library of Congress Cataloging-in-Publication Data

Janal, Daniel S.
    Online Marketing Handbook: How to Sell, Advertise, Publicize, and Promote Your Products and Services on the Internet and Commercial Online Systems / Daniel S. Janal.
        p.   cm.
    Includes bibliographical references and index.
    ISBN 0-442-02058-9
    1. Internet advertising   2. Information storage and retrieval systems—Marketing.
    3. Computer networks.   4. Online databases.
I. Title.
HF6146.I58J36   1995
658.8'00285'467—dc20   95-10014
                                                                        CIP

Dedicated to Florence Janal

CONTENTS

First Foreword

Commerce on the Internet

By Vinton G. Cerf

The conduct of business in an online, computer-mediated environment is not new. In one form or another, it has been a part of the business landscape since computers and communications services were linked on public data networks in the 1970s. But, with the explosive growth of the Internet and the appearance of the World Wide Web, together with the rapid expansion of public access to the Internet, the idea of doing business online has taken on new dimensions and attracted a broad range of business interests.

In the late 1980s and early 1990s, it became fashionable in the business world to have an e-mail address on your business card. As the 1990s passes the midmark, it has become fashionable for companies to have a home web page on the Internet and, in the new century, it may well become a mark of distinction to have a personal home page, as some people today already have discovered.

For many people who have been a part of the Internet's infancy and childhood, the appearance of commercial interest and involvement is sometimes viewed with alarm and dismay. I think this represents a minority of the Internet's users, but it will not hurt to understand how such reactions might come about and how to be sensitive to them. Moreover, the medium of communication which the Internet creates is unlike many other infrastructures used in the conduct of business and practices may have to adapt to make best use of this technology.

In its earliest days in the 1973-1983 period, Internet was a research tool for exploring the use of computers in a distributed environment. The U.S. Advanced Research Projects Agency (ARPA), a part of the Department of Defense, sponsored research into the applications of packet-switched computer networks, starting with the ARPANET which was developed in 1969. During 1973–1983, ARPA experimented with packet radio and packet satellite and demonstrated their interconnection as early as 1977 using a set of protocols first described by Robert E. Kahn and me in 1973 and 1974. These were evolved through about 1980 with the help of several score researchers around the globe and standardized as the TCP/IP protocol suite.

In this same general time period, other networking activities emerged including the so-called USENET based on the Unix-to-Unix Copy Program (UUCP) protocol and the BITNET (Because it's Time Network) based on the IBM RSCS protocol. These private, voluntary networks each evolved key computer-mediated communication methods which are now found in the Internet environment today. In the USENET, a sophisticated network news system evolved allowing tens of thousands of sites to share in the distribution of news feeds to all participants. In the BITNET, a very sophisticated automatic electronic mail list handling system was developed, nicknamed LISTSERV, which allowed for automatic management of list membership through exchange of messages between list members and LISTSERV systems. Members could join and leave lists without manual intervention which permitted considerable scaling of list sizes. Internet now serves as a major underlying communication system for USENET and for access to LISTSERVs, in addition to supporting a widely distributed electronic mail system of its own. All these systems have been made to interwork so that there is a considerable variety of ways to participate in the contribution and exchange of information in these various media.

The government-sponsored Internet effort proscribed the use of the government supported resources for anything but research and academic purposes. In the USENET and BITNET environments, resources were contributed on a voluntary basis and, by general consensus, advertising and job offers were not permitted.

These general proscriptions remain not only a vivid memory for many current Internet users but have become a part of the culture of the community, except where explicitly permitted. The U.S. Government has reduced its role as network service provider/sponsor over the years and one of its major contributions, the NSFNET backbone, is to be retired from service in 1995, to be replaced by a system of competitive Internet transit services. For-profit businesses that plan to use the Internet in the conduct of their operation should be cognizant of this history and also sensitive to the way in which their commercial use may strike some constituents of the global Internet community.

For many users whose access to Internet services is by way of the dial-up telephone network, unsolicited advertising consumes bandwidth and local storage capacity and thus interferes in a palpable way with the user's primary motivation for being connected to a newsgroup or e-mail distribution list. Use of the newsgroups or e-mail distribution lists for the purposes of carrying unsolicited and often irrelevant (with regard to the group or list) content is considered a genuine and serious abuse (as a number of businesses have discovered). There *are* lists and newsgroups that have been set up to include commercial advertising and list members who join do so with that knowledge.

More recently, the passive World Wide Web and Gopher services have emerged on the Internet which support a browsing mode of operation. Here, users have more control over what they choose to examine and have appeared far more tolerant of advertising or other solicitations offered for their consideration. Indeed, many Internet users go to various web sites with the expectation that they can find product and service information at those sites. In an even more elaborate formulation, MCI has developed its marketplaceMCI service, in which virtual storefronts are put into an Internet mall, where customers not only learn about goods and services but can order and pay for them all, through the Internet. Similar explorations of Internet utility in the business world are readily found. A number of bookstores offer their products on the net (e.g., the Online Bookstore, the Computer Literacy Bookshop, O'Reilly). The Internet Shopping Network, recently acquired by the television Home Shopping Network, is yet another example.

The advent of commercial transaction processing on the Internet marks an important new element available to the business community. Digicash, CyberCash, First Virtual Holdings, the NetBank and others are organizations whose services range from Internet-based credit card transaction support to a new kind of electronic money. Many of these new services rely on the widespread availability of cryptographic software, which provides confidentiality and in — some formulations—authenticity, protecting both buyers and sellers. As these new services are tested in the crucible of the marketplace, it is likely that new case law will be developed and new economic thinking will emerge, especially as regards the international velocity of money.

Among the concerns arising in the Internet and more general online environment is the availability of essentially unconstrained content. Parts of the Internet hold content that some users would consider appropriate only for adult access. So far as I am aware, it takes some effort to get to and to display, read or listen to this material. Some newsgroups focus on adult subject matter but one has to take explicit action to join these groups. We are only at an early stage of understanding how access to such content should be handled (dare I say that the jury is still out?) and this will surely be a part of the evolving Internet experience in the rest of this decade and into the twenty-first century.

Nor can one ignore the educational and entertainment potential of the Internet, even in its present, still relatively primitive state. Many users find Internet Relay Chat and various multi-user game environments—Multiuser Simulation Environments (MUSE), Multiuser Dungeons and Dragons (MUDs), for example—well worth the cost of access. Discussion groups are a frequent source of relaxation and stimulation, as the participants in the venerable WELL (Whole Earth Lectronic Link) have discovered. Bulletin Board Systems (BBS) are connecting to the Internet, bringing yet another community into the growing melange of Internet users.

Into this turbulent mix, new business concerns are arising, for instance, in connection with intellectual property which is transportable through the Internet. Virtually anything that can be digitized can, in theory, be delivered through the Net. Protection of such property is a nontrivial exercise. The Software Publishers Association has instituted the practice of scrutinizing public access databases for improper distribution of copyrighted material, and publishers in general will have similar interests. We may find that the practice of charging users per copy or even per view will be augmented, if not displaced, by other models of access (such as subscription). We may discover that the new cyber money models allow "micropayments" to be processed efficiently and cost-effectively so that consumers can enjoy low prices and providers of material can be compensated for their wares.

Finally, we are already discovering that in the online environment, behavioral norms are not the same as in other mass media. Internet is a kind of two-way or multiway mass medium unlike any other. It has weaknesses, such as the lack of visual and aural cues that normally accompany personal, face-to-face discourse. It has advantages in that rebuttal receives the same distribution as original arguments, unlike the usual treatment in the press, for instance. Some of the verbal behavior seen on the Internet is probably a consequence of demographics. Although good data is very hard to come by, it is thought that a large fraction of current Internet users are in the 18- to 28-year-old range. Many are college students because so many universities are on the Internet. This is an energetic, often libertarian segment of the population. As the Internet penetrates more broadly, some of these demographic aspects will probably change, but it isn't clear exactly in what ways.

This foreword has dealt principally with the Internet but it seems appropriate to acknowledge the important experiences of CompuServe, Prodigy, America Online and tens of thousands of bulletin board sysops which have also served to explore the ways in which various kinds of businesses might be conducted in an online environment. Many of these systems are now interconnected with the Internet and are becoming an integral part of its landscape, lending their services and content to an ever-widening body of users.

The creation of a mass medium is nothing new to this century, considering the history of broadcast and cable television, VCRs and radio, for example. Nonetheless, it is exciting to participate in the formation of something as versatile as the Internet and to observe its absorption into the global social and economic fabric. I hope that the potential value this new infrastructure can bring will be achieved in the coming years. And I hope that the readers of this book will help to explore the edges of the medium and, in so doing, help to define the extent of these possibilities by making them real.

Vinton G. Cerf
Camelot
Annandale, Virginia

Second Foreword

Doing Business in Cyberspace

by Cheryl Currid

There's a lot more to doing business in the twenty-first century than remembering to turn over the calendar page. No matter what your business — from banking to banana farming — get ready to start doing business electronically. Organizations planning to stay in business beyond today will likely find a computer and a communications line at the beginning, middle and end of every transaction.

For many, the road to success isn't well paved; in fact, it isn't paved at all. It's the information highway—cyberspace. And, making your business accessible on it could well mean the difference between success and failure of a marketing program.

Experts estimate that 30 million people from around the globe have found a way to hop on the information highway. These are customers and potential customers. They are searching around to see who else is there and where they can get information.

As you read this today, smart businesses are already constructing their marketing plans for cyberspace. They are setting up road signs, shopping centers, office complexes, and rest spots.

The benefits are clear. For a relatively low cost, businesses can establish a name, face and voice direct to the consumer. Even a small business can quickly develop a global presence by making the right moves.

Today, almost anyone with a few dollars and a modem can get to cyberspace. But, for firms trying to understand the marketing potential, the path isn't well marked.

That's where this book and Dan Janal come in. Few people are as qualified to show you the rules of the road as Dan. An experienced marketer and successful entrepreneur, Dan offers you expert advice about sizing up the online opportunity. He has researched the options, dug into the details and presents his findings without a single word of techno-babble.

This delightful primer gives you a chance to see for yourself how the information highway is unfolding, and where you may (or may not) want to stake your space. Read it carefully. This guide will help you make your most important business decision of the decade.

Cheryl Currid
President
Currid & Company
Houston, Texas

Preface

A revolutionary change in the way people buy products and services is taking hold as the world marches toward the third millennium. The Information Superhighway offers rich opportunities for businesses to sell products and services to a rapidly growing market of 25 million highly educated and affluent potential shoppers worldwide.

Shopping by computer will become a natural way of life. Purchasing products online will be as commonplace as picking up a telephone and dialing a catalog's 800 number or driving to the shopping mall—and much more convenient.

However, reaching these computerized consumers with reasons to buy will require new rules and a new way of thinking for marketers because, as Marshall McLuhan says, the medium is the message. Strategies that worked in newspaper ads and television commercials won't work with computer consumers, who demand interactivity, immediacy and information. This book will help marketers reach these consumers with compelling strategies. Read it—marketing will never be the same!

Why You Should Read This Book and How You Will Benefit

Whether you are working out of your home or a corner office on Madison Avenue, this book will help you learn how to maximize your marketing efforts by using the Internet and the commercial online services. You'll learn which tools and tactics to use on each system; how online marketing fits into the marketing mix; how advertising, public relations and promotions differ in the online world and how you can take advantages of these opportunities.

You should read this book if you are:

- An advertising executive who needs to understand the changing dynamics of advertising on the Information Superhighway.
- A small business owner who wants to reach a local market.

- A small business owner who wants to reach a national market.
- A marketing official at a small- to medium-sized business reaching local and national markets who needs to integrate online services into the marketing mix.
- A marketing communications manager at a large company reaching national and international markets.
- A public information officer at a government agency that needs to deliver its message to the public.
- A consultant, author, speaker or seminar leader who wants to sell services, books, tapes or seats at a seminar.
- A software publisher who wants to increase sales.
- A teacher or student of marketing, advertising, public relations and new media.

You will get the essential information you need to become an online marketer. Best yet, the marketing strategies are conveyed in practical, hands-on formats that you can put to use quickly and easily. For example, you'll:

- Find out what other companies are doing to advertise, publicize, promote and sell their products.
- See what works and what doesn't.
- Save time by learning how the Internet and commercial online services operate, what their policies are on marketing and advertising and how to advertise and promote your products and services.
- Ride high on the learning curve of the new media.
- Leapfrog past competitors who aren't techno-savvy.
- Save money by not devoting resources to schemes that other companies have tried and found unproductive.
- Gain insight by reading case studies from companies that are on the leading edge of online marketing.

Also, you should read this book if you need a good overview of the entire field of online marketing. While other books focus entirely on the Internet, this book has up-to-date information on the Internet and the major commercial online services which, in many cases, offer better solutions than the Internet to selling products and services for large and small companies alike.

Do I Have To Be a Technical Guru to Read This Book?

You don't have to be a computer programmer to read this book, which assumes only that you have at least a passing familiarity with computers. For example, you know that when a computer manual says to press "any key" it means any darn key on the keyboard, not a key marked "any key." And that when we say to put a disk into the computer, you don't first try to remove the hard plastic case.

We'll avoid the technobabble and we'll talk about marketing online in terms you can understand. We'll explain the technology you really need to know. In a few cases, we'll discuss technology in detail, such as setting up your own home page on the World Wide Web, one of the most intriguing and groundbreaking methods to marketing the online world can offer. However, the book will not document every niggling keystroke. That is the job of other books, to which you will be happily directed to complete your education. Also, there are some technical procedures that you and I can't possibly accomplish, such as loading the home page onto a server on a computer network. In those cases, we'll give you an overview of what is going on or provide you with questions to ask a service provider so you can get the best deal. In other words, we'll teach you how to buy a car and steer it along the highway, and we'll point you to mechanics' school to learn how to tune up your car.

How to Use the Conventions in This Book

To navigate the Internet and commercial online services, send e-mail to specific people or find commercial sites mentioned in this book, look for text presented in Courier 10 point, like the address displayed below. For example, to reach my home page on the Internet's World Wide Web to learn about my company's services and books, you would type:

```
http://www.janal-communications.com/janal.html
```

You must type the statements exactly as they appear in this book. That means typing a capital letter, not a lower-case one; or a dash instead of an underline; or two forward slashes (//), not one and not a backward slash. If you don't type these commands exactly, you may not reach your destination. When an address is listed as part of a sentence or at the end of a sentence and correct punctuation calls for a period or comma, do not type it.

Another convention worth noting is the use of URLs (uniform resource locators) on the Internet, keywords on America Online, go words on CompuServe, jumpwords on Prodigy and shortcuts on eWorld. These terms refer to the text you need to type to reach various forums, bulletin boards, World Wide Web home pages, Gopher sites and FTP sites. Whenever possible, I've included the address of the services mentioned as close to the subject as good grammar allows. For example:

The Public Relations and Marketing Forum `CompuServe: Go PRSIG` provides a place for people interested in marketing to discuss issues of mutual concern.

Here's the key to the system: CompuServe is the name of the online service. Ignore the colon. Go is the lingo for the online system navigational term that lets you navigate the system. `PRSIG` is the name of the forum. Don't type the name of the service or the colon. To reach the service, you need to access the navigational icon and type the access word.

This convention will reduce tedious wording that would otherwise get under your skin very quickly.

To reach services mentioned in the text, type in the appropriate shortcut word. For consistency, the style is:

For CompuServe	`CompuServe: Go WORD`
For America Online	`AOL: Keyword WORD`
For Prodigy	`Prodigy: Jump WORD`
For the Internet World Wide Web	`http://address`
For the Internet	`ftp.address`
	`telnet.address`
	`gopher.address`

Of course, you would replace the "word" or "address" with the appropriate material. Similarly, examples from online sessions are printed in that typeface.

How This Book Is Organized

This book is organized from the perspective of the marketing executive, not the computerholic. Its purpose is to teach people how to promote their businesses by using the Internet and commercial online services wisely and effectively. I believe that you want the benefits of technology, not technology itself. Therefore, I will adopt the approach that explains these online tools in a context that marketers can use. If a feature of an online system cannot be used for reaching a marketer's goals, I probably won't discuss it.

This book is structured in this manner:

Section 1—Getting up to Speed on the Information Superhighway. This section provides the overview and essential information of online marketing.
Chapter 1—The Electronic Cash Register: The Benefits of Online Marketing. This chapter provides an overview of online systems and how they can help you sell more products.

Chapter 2—Essentials of Online Marketing. A new medium must make its own rules to take advantage of the technology. Radio ads didn't work on TV when it was a new medium. Neither will your current ads work on the interactive medium of online systems. Read this chapter to learn about the new marketing paradigm.

Chapter 3—Overview of the Internet and Commercial Online Systems. What's the straight information on the Internet and commercial online systems? Find out who is online and what tools each system can offer to marketers.

Chapter 4—Netiquette: Rules and Restrictions for Online Marketing. This isn't your grandmother's etiquette. If you don't follow the rules of the road for the Information Superhighway, you will crash and burn in a flaming disaster.

Chapter 5—Market Research. A good marketing plan starts with up-to-date information. Here's the lowdown on where the best data can be found.

Chapter 6—Becoming a Better Marketer. To keep up with the trends, you need to tune into professional marketing and development groups online.

Section 2—Making the Sale. Read this section to learn how to sell products on the Internet and commercial online services.
Chapter 7—Online Shopping. This is where the rubber meets the road. You can sell products online in virtual shopping malls and catalogs. Enhance the shopping experience by learning about the tools and strategies that work. Set up

an electronic store on the World Wide Web and take advantage of other retail opportunities available on the commercial online services. See how the big boys are grabbing attention—and how many small companies can look just as big by marketing smarter! Learn from their examples.

Chapter 8—Forums: Marketing Opportunities for Information providers. The lifetime value of a customer is immense. Smart companies can create forums on the commercial online services to create relationships with customers—and make money at the same time.

Chapter 9—Building Relationships with E-mail. Relationship marketing works one customer at a time by creating relationships through mailing lists, newsgroups, forums and bulletin boards. These marketing strategies will help small businesses and consultants and create a powerful edge.

Chapter 10—Selling Products and Services with Classified Ads. These little blurbs, created in the 1700s, actually paved the way for advertising as we know it today. Here's how you can take advantage of the high-tech classifieds.

Section 3—Marketing Tools. Learn how to use advertising and public relations in the online world.

Chapter 11—The New Advertising. Forget the old rules. Online advertising is writing new ones every day. Learn how to create interactive ads to sell your products.

Chapter 12—Public Relations. These tools will help you gain the aid of reporters to tell your story. Guerrilla strategies will show you how to reach your audiences directly.

Chapter 13—Building Relationships with Customer Service. Good marketing doesn't end with the sale. Customer service can help build loyal customer relationships. Learn how.

Chapter 14—The Future. Every day is like a year to an online system and interactive marketing—there is so much going on! Despite the advantages today's services offer, they can be even better as technology gets better, faster and less expensive. See what the future holds—and how it can help you.

Appendices will lead you to other resources that will enrich your lives as marketers.

Updates

A word of caution: The field of online marketing is shifting rapidly. While this book was being written, Home Shopping Network announced its plans to turn the Internet into an online shopping mall, America Online declared its intentions to begin offering advertising and commercial shopping services, and McDonald's placed its own promotions online. New players are entering the field and new software is being written to make online shopping more interactive and thus more accessible to people. New rules are being written all the time. This book presents a snapshot of the online world as it exists at this time. Look for future editions of this book to provide updates on new trends.

You will note that I have devoted a great deal of space to CompuServe, America Online, Prodigy and the Internet. When this book was being written other systems were either in the early rollout stage or preintroduction phase (e.g. Apple's eWorld, AT&T Interchange Online Network and Microsoft's Network). Future editions of this book will include relevant information on these services. If you can't wait, you are invited to send for a subscription to my marketing newsletter, *Online Marketing Update.*

For information, please send a note to the author at the following addresses:

```
CompuServe: 76004,1046
MCI Mail 341-8158
Internet update@janalpr.com, 76004.1046@compuserve.com
America Online djanal
Phone: 510-831-0900
World Wide Web: http://www.janal-communications.com/janal.html.
```

Disclaimers

Although the commercial online services have cooperated in providing information for this book, they have to protect proprietary information and would not discuss several things, including forum pricing for information providers.

A word or two about redundancy. If you read the book from cover to cover you will experience literary déjà vu: Haven't I read this material before? Yes, you have. I am assuming that people are going to jump to the chapters that interest them most and skip other chapters that have good anecdotes, quotes, background material or netiquette. Rather than risk sending you out in the cold, hard online world, where one false move can get you flamed, I've repeated information that is absolutely essential or simply fascinating. If you do read the book from cover to cover, this redundancy will actually help you because, as educational specialists will tell you, we need to visit a topic more than once to get a clear grasp of it.

Throughout the book I refer to "The Internet and commercial online services" instead of lumping the Internet in with the other services. While the wording may seem tedious, it is necessary because these are different cultures with different business procedures. When necessary, I've discussed Internet-only strategies and commercial online services-only strategies.

The success of online marketing depends on interactive communications. Therefore, when possible, I've listed phone or e-mail addresses for the people and companies quoted in this book. If you wish to contact a person, please try the e-mail address first.

Finally, I've taken great pains to avoid hype and overused terms like "Information Autobahn," "The I-bahn," "digital" this and "cyber" that, and I pledge to use the term "Information Superhighway" as sparingly as possible.

About the Author

I have spent my entire professional career in the media and have seen that world from its two sides—editorial and advertising. For seven years I was a prize-winning reporter, news editor and business editor for daily newspapers in Florida and New York. I've also worked for several New York City public relations agencies and have operated my own PR agency for nearly a decade. I've consulted for AT&T, Bell Atlantic, Prentice-Hall, Grolier Electronic Publishing and nearly one hundred other computer software companies, including many start-ups. From those perspectives, I know how a company must employ and deploy innovative guerrilla marketing programs.

For nearly a decade, I have also been a sysop (for systems operator or host) for the PR and Marketing Forum, CompuServe's forum for public relations and marketing executives. I also was part of the team that launched a new online service originally called QuantumLink and now known as America Online, one of the fastest-growing online services. I also teach public relations at the University of California at Berkeley. I've written another book, *How to Publicize High Tech Products and Services*, and developed the *Publicity Builder* software published by JIAN Tools for Sales.

From this concentrated and balanced perspective—writer, editor, marketer, small business owner, consultant for large businesses, teacher and online veteran—I can provide you with a tour of the landscape of the Information Superhighway as no one else can. So buckle up your seat belts. Let's hit the road.

Acknowledgments

This book is a collaboration of great minds who consented to share their wisdom and experience with an old newspaper reporter and editor turned marketer. I'd like to thank:

Leslie Laredo, Michael Kolowich, Jennifer Christensen, David DeJean at AT&T Interchange Online Network. Steve Case, Pam McCraw and Doug Rekenthaler at America Online. Regina Brady, Keith Arnold, Michele Moran and Kathy Gerber at CompuServe. Carol Wallace at Prodigy.

Pam Alexander, Christina Tavella, Tonya Mazarowski and Brian Johnson at Alexander Communications, Connie Connors and Lydia Trettis at Connors Communications. Marcos Sanchez, Skye Ketonen at Niehaus Ryan Haller. Kim Bayne of wolfeBayne Communications. Marty Winston of Winston & Winston.

Dan Fine of Fine Communications, Marc Fleischmann of Internet Distribution Services, Joe Andrieu of Presence and Bill Linder of Columbus PBX, Mike Voss and Tamara DeGenaro of Digital Express.

Ron Solberg and Bill Lutholtz of PRSIG.

Greg Jarboe at Ziff-Davis Publishing Company. Charlie Cooper at *PC Week*. Ryk Lent at Ziff-Davis Interactive. Chris Shipley of *Computer Life*. Robin Raskin and Bill Machrone of *PC Magazine*.

Lorraine Sileo and Chris Elwell of Simba Information. Jeff Silverstein and Maureen Flemming of Digital Information Group. Kristin Zhivago at Zhivago Marketing Partners.

Special thanks to the Internet Roundtable Society—Bob Lash, Wendi Bernstein Lash, Michael Fremont and Scott Shanks for invaluable assistance.

Ameet Zaveri of InfoPlace and Christina O'Connell of O'Connell and Associates for reviewing the manuscript.

Maurice Hamoy of Inset Systems for providing a copy of Hijaak to take the screen shots for this book.

Michael Krieger of law offices of Michael Krieger, Ken Skier of SkiSoft Publishing, Brad Peppard of Quarterdeck, Tom Stitt of SoftKey, Gary Jose of Individual Software, Keith Hendrick of Road Scholar Software, Eric Robichaud of Rhode Island SoftSystems, Lynne Marcus of Marcus and Company, Mark Bruce of GHB, Mark O'Deady of Full Circle Productions and Peggy Watt of many magazines, Sharyn Fitzpatrick of the Learning Company, Pat Meier of Pat

Meier and Associates, Charlie Valeston of AT&T, Susan Morrow of Morrow and Associates, Leigh Mariner of Mariner and Associates, Ivan Levison of Ivan Levison & Associates, Larry Parks and Jonathan Parks of Productivity Software International, Howard Zack of Clark Boardman Callaghan, Dave Arganbright, Joe Szczepaniak and Maryanne Piazza of Grolier Electronic Publishing, Alan Penchansky of Edelman Inc., Tim Bajarin of Creative Strategies, Steve Hersee of Copia International, Richard Goswick and David Toner of Goswick Advertising, Jeff Tarter, Jane Farber and Allison Shapiro of Soft-letter, Bob Kersey and Colleen Coletta of Optical Data Interactive, Keith Hendrick, Jim Nichols and Jackie Clark of Road Scholar Software, Jerry Duro of Roman Marketing, John Cole of John O. Cole and Associates, Greg Doench of Prentice-Hall and Carol Rizzardi of *Advertising Age*. Thanks to Joel Strasser and Tom Richmond who gave me my start in PR.

Thanks to reporters who like a good story. Lance Elko, Selby Bateman, Pete Scicso, David English, Mike Hudnall, Bob Schwabach, Larry Shannon, Pete Lewis, Steve Manes, Keith Ferrell, Kathy Yakal, Ted Needleman, Bob Scott, Kerri Karvetski, Heather Clancy, Dave Haskin, Jerry Olsen, Barry Brenesal, Gayle Ehrenmann, Ephraim Schwartz, John Blackford, Arlan Levitan, Matt Lake, Yael Li Ron, Jon Zilber, Scott Finnie, Adam Meyerson, Donna Meyerson, Michael Penwarden, Gina Smith, Leo Laporte, John Dvorak, Fred Fishkin, Mike Langberg, Michael Antonoff, Fred Abatemarco, Nancy Trespasz, Fred Langa, Jim Forbes, Paul Schindler, Phil Albinus, Donna Tapellini, Rich Malloy, Dan Rosenbaum, Dennis Allen, Rick Manning and Scott Mace.

Friends for life, Steven Kessler, Stuart Gruber, Barry Block, Alan Dauber, Alan Penchansky and Len Zandrow.

Matt Wagner at Waterside Productions and David Clark of Microsoft Press.

The excellent staff at Van Nostrand Reinhold, Neil Levine, Mike Sherry, Lesley Rock, Chris Grisonich and Chris Bates.

Thanks to Vinton Cerf and Cheryl Currid for their excellent forewords.

Thanks for feedback and encouragement from George Thibault of Revolution Software and Steve Leon of Technopolis Communications.

Special thanks to Susan Tracy. May all your fortune cookies come true.

SECTION 1

Getting Up to Speed on the Information Superhighway

This section explains why your company should consider selling products online and what steps you should factor into your marketing plan to ensure that online adds value to your entire marketing program. You'll learn about the tools and services available to market products on the Internet and commercial online services. You'll find out the demographics of members of the major commercial online systems The new rules of marketing in the online world will be explored and you'll be provided with a road map of online resources that will make you a smarter marketer and connect with your peers online.

CHAPTER 1

The Electronic Cash Register: Benefits of Online Marketing

In this chapter, you will learn:

- How large and small companies are using the Internet and commercial online services to sell products and promote their companies' good will to consumers and to other businesses.
- What online systems are and how they can benefit your company.
- Market figures and statistics for the major online systems.
- Why the online market will grow.
- How to separate the hype from reality regarding online statistics.

Within five days of posting a one-line message on the Internet, eWorld, America Online and AppleLink, Keep It Simple Systems, of Helena, Montana, received 400 requests for information about its solar charging units for portable computers that led to numerous sales in the United States and more than 35 countries.

By placing its catalog on the Internet's World Wide Web, Hello Direct provided much more information to its phone systems customers—and dramatically cut its costs of printing and mailing expensive 72-page catalogs.

Simply by answering people's questions in an online forum, author, speaker and consultant Wally Bock sold 50 copies of his book on police management systems to an East Coast police department—and he expects reorders from that police department every 18 months for the foreseeable future.

Many major music companies, including Warner Bros. build excitement for new albums by prereleasing singles that fans can download from the Internet and every major commercial online service.

Paramount Pictures created a Web home page promoting the release of *Star Trek—Generations,* http://generations.viacom.com/. More than 17,000 people visited the site in the first ten days and 3,600 placed orders for products.

From the convenience of your home computer, you can order a dozen roses for Mother's Day, a lobster dinner, a best-selling book and hard-to-find collectibles.

Large and small companies are beginning to seize the tremendous opportunities to sell products to consumers and other businesses through the Internet and commercial online systems, like CompuServe, America Online, Prodigy and others.

Small companies are finding that online services are the great leveler; they can command the same attention and respect as major corporations.

Consultants are prospecting for clients by offering free information and advice and finding long-term clients as a result.

Savvy marketers are tapping into online services to initiate a new era in relationship marketing to create one-to-one relationships, as well as one-to-many relationships to increase word-of-mouth advertising.

Marketers of every stripe are integrating online marketing into their marketing mix for positive results in sending a single, unified message along multiple channels of communication.

Online shopping is estimated to be a $50–$200 million business today and will grow to at least $2.5 billion by 1998, according to SIMBA Information Inc., of Wilton, Connecticut. Consumers are taking advantage of online shopping services in greater and greater numbers and spending significant amounts of money. The average sale on CompuServe's Electronic Mall is over $70. Prodigy is the largest seller of airline tickets in the country, and it processes more stock transactions than many brokerage houses. Clearly, online commerce is hot. Selling products and services along the Information Superhighway is the next great growth opportunity for today's companies.

Mind you, online sales are not the be-all and end-all of selling. They constitute another channel of distribution that will work well for many companies. But the importance of commerce on the Information Superhighway is revving into high gear.

While the first travelers on this virtual roadway of the Internet were educators and students who hopped aboard school buses paid for by their educational institutions, defense department personnel who command military vehicles provided by the Defense Department and scientists who rode mobile labs from research institutions, today's travelers are more likely to be cruising the digital highway in souped-up Range Rovers, Mercedes, Porsches and other vehicles of the educated and affluent—a potent market for today's online marketer.

The consumer has learned to cruise the digital highway—and life will never be the same for marketers. Imagine an audience that is highly educated, fairly affluent and open-minded. Now you have the picture of the average person in the driver's seat. It is a marketer's dream.

The Information Superhighway is more than a place to take a Sunday drive in the country and chat with new neighbors near and far. It is becoming a mobile mall filled with opportunities to buy new products. In a matter of moments, customers can first become aware of your product from a positive endorsement read on an online bulletin board, conduct research by reading files on your CompuServe forum or World Wide Web home page and purchase the product by sending you their credit card information online or calling your order center via the phone lines. With the right messages and tools, your cash register will ring as you complete the four great rules of selling—attention, interest, desire and actions in cost-efficient and cost-effective manners.

The best news is that the number of these customers is growing.

Online Shopping: The Raison d'Être for Online Marketing

Sales of products from the commercial online services ranged from $50 million to $200 million in 1994, according to SIMBA Information of Wilton, Connecticut. Since the commercial online services keep sales figures private, it is difficult to have more accurate numbers. The Internet does not gather statistics on worldwide sales of the merchants who are coming online.

Sales of goods and services over online networks will total between $2.5 billion and $5 billion by 1998, according to SIMBA.

Home Shopping Network in 1994 legitimized online shopping when it purchased the Internet Shopping Network http://internet.shop.net, one of the first companies to sell merchandise over the Internet. At the time of the purchase, ISN, founded in 1993, offered 20,000 computer-related products from nearly 1,000 companies. While online sales have been a good business for CompuServe and Prodigy, this transaction gave online shopping additional visibility in the traditional consumer marketplace. Analysts say the deal allows Home Shopping, with its state-of-the-art backroom and order-fulfillment operations, to greatly expand Internet sales opportunities.

According to a company spokesperson, the goal is for ISN to become a full-scale electronic mall that can carry advertised products as well as catalogs of independent name-brand retailers. Promotional tie-ins will exist between Home

Shopping Network's Home Shopping Club cable and broadcast television services and the computer-based Internet service. Home Shopping executives declined to make sales projections. For information, send e-mail to `info@internet.net`.

One reason vendors want to sell on the Internet and commercial online services is that computers can provide consumers with interactive shopping tools. Those tools don't exist for TV—yet. Major deals, however, are in the works, with such companies as Microsoft and TCI.

Online services can offer these benefits to consumers and marketers:

- *Convenience:* Customers can order products from the comfort of their home or office 24 hours a day, 7 days a week.
- *Information:* Computers can store and display reams of product descriptions and prices, much more information than can be found in a billboard, newspaper or magazine ad, TV commercial, radio spot or even a catalog.
- *Respond to market conditions:* Companies can quickly add products, descriptions and prices and keep them up-to-date.
- *Reduce printing and postage costs:* Production costs for digital catalogs are far less than printing and mailing catalogs.
- *Reduce expenses:* Online stores don't carry the huge expense of traditional storefronts, with rent, utilities and insurance.
- *Fewer hassles:* Consumers don't need to deal with pushy salespeople.
- *Build relationships:* Merchants can interact with consumers to create dialogues that lead to long-term relationships.

"In many ways, electronic shopping is the ideal medium for the '90s, from both the merchant's and the consumer's points of view," says Regina Brady, CompuServe's director of customer promotion. "Consumers, particularly those who work full-time, appreciate the sheer convenience of being able to sit down at their computers at any time of the day or night and order top-quality merchandise from well-known retailers.

"Most consumers today are looking for ways to streamline their shopping—to get it done quickly without compromising on price or quality," she says. "At the same time, they demand a high level of service and they really appreciate personalized contact. The online medium allows even small retailers and catalogers to deliver that kind of service cost-effectively."

Merchants can forge tighter bonds with consumers through the use of e-mail and interactive communications. "Electronic mail is an important channel of communication between shoppers and merchants. Members who can't find what they're looking for or have questions about the merchandise can send a message via CompuServe Mail and expect a prompt response. By tracking orders and electronic mail inquiries, merchants can maintain lists of their best customers and notify those members by electronic mail when they hold special sales and promotions," says Brady.

Marketers should take a serious look at online systems for another simple reason—the cost of doing business is relatively low. E-mail is inexpensive, or free on some systems, as is the electronic distribution of products, such as software, information, reports and surveys.

People clearly want to shop online. How do you reach and persuade them? That's where online marketing comes in.

Who Is Online?

Merchants are tapping a large and affluent audience. More than 25 million people use the Internet and another million are joining every month—"a very conservative estimate," according to Jake Kirchner, editor of *Communications Week*, a trade newspaper. According to John Quarterman, editor of *Matrix News* and *Matrix Maps Quarterly*, some 27.5 million people can exchange e-mail messages on the Internet, while 13.5 million people have computers and software that can access the Internet's commercial center, The World Wide Web as of October 1994 `http://www.tic.com`. Another 5 million people subscribe to commercial online services, according to SIMBA Information. The growth rate is exploding at 76% from 1994 over 1993, with 5.1 million people online compared to 2.9 million. These commercial services are beginning to offer access to the Internet as well, which means that the more affluent users of these services are gaining access to commercial stores on the Internet's dynamic World Wide Web without having to learn complicated commands.

Consumer online services grew their customer base 28.7% from 1992 to 1993, according to SIMBA Information. At the end of 1993, there were more than 5.0 million subscribers to online services compared to 3.8 million in 1992. Nearly 1.3 million subscriptions were sold in 1993, the second consecutive year in which more than a million new subscribers were added. Final figures for 1994 were not available at press time, but each major service reported large increases in memberships which brought the total number of subscribers to approximately 6 million.

Table 1-1. Membership figures of commercial online services. Figures as of December 1994.

Service	**1994**	**1993**	**1992**	**1991**
CompuServe	2,400,000	1,600,000	1,130,000	900,000
America Online	1,750,000	531,000	200,000	156,549
Prodigy	2,100,000	2,100,000	2,000,000	1,135,000

Source: SIMBA Information Inc., Wilton, Connecticut.

The report predicts that, with new services from Apple, Microsoft and AT&T, the consumer market will grow more than 20% annually through 1998. All these systems plan to offer full access to the Internet's services and users. By the end of 1994, subscribers to commercial online services can send e-mail over the Internet, as well as participate in newsgroups and mailing lists. By mid–1995, they will be able to explore the Internet's World Wide Web, home to the growing commercial center of the electronic shopping mystique.

Clearly, the trend is for people to get online. What is fueling this trend?

"Lower hardware prices and easier-to-use systems contributed to growth in both the consumer and business-to-business markets," says SIMBA analyst Lorraine Sileo.

The move of people going online could explode in 1995 when Microsoft undertakes two activities. When it ships Windows 95 in late 1995, the new operating system will include the tools to access the Internet painlessly. To use the Internet today involves a complicated procedure that even experienced network technicians find cumbersome. With this barrier removed, more people will go online. Second, Microsoft will unveil its own online system in late 1995, called Microsoft Network, which will allow people to go online with ease.

SIMBA's report goes on to predict: "The potential growth for online services lies in serving new customers in both the consumer market and business-to-business markets. As these segments of the population are more fully penetrated, there will be an opportunity to generate revenues from advertising and transactions—revenue streams that have been only a minimal part of the sales mix for online services to date."

Barriers to acceptance are falling rapidly. Subscription prices are plummeting, services are easier to use and prices of high-powered computer hardware are falling. According to the author's anecdotal research, small companies are getting rich by selling products and services to other companies.

Subscriptions to online services are about $10 a month for basic services. Consumers seem to prefer this pricing method, which is similar to cable TV's model. Previously, online systems charged by the minute, which scared away new subscribers who faced sticker shock when they saw their first bill. Often, easy-to-use software to navigate the system is given free to the subscriber.

Other signs for growth are positive as well. The installed base of personal computers in businesses and homes has skyrocketed in the past 10 years. More than 29% of American homes now have personal computers, according to the Software Publishers Association. Modem use is growing rapidly. Many computers come equipped with modems that can sign on to online services, as well as send faxes. Standalone 14.4-kilobaud modems cost about $100 at the end of 1994, about half the price at the beginning of the year. And prices continue to fall. A 2400-baud modem, once the cream of the crop at $500, can be purchased for only $9.95 in computer stores. Clearly, the barriers to online entry are falling.

According to a Harris poll, the percentage of Americans who are aware of the term "Information Superhighway" has increased sharply to almost half the population in September 1994 from one in three people in April. However, the poll says that a quarter of all adults have a reasonable understanding of the term.

Growth will continue to be rapid. Using the classic marketing strategy of giving away the razor and making money on the blades, all commercial online services have a variety of free giveaways to spur growth. You can hardly pick up a computer magazine without a disk from America Online falling onto your lap. Most computers are shipped with at least one commercial online service vendor's software placed onto the hard disk. These freebies allow consumers to try the service free for a period of time before paying the monthly access fees.

Clearly, the trend points toward increased use of online systems and a phenomenal potential for growth. Not only are people coming online, but they are shopping as well.

Despite phenomenal growth, much of America is still unplugged. Only 2.6% of American households subscribe to online services, according to SIMBA's 1994 report. The same low percentage applies to business users as well. Only 2.7 million subscriptions to business-oriented online services were in place in 1993—

even though there were more than 120 million white-collar workers in the United States alone. Rather than look at these numbers as negatives revealing low penetration, marketers can revel in them, knowing that the early adopters belong to high demographic profiles and are clustered in certain easily targeted job categories, which makes target marketing easier, and, that they can look forward to an unprecedented growth rate.

Critics have taken aim at the Internet's 25–million–user figure, claiming the number is much lower, perhaps 20 million. It should be noted that no one has accurate subscriber figures because the Internet is not a regulated business and does not maintain subscriber numbers. This can lead to massive overcounting of subscribers. For example, a company can set up a connection to the Internet for its 1,000 employees. Some of these people, however, might never sign on, or might use the service only for sending e-mail to co-workers. They may never visit the World Wide Web or shop online. Please take this information as a warning if someone tries to sell advertising space on the basis of cost per thousand (CPM in advertising lingo). Instead, ask for the number of accesses (the number of times people visit the site and read information) or sales. However, don't lose sight of the fact that the Internet and commercial online services attract people who have sought out merchants and are ready, willing and able to make purchases.

Demographics

Who is the typical online user? That's impossible to say. Commercial online services, which account for perhaps 5 million people, have conducted studies of their customers, but the Internet, which is reported to have 25 million users, has not. Therefore, most of the people who use online services have not been studied. If we look at the figures from the commercial online services, a profile of the highly educated, high-income consumer emerges.

Subscribers to online services are young, affluent, highly educated and overwhelmingly male. Each major commercial online service reports that its subscribers' are college graduates, married and have an average income of over $60,000. On male–female ratio, only Prodigy comes close to an even balance. Other services are trying to attract women.

These figures, however, must be viewed with caution. Please note that some well-intentioned statistics can be misleading. Let's look at John Newbie, who opens an account on an online service. He is a highly valued member of the 35–45 male group that earn $75,000 a year. Now here are several scenarios that affect the reliability of demographics.

1. John signs on once, gets frustrated and never signs on again. He keeps his subscription because he feels that he might need it some day. That's bad, because he is missing in action and therefore a misleading statistic.

2. John signs on, uses the service only to check his stocks or the day's headlines and never ventures into a shopping area. He is still counted as a consumer and a highly placed one at that. However, he might as well not exist for commercial purposes.

3. John orders a commercial online service and gives the account to his 16-year-old daughter, Jennifer. That is okay, since teenage girls buy lots and lots of products. However, the marketing information doesn't know about Jennifer; it knows only John.

4. John signs the credit card and gives the account to his whole family. His wife, Christine, daughter Jennifer and son Jim use the system around the clock. They might buy lipstick and rap CDs and spend time in the college SAT preparation area. Now, what do your demographics mean? Prodigy would assign a different password to each member of the family and list this family as four separate individuals. The other services do not recognize four distinct users. Instead, they would present a very interesting portrait of a middle-aged man who buys lipstick and rap CDs and studies for the SATs!

So what does this do to the traditional cost per thousand (CPM) yardstick used by advertisers and publishers to set and compare rates? It wreaks havoc. A new method of measuring subscribers must be used based on hits (the number of times information is accessed by consumers) and the placement of the information and other factors. Until that happens, online marketers must use a degree of skepticism when looking at certain demographic figures.

Mass Market or Niche Market?

A great debate is stirring over whether the online customer is part of the great mass market or a niche market. The answer is that both are true. Just as you might be a member of the select group of people who like to discuss the beauty of creating anagrams from people's names (a very select group indeed), you also might watch *Seinfeld* on TV (a group that comprises about 20% of all households) and drink a brand of soda that has a 58% market share. You are truly a resident of both mass and niche markets.

A careful survey of the forums on various systems might reveal an audience that is just the one you are looking for, regardless of whether the online system has 2 million users or 20 million users. For example, if you needed to reach senior citizens, you would do well to investigate the forum run by the AARP, the association for retired persons `AOL: Keyword AARP` and `Prodigy: Jump AARP`. You could also find seniors on other online services: `CompuServe: Go RETIRE`, `Prodigy: Jump SENIORS`. If you wanted to reach people with bicycles, you'd find a direct hit with the BikeNet forum `AOL: Keyword BIKENET`. Please remember that advertising is *not* permitted on these forums. You could, however, conduct informal market research by finding out what topics are hot as seen by what people are talking about and build relationships with members by conveying information in answer to their questions. However, knowing that 40% of AOL's members use bicycles might lead you to want to target that service's retail outlets.

Certain consumer market segments are well represented on the Internet. Virtually every college professor, staff member and student is on the Internet with a free account. That creates markets for everything from books to jeans to beer to music CDs. The three major commercial services report very high demographics, mostly male, between 30 and 50, mostly with incomes in the $50,000 to $90,000 range and mostly college graduates. More detailed statistics are in Chapter 3.

Optimistic marketers look at the 27% penetration of computers in the home and say that number is high enough to indicate that a mass market exists. That could very well be true if you look at the types of products that are being purchased online: camera film, flowers, stocks, travel services. These are all products that reach out to a mass market.

The Internet and commercial online services also are good places to attract sales to consumers and business to business. Computer equipment, software and supplies are an attractive audience for online marketers.

Case Study: Racer Records

Racer Records, a small, independent record label with eight releases by six artists, gives away free sampler CDs and cassettes, conducts live conferences and uploads sound files on two online services as a way of promoting sales. "We're very active in the online world; we're the only American indie label to have a section in the

Recording Industry Forum here on CompuServe, and we released both of our most recent albums with online record release parties," says owner Kristi Wachter. "We also have an Internet mailing list, an Internet FTP site and the beginnings of an Internet World Wide Web page.

"According to my records, I've gotten 834 requests for free samplers from CompuServe members, and 1,036 requests from Internet users (out of a total of about 16,000 sampler requests). The real numbers are probably slightly higher, since some people request the sampler by phone instead of e-mail, and some of them neglect to tell me where they heard about Racer. If you assume a cost of 15 cents per incoming call on my 800 number, getting the bulk of these requests via e-mail has saved me over $250," she says. "More significantly, I got over $1 in sales for each sampler I sent out to a CompuServe user; I got nearly $1.25 in sales for each sampler sent to an Internet user. By comparison, the highest sales rate I got from a print ad was 47 cents in sales for each sampler sent," she says, "I also discovered that my total sales from 'free' advertising (CompuServe, Internet, and word of mouth) combined were *greater* than my total sales from all combined paid advertising," says Wachter.

"I also find that people who use the Internet and CompuServe are more accustomed to buying things through the mail. I get very good purchase rates from CIS and Internet folks, compared with people who requested the sampler after seeing a print ad."

Creating information, not advertising, is her strategy for online marketing.

"I hope (and suspect) that you're emphasizing the importance of not actually advertising on the Net—that's the fastest way in the world to get a bad name. All of my 'ads' have been strictly informational and have given ways for people to find out more without incurring any cost. I'm also scrupulous about not sending unwanted mail to people. I am completely convinced that my low-key, try-before-you-buy approach has had everything to do with my success and popularity on CompuServe and the Internet."

Case Study: Deluxe Business Systems

Deluxe Business Systems, a division of Deluxe Corporation and a leading business forms supplier, has put its catalog of more than 2,000 products on the World Wide Web, `http://deluxe.com/`.

"This is the latest, most advanced way to order products," says Michael Eagan of Deluxe Business Forms. "Products—including forms, checks, software, and office supplies—can be viewed on more than 1,000 linked screens.

The Deluxe catalog allows users to browse through a home page menu without downloading to disk space. After accessing the catalog through the `deluxe.com` address, users see a menu of 18 icons offering access to product groups, an index, and a guide to frequently asked questions. The catalog also has interactive features: Users can have questions answered on-line and can pay for purchases by completing an on-screen order form and using a credit card number.

To protect card numbers, Deluxe will use PGP encryption to scramble the card data in a format indecipherable to other Internet users.

In the first week of operation, the site reported 12,500 visits. Sales figures were not available.

Technical Backgrounder: Lite Version

Before we get ahead of ourselves here, many readers are probably asking "What is a commercial online system. What is the Internet?" Let's take a brief pause to make sure that we are all know what we are talking about.

An online system is a computer network that contains databases of information, such as current and historical news from newspapers and magazines, research reports and stock quotes; forums of professionals who discuss matters of common concerns; forums of people who discuss lifestyle issues, such as health, sex, religion, current events, sports and hobbies; entertainment such as music and computer games; files of computer software; service areas operated by companies who want to maintain a closer relationship with customers by answering support questions; and by offering free information, software upgrades and camaraderie with other customers. Companies can also sell, advertise and promote their products on these systems provided they follow the rules created by the owners of these systems. Subscribers can order products as well. CompuServe, Prodigy, America Online, Microsoft Network, eWorld and AT&T Interchange are some of the largest commercial online services.

The Internet is a network of networks. Although it was created by the government for use by the military and educational institutions, the past year has seen a tremendous growth in its use by the consumer public. Consequently, merchants have begun selling products on a portion of the Internet known as the World Wide Web.

Equipment and Software That You Will Need

To use an online service, you will need a computer, modem and special software provided by the commercial online service, such as CompuServe, America Online and Prodigy. This software is easy to use, thanks to its graphical user interfaces, which allow you to navigate easily to find topics of interest, write e-mail to customers and prospects and maintain and update company-sponsored forums.

To use the Internet, you need a computer and modem, a subscription to the Internet through a privately owned service provider and software that lets you browse the World Wide Web, such as NCSA Mosaic `order@ncsa.uiuc.edu`, Netscape Navigator `info@mcom.com`, or Netcom's NetCruiser `info@netcom.com`. Windows users may also need Trumpet Winsock, a software program that must be installed and configured properly on the computer.

Microsoft's Windows 95 operating system will include these tools, which will save millions of people about a billion hours of anger and frustration. An easy way to get full Internet access is to use Netcom's NetCruiser software which is as painless to install and use as any of the software provided by the commercial online services. With NetCruiser, you can perform all Internet functions: from reading mail and posting messages to the newgroups and mailing lists, to browsing the World Wide Web and retrieving files from Gopher and FTP sites.

Summary

Bright times are coming for vendors on the Information Superhighway. Online systems are attracting subscribers in record numbers, and they appear to want to buy products and services. However, these online consumers want to buy based on information, not emotion, which forces marketers to devise new marketing messages. Also, the new technology creates new opportunities for creating these messages in a highly interactive manner. Marketers, start your engines

CHAPTER 2

Essentials of Online Marketing

While the potential to reach large audiences is real, so is the need to use solid marketing strategies and tactics.

"It's not magic. If you ask 'Can I spend $100 and make a million?' I'd say 'No.' It is work. You have to have a good business plan, be price-competitive and promote yourself," says Marc Fleischmann, president, Internet Distribution Services, Inc., of Palo Alto, California, a marketing design technology company that helps companies market service on the Internet `marcf@netcom.com`, `415-856-8265`. "Companies with bad ideas, poor marketing or products that didn't work in the real world won't work online either. If it will sell in a mail order catalog, it will work on the Internet."

An online presence will help successful companies become more successful if it is used as part of the marketing mix. "The Internet," he says, "is another channel for successful companies."

In this chapter, you will learn:

- What online marketing is.
- How it differs from other forms of marketing.
- Benefits of online marketing.
- What it takes to become a successful online marketer.
- Questions you need to consider to create an online marketing plan.
- Benefits and limits of technology.

Definition: Online marketing is a system for selling products and services to target audiences who use the Internet and commercial online services by utilizing online tools and services in a strategic manner consistent with the company's overall marketing program.

Benefits of Online Marketing

Companies can benefit from online marketing in many ways, including:

- Reach a defined audience in an environment that is not yet crowded with competitors.
- Target a defined customer group with precision and develop a continuing dialogue.
- Transact business electronically and at a lower cost. E-mail and data files can be transmitted to selected customers or entire lists in seconds, for pennies.
- Streamline the selling process by allowing manufacturers to communicate and sell directly to end users without going through classic distribution channels
- Act quickly by adding products and changing selling propositions at a moment's notice.
- Track the sales interaction, steps and results.
- Keep an eye on competitors.
- Create a responsive dialogue with customers.
- Distribute software and information products quickly through e-mail and file transfers.

"Being the first online will not only establish initiative, but will accelerate the learning curve of conducting business online," says Leslie Laredo, director, Advertising Development, for AT&T Interchange Online Network, a leading analyst and a recognized expert on online advertising. "As the old lottery ad stated, 'You've got to be in it to win it.' Participation at almost any level is fast becoming necessary."

Case Study: Gazillionaire Software from LavaMind

The Internet has all the tools needed to design, create, market and support a software game, according to Naomi Kokubo and Steven Hoffman of LavaMind Productions, of San Francisco `lavamind@ix.netcom.com`, `415-566-3808`, which created a Monopoly-like game set in outer space called Gazillionaire. Here's their story.

"We're a husband and wife team, who have just developed a new multimedia CD-ROM game working out of our apartment on a zero budget. A year ago, we had no experience producing CD-ROM titles but, after 9 months of working 14-hour days, seven days a week, we not only created a new CD-ROM game, but we are marketing it ourselves over the Internet.

"We had to do everything ourselves. We learned how to program for Windows. We created 80% of the artwork. We designed the sound ,and now we're marketing it over our modem on a shoestring budget. And you know what, we're doing better than we could have possibly imagined."

They released a scaled-down version of Gazillionaire as shareware over the Internet. Shareware is a marketing strategy of selling software in which consumers try out the software and buy it if they like it.

They sent copies of the game to FTP sites on the Internet, along with a letter to the site operator asking for permission to place the software on their server. Most sites granted permission because it cost them nothing and their users would have more programs to play with.

"We've been flooded with e-mail from all around the world. Everyone seems to love our game. Its incredible! We've been receiving checks and money orders from Australia, Denmark, England and Japan. We've even been contacted by dealers in Korea and Denmark. It's fantastic. Every day we receive orders for the full version of Gazillionaire along with dozens of e-mail messages asking for information on the shareware version of Gazillionaire. Without the Internet, we would never have been able to accomplish what we have," they say.

"The thing that saved us is the Internet. For only $20 a month, we can run a global company out of our apartment. We don't have a virtual stranglehold on the retail outlets or billions to invest in interactive TV, but we have a $100 modem and we can reach an audience of 25 million people from our home.

"We used the Internet for everything. The Internet made all the difference in the world. It has helped enormously in the following areas:

"*Publicity*: We have used the Internet to gain access to magazine editors, newspapers, TV and radio stations. So far, we've been featured on national radio, in several local newspapers and in several national magazines just by contacting publishers and writers over the Internet.

"*Advertising*: We try not to advertise directly over the Internet. People get annoyed if you send them junk e-mail. Instead, we post notices about our game on the appropriate newsgroups. Because we are giving away a free game, which is scaled down but fully playable, we can post notices. After all, one of the main functions of the Internet is to distribute shareware, and nobody objects to a posting about legitimate shareware, just as long as you post it in the correct newsgroup. If we weren't giving away shareware, then we would be limited to posting notices in only a few DEMO and BIZ newsgroups which allow blatant advertising. [Please see Chapter 4 for a discussion of Netiquette.]

"***Tech Support***: We have been providing all of our tech support over the net. This keeps our cost low and is viable because 99% of the people purchasing our game have access to the Net.

"***Research and Development:*** The Internet has been an invaluable source of research and development for future game titles. We read the game Newsgroups and try to find out what gamers want out of a game and what gamers hate about existing games. This helps to stimulate our imagination and provide a basis for developing our future entertainment titles.

"***Testing***: By distributing our game as shareware, we were able to not only test the market, but we were able to discover and fix a number of bugs in our code. People would tell us what was wrong with the shareware game, and then we could implement their advice to fix the full version of Gazillionaire.

"***Expert Advice***: The programming newsgroups on the Internet have provided us with help solving a number of major technical problems. We constantly monitor the comp.sys.lang.basic.visual newsgroup to find out the latest info on Visual Basic and other programming tools which we used to create our game.

"***Test Marketing***: By looking at the price associated with other shareware products on the Internet, we were able to determine a suitable price for our product.

"If it weren't for the Internet," they say, "we could not do what we're doing."

LavaMind's strategy works because Naomi and Steven became part of the community, created relationships with people in many different newsgroups, asked permission before being commercial and created a product that lends itself to sales on the Internet.

Secrets of Online Marketing

The Information Superhighway is a new medium, as different from TV as newspapers are from radio. Just as you wouldn't take a radio advertisement and play it on television, you wouldn't take a print ad and place it on an online service. The old rules don't apply. Forget about customers buying on emotion and justifying on logic. Don't believe the 90/10 rule of 90% persuasion, 10% information. That strategy won't cut it when you appeal to this audience because:

- The Internet and commercial online services offer new technological tools that require new marketing rules to appeal to audiences.
- The online audience is influenced to buy based on objective information, not classic advertising and sales persuasion. This is the key difference in creating advertising messages compared to other media. Consumers have a strong negative reaction to hype when it is online.

Marketers will be most successful when they follow the 13 keys to success with online marketing, as defined by Leslie Laredo of AT&T Interchange Online Network and other online experts interviewed for this book.

1. Appreciate the new paradigms in online marketing and advertising.
2. Online marketing supports the integrated marketing program.
3. Mass market is over. Customization is in.
4. Build relationships one at a time.
5. Appreciate the long-term value of the customer.
6. Advertising must be interactive.
7. Provide reams of information, not persuasion.
8. Create interactive dialogue.
9. Contribute to the community.
10. Adjust to the compression and distortion of time.
11. Blend advertising, public relations, promotions, catalogs and sales.
12. Online is a competitive advantage.
13. Company size is irrelevant online

1. Appreciate the New Paradigms in Marketing and Advertising

Online marketing is a new branch of an old tree—marketing, which can be defined as the process of satisfying human needs and wants with information, services or products through the exchange of money. To be a successful online marketer, one needs to know the basics of the marketing process. These basics include needs assessment, market research, product development, pricing, distribution, advertising, public relations, promotions and sales.

Online marketing has its roots and basis in traditional marketing concepts but branches out in a most important manner—interactivity. Vendors now have the ability to deal interactively with consumers at any time of the day or night in their home or office. Conversely, buyers can interact with vendors in a new way. Communication is two-way, not one-way.

However, the most striking difference between online marketing and other forms is the technology itself. Communicating messages on computers replaces paper with the on-screen displays of information, text, art and sound. Principles of layout, design, typography and art need to be reconsidered when communicating with an online audience. Also, computers allow communication to become an interactive, two-way process, unlike print and television advertisements, which are one-way processes. Simply uploading ads to online services will mean your company will miss the chance to take advantage of technology and its tools to empower your messages.

Online marketing can take advantage of presenting interactive sale materials that meet the needs of every type of buyer. Instead of creating a message for the lowest common denominator, as does broadcast advertising, for example, online marketers can create interactive brochures that allow the consumer to choose the information she wants to see, when she wants to see it. Companies can create individual sales presentation to match the needs of each buyer.

"Cyberads must leverage the online medium by providing more and deeper information, more entertainment value and faster and more personalized fulfillment than what can be jammed into a 30-second TV commercial or a single page print ad," says Laredo. "What's more, online advertising dictates customized communication, not broad general messages. Target marketing can be exercised in a much finer fashion. Individual message management or one-to-one selling, with ad placement in the context of relevant, sought-after content, is the new rule. Online advertising is more like personal selling than anything else."

2. Online Marketing Supports the Integrated Marketing Program

Online marketing should support the entire marketing program. Online marketing does not and should not exist in a vacuum. That's because the online component is but one part of the marketing solution—not the only solution. To conduct a successful marketing campaign, online services should be thought of as another distribution channel that generates sales. In that way, the key marketing messages of your company should be seen in the online advertising, publicity and promotion that your company employs. Companies must use a consistent message, typeface, logo and other elements of the marketing campaign.

The difference comes when you analyze the delivery mechanism. For example, a trifold brochure printed on 80# brilliant white card stock might look great in print, but it doesn't work on a computer screen, which cannot transmit the rich feel of paper, nor accommodate text and graphics.

Marketers must figure out how to transmit the brand image and message from a one-way media to an interactive media.

Integrated marketing, a hot buzzword in business schools these days, has three components:

- *Message consistency:* The consumer finds the same message regardless of the media used.
- *Interactivity:* The consumer has a way to conduct a meaningful dialogue with the company.
- *Mission marketing:* Everything the company does stems from its definition of what the company is and what its purpose is.

Examples of companies with good integrated marketing programs are Ben and Jerry's, Saturn, Snapple, Coca-Cola and United Airlines (even their planes and ticket envelopes match!).

Online services can be promoted in print advertisements. Astonishingly few companies do this. While browsing through a recent issue of *NetGuide*, a magazine that highlights online services, only a handful of advertisers included their e-mail addresses, forum locations or URLs for World Wide Web home pages. Ironically, two car companies did include references to their online locations, while several software publishers did not!

3. Mass Market Is Over—Customization Is In

Online marketing allows companies to target customers in a way that other media cannot.

"For the last 30 years, mass marketing has torn the business away from the customer. We've been advertising mass-produced product to a mass audience. We end up counting the people we reach, not reaching the people who count," says Dan Fine, president of Fine Communications, a database marketing company based in Seattle. "Customers have been bombarded with more advertising messages than they could stand. As a result, they've become increasingly selective as to which messages they give their attention to. We have come to a time when the consumer wants to talk back to the marketing message and a place where individual relationships must be re-established."

To get an even better perspective of online marketing, perhaps it is best to compare it to mass marketing and direct marketing:

- Mass marketing needs a mass market to survive. It reaches consumers through television and magazines. It does best when it sells food, health and beauty aids, beer and cars.
- Direct marketing needs a highly targeted audience. It finds consumers through mailing lists. It is a good vehicle to sell credit cards, travel, software and catalog goods.
- Online marketing targets individuals through online services. It sells travel, stocks, upscale consumer goods and computer equipment and software.

4. Build Relationships One at a Time

Successful online marketers know that you build a business one customer at a time and that the lifetime value of a customer can be significant.

"You must get personally involved in the virtual community. You must invest the time to start relationships," says Carol Wallace, program manager, communications, for Prodigy. "Through that process, you will begin to understand how this society operates. Then you will be in a better position to sell to them."

5. Appreciate the Long-Term Value of a Customer

For marketers, a major change in thinking must occur regarding the value of the customer. For too long, companies have regarded consumers as replaceable commodities. Marketers must look to the long-term value of a customer. This concept will be a stretch for many salespeople.

For example, when was the last time you got a call, card or note from the person who sold you your car? Probably never. Do you have any sense of loyalty to that salesperson or dealership? Probably not. That's too bad for them, because you probably will buy a new car one day and it won't be from them!

What does this cost the company? Let's look at the figures. If you are an average consumer, you'll buy a new car every three to five years. You will be influenced by peers, ads and other factors. One factor that will not influence you is a sense of loyalty or commitment to the salesperson or dealership. If the average car costs $20,000 in today's dollars and if the average car is held for five years, that means the lifetime value of a 30-year-old customer for a car dealership is $160,000, that based on the assumption that person buys a new car every five years until he is 70. You'd think it would be worth $1.50 to send a birthday card or personal note once a year to build a relationship worth that much money. Few car salespeople do this—even though they make their living by commission.

For the online marketer to succeed with the online audience, this scenario needs to change.

Case Study: Wally Bock

Wally Bock, an author, speaker and consultant who trains police departments on human relations and procedural issues, uses online services to reach his target audience: police chiefs. He participates in discussions on online bulletin boards and answers questions such as "How do I deal with sexual harassment?" He replies with a message that provides a few examples from his book.

"The last time I did that, I got an individual order from a police chief in Wisconsin. He posted a message praising the book," says Bock. "This led to more orders. An East Coast police chief asked for a review copy and then ordered 50.

He promotes his staff every 18 months, so I expect to sell 50 new orders every 18 month. That's the value of long-term customers."

Bock also publishes two newsletters for businesses going online, *CyberPower Alert*™ and *CyberPower for Business*™ wbock@cyberpower.com, that places the lifelong value of a customer at $500–$5,000.

"That's what the future of this marketing is about," he says. "I am not in the business of one-time sales. That is not smart. If you are a customer of mine, you will be a subscriber for years. You become a prospect for additional businesses and products and consulting. My primary focus is getting quality people who stay a long time. Secondarily, get as many as possible."

For Bock, the key to success is target marketing.

"We tailor what we have to specific people," Bock says of the forums and newsgroups and mailing lists that have tightly defined readers. "What I can do on the Internet I can't do with paper mailing lists. There is no other technology that lets me do this as well."

6. Advertising Must Be Interactive

Customers of online systems have a style all their own. They are not typical consumers. According to demographic information supplied by the commercial services, the average online consumer is better educated and has more disposable income than the average American. These consumers also have little tolerance for in-your-face advertising, ads that suddenly appear on their computer screens and ads that masquerade as messages.

Because the online consumer is not the average consumer and because the technology of online systems offers different message formulation possibilities, the entire advertising/marketing focus must undertake a major paradigm shift from traditional methods.

In traditional advertising, the purpose is to disseminate the message to as many people for the lowest cost. Generally speaking, the advertiser buys space in a medium that claims to reach the desired demographic audience. For instance, the advertiser places an ad in a skiing magazine to sell ski equipment or airs a commercial on a children's cartoon show to sell a doll. The communication is one-way: The advertiser presents information and persuasion to convince the consumer to purchase the product. Appeals to logic and emotion are made. If the ad is successful, the consumer buys the product. If the consumer has a question, she can ask the company for more information, receive it in two weeks and make a decision.

The online medium uses a different strategy. Consumers request information from companies, which respond quickly. Consumers search for more data, pictures, testimonials and the like, which the company has carefully placed in accessible places online. A company representative might even interact personally through private e-mail to answer questions. When the consumer has finished her research, she has built a relationship with the company that propels her to want to buy, and she places the order.

This strategy works because the request for information was created by the consumer, not the advertiser. The two keys to remember are that information is at a premium and that information must be requested.

"Interactive advertising would best be defined as a sort of 'digital infomercial,' if you will," says Jonathan Pajion, executive vice president, marketing, for 2-Lane Media, of Los Angeles, which has won wide acclaim for its *Forrest Gump* advertisement that is available on the Hollywood Online forum AOL: Keyword Hollywood. "A typical digital ad, if done properly, will convey much more information than an ad in any other media and do it in a much more friendly manner. An interactive ad will allow the consumer to pick and choose what information he/she wants to view and the order in which it is viewed. Additionally, if properly executed, the ad won't really seem that much like an ad that the typical consumer is used to."

2-Lane Media has created promotions for such films as *Undercover Blues*, *Fatal Instinct*, *Addams Family Values*, *Naked Gun 33 1/3*, *NBC Spring/Summer Preview*, *City Slickers II*, *Angels in the Outfield* and *The Mask*.

"With Gump and the other Hollywood Online kits, you don't really feel like you're viewing a blatant ad for the film, though you are. Instead, you feel like you're exploring and finding out exciting preview and insider information about the film and the stars and crew. Under the guise of obtaining information and perhaps playing a game, the consumer is also repeatedly given the sales message in some form or another. Any of these kits we've done for Hollywood Online fit the above description very well," he says. "As other examples, there are interactive kiosks that promote certain sales messages and other online and floppy-based kits for music and ads on the new generation of digital magazines."

Case Study: DayTimer Technologies

DayTimer Technologies is publishing the software version of the famous DayTimer appointment calendars. They are planning a Web home page and forums on CompuServe and America Online.

"The question was 'How do we provide information instead of sales material that will draw people to our area?" says Craig Settles, senior strategist, Successful Marketing Strategists of Berkeley, California, which created Online Marketing efforts for DayTimer. "The product lets you know what's going on. From that came the idea of creating a reminder service. Consumers can enter 20 birthdays and anniversaries. The Internet will send reminders to your e-mail box. It is very simple and straightforward and very important. Anyone who has forgotten an anniversary will consider this very important."

The strategy involves presenting a valued service instead of a hard sell. Best of all, it is free.

"This is an indirect way of introducing them to the product," says Settles, who notes that a large percentage of Daytimer users have a computer. Additional free information will include papers on the subject of time management, why group scheduling software saves time and why electronic organizers enhance the value of software.

The company hopes to make money on the venture in several ways. They will have a joint effort with FTD on the Internet to send flowers. Eventually, the entire Daytimer catalog will go online and consumers can order products.

This strategy works because the promotion is information-oriented and it allows consumers to order products.

7. Provide Reams of Information, Not Persuasion

The stereotype of the overbearing salesperson is the antimodel for online marketing. Online consumers are information seekers and are persuaded by facts and logic. The medium itself is mostly text-based, which attracts an educated audience that is used to making decisions based on reading reports. They go online to find information from company databases and discussion groups of peers. These are not people who are persuaded by the classic techniques of image advertising, which is based on irrational and emotional messages, such as appeals to ego and sex. Online consumers are turned off by hype and oversell. The successful online marketer will have a better chance to succeed if she offers information and rich content instead of self-serving materials.

This is good news for online marketers because space on the Internet and forums on commercial online services are inexpensive or free. Companies that have been forced to condense their messages to fit inside printed advertisements that fit on half a newspaper page will enjoy the freedom of virtually unlimited space online to post file after file of product information, complete with text, picture and sound.

"You are not constrained by pages like print magazines. Advertising becomes more interactive and creative," says Marcos Sanchez of Niehaus, Ryan, Haller, a public relations firm in South San Francisco that represents several Internet information providers. "With magazines, you had to match your message to a limited space. On the Net, you can use an inverted pyramid. Start with overview and then go very broad. The ad becomes an amorphous space."

Another advantage is that you can find out what people are really interested in. Let's say you are selling cars and have information stored on separate pages that list different options, such as air bags, stereos, J.D. Power ratings, safety tests and colors. By looking at the hits (the number of times a page is read), you can see that more people are interested in air bags, than say, colors. This data can be used to fine-tune advertising messages online and in other media as you begin to realize what information people are really interested in.

"This changes the model of how we look at advertising," Sanchez says. "It is no longer a 3- by 5-inch ad that goes out to 20,000 people. It is unlimited space going out to the world, limited only by the capacity of your server."

Companies can also use information to build relationships with existing customers. For example, NBC and ABC both have forums on America Online `AOL: Keyword NBC, ABC`, in which readers can find out which guests will be on *Good Morning, America*, download pictures of their favorite actors and find out how to get tickets to the *Seinfeld* show being taped. The CBS forum on Prodigy allows viewers to read about David Letterman. All these services build interactive relationships with viewers by allowing them to send e-mail to the companies.

Another example of information content is GE Plastics `http//www.ge.com`, which has placed more than 1,500 pages of information onto its site on the Internet's World Wide Web. Customers can find information and answers to their questions 24–hours a day from any spot in the world.

Remember, hard sells don't work.

8. Create Interactive Dialogue

After the prospect has read your online information, you must create a way for her to continue developing a relationship with the company. Electronic mail provides a great way to create a new dialogue. Customers should be encouraged to send questions to the company—and the company should be equipped to send a prompt reply.

Technology allows several methods for replies. Customer support representatives can respond to electronic mail on a timely basis to individual questions as soon as they are received in the company mailbox. Automated mail responders on the Internet (called mailbots) act like fax-back systems, which send the desired information immediately to the requester at any time of the day or night.

Companies can also create relationships by having representatives scan online forums for conversations concerning their company, products or product area. When they find these messages, they quickly provide information, answer questions and dispel rumors with the goal of finding new prospects and building loyalty to the company and brand.

9. Contribute to the Community

Online marketing is a two-way, interactive process. You are asking for the consumer's time and money. In return, you must offer valuable information free. Companies can contribute by releasing surveys, reports and impartial information packets that contribute to the greater good of the online community. For example, an insurance agency could post files about how to save money on insurance, a real estate agency could explain how to choose a house and a swimming pool installer might post an article about how to select a pool manufacturer.

Companies can also offer free samples of their products, such as online newsletters and reports and demo versions of software. In addition to being useful to the consumer, these products cost nothing to deliver to the consumer via online delivery systems, such as e-mail and file transfers. Software is a popular freebie. Several companies offer free screen savers to people who visit their online stores and World Wide Web home pages.

10. Adjust to the Compression and Distortion of Time

Remember the first time you searched your computerized address book for the name of a colleague? You were so amazed that the computer could sort through so many names so quickly. The same act would have taken much longer if you had done it by hand. Then you got used to the speed of the computer and would complain if the operation took longer than two seconds. This example shows how people's perceptions of time have changed thanks to the computer.

"Fast" is a relative term. In the world of online marketing, fast can be measured in seconds. People get impatient when their questions aren't answered by support staffs in minutes. These same people might have been happy to grant a 24-hour call-return policy from a customer service representative. Companies that conduct business online must expect to deliver information quickly because the customer demands it and because the technology can make it possible. For example, automated mail systems, similar in concept to fax-back systems, can automatically send information-packed files to customers who request specific information. This is the norm, not the exception.

11. Blend Advertising, Public Relations, Promotions, Catalogs and Sales

While researching this book, I was constantly asking questions that turned into conundrums. Is a Web home page an advertisement or a catalog? Is posting a message on a forum public relations or a promotion? Is information an advertisement? The answers are that the lines of distinction between these forms of marketing blur in online environments. Online marketers must get used to new definitions and new uses for trusted strategic marketing elements of advertising and public relations as they undergo a metamorphosis in the online environment. Time will shake out these strategies and determine what works and what does not. Undoubtedly, new communication forms that we can't even comprehend today will be created and will seem obvious in 18 months. Online marketers must keep their minds open. Probably the best strategy is to see what other companies are doing online and adapt the most reasonable tactics to your own use.

12. Online Is a Competitive Advantage

Having a commercial presence online presents a competitive advantage to companies. It provides them with an alternative and additional distribution channel for its products and services. For computer and software companies, *not* having an online forum to offer customer support can be seen as a distinct disadvantage. However, online is just one channel; it is not the only channel. Companies should give careful consideration to how they use online services. Do you want to sell products, create an image and/or support customers' queries? Each channel should support the company's main goals and messages.

13. Company Size Is Irrelevant Online

When you drive past a shopping center, you can tell the big players from the start-ups. Online, you can't. In many ways, online services are the great levelers of companies.

"Small companies with a well-designed home page can look every bit as professional and credible as a large, multinational company. Small companies can build instant credibility with a Web home page," says Wendie Bernstein Lash, president of the Internet Roundtable Society, an Internet presence provider. "People can't tell if you do business from a 90-story office building or a two-room rented suite. Web home pages level the playing field for small companies."

Although online marketing is still in its infancy, quite a few small companies have become big companies by using online marketing to sell flowers, T-shirts, novelties and computer software. In some cases, online marketing was their only sales method and distribution channel.

The Marketing Process

Planning is essential for any successful marketing program. This is certainly true of online marketing. This section will raise questions you should consider as you plan your online venture. We'll look at these three main areas:

- Planning to go online.
- Creating messages.
- Disseminating the message.

We hope that questions in this section will help you to think through your online marketing plan and keep you from jumping online before you know where you're going and what you will need when you get there.

Planning to Go Online

Successful online marketers begin by asking these questions:

- ***Should your company be online?*** What does it hope to accomplish? Are these objectives reasonable? Doable? Reachable?
- ***Is there an online audience for your products?*** Determine if the audience is there. Just because you can reach 25 million people on the Internet doesn't mean that they are all interested in your product. How many of them are at all likely to be interested? Is that a large enough market to justify the expense?
- ***Which online service or services attract that audience?*** Don't limit yourself to just one service—your customers might be users of several services. Should you even use the Internet, or does another service have better demographics for your product? The commercial online services can provide detailed demographics on its audience. The Internet cannot. This will change as studies are commissioned by companies interested in marketing on the Net.
- ***Does the product line appeal to an audience that is accessible through online services?*** Certainly, there are many people online who need to purchase computer equipment, software and supplies, but they also have needs like every other consumer. Online subscribers are among the largest purchasers of stocks, flowers and travel services. Nontech companies like the Vermont Teddy Bear Company, Godiva Chocolatier and Warner Bros. Records find customers online. Online marketing know-it-alls might say that the Internet is the hallowed ground of scientists and college students involved in serious research, yet there is room for

USENET newsgroups that discuss Barney the dinosaur, Lego toys, Mighty Morphin Power Rangers, Melrose Place and sex.

- ***Which products should be featured online—all or some?*** With information, more is better, so you can tell a complete story. Storage space online is cheap compared to display advertising space, which is expensive. Therefore, you can put your entire catalog online without incurring the same expensive charges associated with printing a catalog.

- ***What is the budget?*** More important, whose budget does the money come from? Advertising? Publicity? Technology? Create a budget that allows you to take advantage of these online tools.

- ***How can you take advantage of online technology to create marketing materials that embrace interactivity?*** Customers must be able to find information quickly and at their own pace. Programmed sales pitches and canned presentations won't work as effectively. You will need to think how to make your information interactive. On the Internet's World Wide Web, you can accomplish this by linking text to related elements. For example, when the customer sees the word "toaster," she can click on that word and see a picture of the toaster, or see all references to toasters in the database. "Interactivity will quickly mean much more than this," says Michael Fremont, executive vice president of the Internet Roundtable Society, an Internet presence provider. "People will be able to try certain products (like computer software) online. Search engines will start to help customers find products and information in an active way rather than just searching databases."

Creating Messages

- ***What is your message?*** Are you trying to sell a product, build loyalty to the brand and company, dispel rumors? The Internet and commercial online services can help you accomplish these goals and others.

- ***Do your online marketing materials carry over the same image, message and tone of your other marketing materials?*** Do they add multimedia, virtual reality and other forms of interactivity that enhance the shopping experience? The online message should be consistent with the rest of the marketing program.

- *What materials will be needed to support the message?* Sales sheets, customer testimonials, reports from testing labs, awards and the like can help build credibility.

- *How can these materials be interactive?* By using hypertext, e-mail, contests, surveys and free products, you can create an interactive dialogue with customers.

- *Why would customers buy online instead of through another channel?* You need to create a "reason to buy online" statement. Also consider if you want them to buy online, or if you want them to go to the store. Will you damage channel relationships if you sell direct? Should online marketing be a stimulus to generate in-store traffic?

- *Who will create the campaign, including message, art and technology?* Does your in-house staff have the expertise to plan a campaign, or should they manage an outside agency that understands the nooks and crannies of online marketing? Should part be conducted in-house and part farmed out?

- *Will the materials be updated? How often? By whom?* Updating a print catalog can be expensive, with production and mailing costs. However, online catalogs can be brought up-to-date with new prices and products very quickly and usually at a lower cost. Sites should have new information added on a regular basis to attract customers and encourage repeat visits.

- *How does this message reinforce the company's mission?* Is the message consistent with the company's goals? Does Online Marketing campaign tie in with the entire marketing program?

- *How should the material that is not online reference the online material?*

- *How do you respond to questions?* With a short message or a multipage information kit? "The more you tell, the more you sell," is the operative phrase online.

- *Which delivery medium do you use to respond?* E-mail or "snail mail"? People buy when they are motivated. With online services, companies can close the sale while the customer is still hot. If they send information packets by mail or overnight courier, part of the customer's thirst for the product might be quenched.

- ***What do your materials look like?*** Do they take advantage of interactive tools and multimedia? Are they static text documents reprinted for mass consumption? Truly innovative companies that understand the medium will use it to its potential.
- ***How do you ask for the order?*** What persuasion techniques can be applied without going over the top? Remember that hard sells don't work online.
- ***Do you use special promotions, discounts, refunds and upselling techniques?*** Online consumers like free samples of products.

Disseminating the Message

Letting the world know about your online presence is discussed in detail in Chapter 7, Online Shopping, and Chapter 12, Public Relations.

Technology and the Online Marketer

Technology has never been more conducive to online marketing and to online shopping—and yet it still has a long way to go! Online marketing is both benefactor and victim of today's computer technology. Let's look at what technology enables marketers to do today—and what the future will bring.

In this section you will learn:

- How technology enhances shopping and marketing.
- What the limits of current technology are.

Benefits of Technology

Shopping becomes interactive—highly personal—with online systems. The World Wide Web of the Internet allows companies to create virtual catalogs and showrooms, complete with a beautiful home page filled with colorful artwork that entices the customer. If the reader needs assistance, she can click on an icon to reveal additional information, pictures and order forms or to send e-mail. It is a marketer's dream. In technical parlance, the Web is a "hypermedia" system, sort of multimedia on steroids, in which text, pictures, video and audio files are interlinked, so that customers can find the information they need when they want it. Unlike a menu system in which customers drill down from one menu to the next to find information, Web users can find information simply by clicking on the hyptertext link (text or picture).

Sales pitches can be tailored by consumers to meet their individual needs, as they select the path of information they need to make an intelligent buying decision. For example, browsers in an online appliance store might select toasters, then choose between residential and business models, see a data sheet on a model that meets their needs, view a picture of the unit, hear the bell and timing unit, and finally order it. This can't be done on TV, as you would have time only to present an image of the store on broad issues, such as reliability, price, selection or location. The only opportunity TV gives an advertiser to go into great detail is with an infomercial, which costs a great deal of money to produce and broadcast.

Space is not a problem on the Information Superhighway. You can create as many pages of data or files of pictures as you like because space is cheap. This is not so in, say, a newspaper advertisement. In contrast to our previous example, the appliance store might place a full-page ad in the daily newspaper that features 50 products with a thumbnail picture and price, before running out of space. Or an advertiser might place an ad in a trade magazine that lists only the product model number and price in order to cram 500 items on a page with ordering information. On the Web, for example, each product can be viewed and demonstrated, along with complete product specifications and pictures. Technology clearly can overcome those barriers to other media—at a price print ads can't begin to match.

With online shopping, ordering and customer verification can be done quickly and privately on the commercial online services, while new tools are being developed for the Internet.

Information access and retrieval by customers is fast—much faster than snail mail, overnight delivery, or even fax-back systems. On all online systems, messages can be sent by the reader and received by the recipient in the blink of an eye—even if the sender is in St. Petersburg, Florida and the recipient is in St. Petersburg, Russia. Messaging is quick and efficient so that customers can ask questions and receive answers to make an informed buying decision. Files containing text or art can be stored online for readers to view when they want.

Graphic quality for static pictures is quite good on today's monitors. That means customers can see what the product looks like. If a picture is worth a thousand words, or seeing is believing, then computer images can help make the sale. The quality is inferior to print or television, however. Computers also transmit pictures and sounds slowly, which turns off consumers.

Text display looks great. That means you can display your messages in different-sized fonts, align them with photos and choose from a wide range of colors—much as you would with a printed magazine or newspaper advertisement. It wasn't too long ago that text-based systems ruled the land and all messages looked alike, with one boring font to tell the entire story and no art available!

Smart systems, built with menu structures or push buttons that play the options, can be created so that advertisements, including text and photos, can be played either at the customer's request or as part of an automatic cycle. Vendors can create multimedia presentations that rival any advertisement on television in the opportunity for interactivity, if not in picture quality.

Clearly, technology offers a lot of options for today's marketer to create and deliver a message to help create sales.

Technology levels the playing field between large companies and small ones. Because technology imposes barriers to entry from the techno-illiterate company, the techno-savvy company—large or small—will get a faster start as well as a fresher approach to consumers. Smart companies will look better than companies that are merely big. Also, there are no established rules about what works. The field is emerging. The technology is so new that no one really has a good handle on how to master it. That means that everyone enters the game on a relatively even playing field. The smart will survive; size is irrelevant. Small companies can look big. A cartoon in the *New Yorker* magazine shows two dogs typing at a computer terminal. The caption reads "On the Net, no one knows you are a dog." The same is true of advertisers. You could be a multinational corporation or operate a mail order business out of your basement. If your messages look, sound and read professionally, the public will grant you the credibility you seek.

Limits of Technology

Today's technology imposes limits on merchants in terms of:

- Ease of use.
- File size and compression.
- Modem speed.

Ease of Use

Online systems aren't of much use if people can't install them quickly or find things easily. While most of the commercial online systems now feature easy-to-use graphical interfaces, the Internet remains a problem area. It is inherently difficult to navigate and there is no master index of services, as more areas are added almost every day. Several publishers have developed graphical interfaces, like Mosaic, Cello and NetCruiser, that make navigating the Net much easier. However, the first two programs require several software programs that take a great deal of time and patience to install for even the most technically literate computer user. Happily, this situation is changing radically for the good. IBM has Internet tools built into its OS/2 Warp product. Microsoft's new Windows 95 operating system contains the software tools to make Internet access a snap. As this product penetrates the marketplace, growth on the Internet should expand considerably.

File Size and Compression

While online shopping can be conducted quite nicely in a text-only mode, the graphic qualities of computers can really make this medium shine. The stumbling block is the time it takes to transmit the data from the retailer's computer to the consumer's computer. Speed of transmission is based on several factors, including file size and modem speed. Text files, even large ones, transmit quite fast. Files containing pictures, sound and video are much larger and take a longer time to transmit. People like instant gratification. If they have to wait 10 minutes for a picture to display on the screen, they could become impatient and cancel the transmission. For example, McDonald's placed a 60-second TV ad on the NBC forum on America Online. It would take 57 minutes for the file to download on a 9600-baud modem. Since people pay for the time they spend online, they very well might have to pay more to see the ad than to buy a large order of French Fries! It is no wonder that only 53 people retrieved the file in the first two weeks it was online. By contrast, a McDonald's coloring book took two minutes to retrieve and was seen by more than 400 people.

This problem can be solved in three ways. Computer scientists will create compression programs that make files that are smaller and that therefore will transmit faster.

Second, the transmission speed of a modem, the device that allows a computer to send and receive files, will become faster. Most computers being shipped to homes today are equipped with modems with speeds of 14.4 kilobaud, a radical leap from the 9600-baud modems that were state-of-the-art only a few years ago, but still too slow to deal with large graphics files and multimedia transmissions.

The good news is that improvements in technology occur quickly. In the last nine years, modems have increased from 300 baud to 28.8 kilobaud, a factor of 96 times. "It will be a few years before slow speed isn't slow speed anymore," says Mike Voss, an Internet consultant. The average Internet provider uses a T1 telephone line today, but will switch to T3, which offers faster transmission speeds to consumers, when prices fall. ISDN technology eventually may replace modems. Cable operators are also exploring ways to deliver the Internet and commercial online services into the home via TV set.

The commercial online systems are at fault here as well. Forced to deal with the consumer with the lowest common denominator equipment, they readily provide access to consumers with 9600-baud modems. However, they have been slow to adopt 14.4-kilobaud access to users across most of the country. On the good side, they realize that they must keep in step with their consumers' demands—and their competitors' promises to provide speedy access quickly. The landscape should change by the end of 1995 so that people can have access to large files in a timely manner.

A third possibility is to reduce the number of colors in the file, which will reduce the file size considerably.

Multimedia Quality

Video clips can be created and played back on the computer; however, the images are jerky and the voice/action synchronization is not quite up to speed. Tighter coordination should come in the near future as technology improves. However, it could be a while before consumers have computers that can run these memory hungry applications.

The Future of Technology and Online Marketing

Technology will improve over time. As computer hardware prices fall, people will be able to buy better equipment, including monitors that display more colors and modems that transfer files quickly. Computers will use faster chips, display more colorful graphics and sport faster modems—all for a lower price than today's models. Software developers will improve compression of files so that customers can receive information faster. Data encryption standards will evolve so that people will feel more comfortable putting their credit card data online.

When that happens, a critical mass will be formed and marketers will find it cost-effective to transmit information faster.

As more people get online, service providers can offer lower rates to stimulate more growth. As more people buy products, online merchants will be able to reap profits and invest in better technology that provides more service to consumers. It is a wonderful cycle that is beginning today.

This means that you must use the technology that exists today—and plan for the technology to come—to get your message across. These are exciting times for creative people willing to push the envelope of interactive communications.

Summary

Technology offers many opportunities for marketers to showcase their products, create interactive sales sessions and deliver as much information as consumers need to make up their minds. As technology improves and prices for equipment fall, marketers will be able to make full use of multimedia elements of pictures, sound and video. In the meantime, the technology available today offers phenomenal opportunities for companies to get their messages across to consumers. Merchants, however, need to be mindful that the online consumer wants information, not persuasion, in order to buy products. Online tools can help to build and foster relationships with consumers in a cost-effective manner. The old rules of advertising and sales don't apply to the online world, and merchants must heed new paradigms needed to attract and convert prospects into customers.

CHAPTER 3

Overview of the Internet and Commercial Online Systems

Every online system has its own personality, rules of procedure and advertising policies. It is important that marketers know the demographics of each system so that they can find which one(s) attract their target audiences. This chapter presents an overview of each major system, including its demographics where available, its ability to provide marketing opportunities, its technical prowess and the attitudes of its subscribers toward advertisers. At the end of this chapter, you will have a better understanding of which online services can meet your marketing needs.

In this chapter, you will learn:

- What an online service is.
- Overviews of the Internet and the commercial online systems.
- Which tools are available for marketers.
- Who is online.
- Commercial features and marketing opportunities of each major online system.
- Customers' attitudes toward electronic retailing and advertising.

What Is an Online Service?

An online service is a computer network composed of information libraries, shopping and commercial services and e–mail that can be used by consumers who have personal computers, modems and software. CompuServe, Prodigy and America Online are examples of commercial online services. The Internet is a network of networks.

Online marketers can use several vehicles to reach consumers. We'll go into each topics in greater detail later in the book. Here is an executive overview:

Forums are company–sponsored areas that allow the company to interact with its customers and prospects. Forums can include message areas, libraries, conference centers and online stores. Companies can create strong bonds with customers, who become lifelong buyers of products. There are private forums and public forums. Private forums, like the Toyota forum on Prodigy can be used only by current customers. Public forums, like *Time* magazine on America Online, can be accessed by any online subscriber. Both types of forums can be profit centers for information providers, who make money by receiving a percentage of the connect time (the amount of time each consumer stays on that forum) and a "bounty" for each new customer it lures to the online system. Companies can also sell products on some forums.

Message areas enable consumers to talk with one another and with company officials to create relationships. These message areas are called by different names by the online services. CompuServe features forums, America Online calls them forums and clubs, Prodigy names them BBSes and the Internet has newsgroups and mailing lists. These message areas are powerful communication tools that online marketers can use to cultivate goodwill, dispel rumors and build brand awareness. Although advertising is prohibited, there are several subtle ways to create the kinds of dialogues that are permitted. For small businesses and consultants, these informal chats can lead to long–term clients. Tactics are discussed in Chapter 9, E–mail.

Libraries are repositories of files that contain materials the company wants its customers and prospects to read, such as press releases, data sheets and advertisements. Libraries can also be used by software companies to house software programs, demos, updates and fixes that consumers can retrieve.

Electronic mail is the primary communications vehicle between consumers and companies. Online services offer a tremendous amount of flexibility for online marketers, who can automatically respond to customers' e–mail requests for information 24 hours a day. Consumers can also place orders via e–mail. You won't lose sales, because your e–mail operator is always on duty.

Electronic malls are places where marketers can sell products. They can be part of a commercial online service or part of the Internet's World Wide Web. Merchants can also lease space from a new breed of electronic landlords who package offerings from companies. Electronic malls give consumers the opportunity to read about products and see a picture or hear a description before placing their order. Consumers can also send e–mail for more information—and read it almost instantly, thanks to automated mail systems.

Conferences enable marketers to build relationships with consumers by providing information, speakers or famous personalities (such as Mick Jagger and William Shatner).

News and financial services provide consumers with information from wire services and newspapers.

Online marketers can also use the traditional tools of their trade to reach consumers, including advertising, public relations and promotions. However, each needs to be adapted to take advantage of the dynamic, interactive and responsive nature of the online community—an upscale market of mostly college–educated males who seem not to suffer fools (or advertisers) lightly. Each of these topics will be explored in greater detail throughout this book.

Advertising (Chapter 11) can take advantage of the technology to deliver highly interactive messages in which consumers can learn of new products, comparison–shop and buy in a matter of minutes. By using sight and sound, advertisers can create a personal interactive selling relationship in a way that catalogs cannot.

Public Relations (Chapter 12) can create exposure to products and services subtly and intelligently. Tactics can be used to create an identity and boost sales for a product, service or consultant. An important advantage of online systems is that marketers can reach consumers directly without the intervention of the media.

There are many tools available to the online marketer. To be effective, online marketers must create an informative, entertaining and interactive experience for consumers.

The Name Game

Each online service has different names for virtually every function it offers. Strip away the technobabble and all the online services have the following element in common: Customers and companies can communicate directly with each other through electronic mail and files stored on the computer system. From this marvelously simple starting point comes a great confusion of terms.

The Internet and commercial online systems don't like to speak English. In fact until recently, you had to know how to use UNIX to use the Internet. Even today, as more and more systems are becoming easier to use with the help of graphical interfaces that let users point and click on menu items and icons to find information, each system prefers to use its own terminology for different aspects of the system. For example, the place where you find people with similar interests on the Internet is a USENET newsgroup, on CompuServe a forum, on America Online a forum or club and on Prodigy a bulletin board. Why? Don't ask. Will systems ever use the same terminology? Not likely.

This chart compares the various terms to one another so that you can see at a glance what each system is trying to say. It is sort of like seeing a foreign language chart that shows you how to say "bread" in English, Spanish, French, German and Italian.

Table 3–1. Terms used on the Internet and commercial online services.

What You Do	Internet	CompuServe	America Online	Prodigy
Send/receive files	FTP	Upload, download	Upload, download	Upload, download
Find people with similar interests	Newsgroups, mailing lists	Forum	Clubs, forums	Bulletin board
Buy things	The Web	The Electronic Mall	Marketplace	Everywhere
Place classified advertisements	Selected newsgroups	Classifieds	Classifieds and online newspapers	Classifieds and online newspapers
Person who runs the place where people meet	Owner (list) moderator (newsgroup) webmaster (World Wide Web)	Host, Moderator, Sysop (Systems Operator), Host	Host	Board Leader

Targeting Your Audience

Marketing has been described as the process of making selling easy. That can be especially true with online marketing. Convincing consumers to buy can be easy if you know which service your consumer uses and which messages will influence her. You will fail if you don't understand how the services differ and how they attract different audiences or if you present a message that is inappropriate for that community or the online media.

One of the first steps in putting together an outstanding marketing plan is to determine what audience you want to attract and find the appropriate places to reach that consumer. To do otherwise would lead to a tremendous waste of time, money and energy. By carefully targeting your market, you will get more bang for the buck.

This is especially true of the evolving field of online marketing. One of the great benefits of online marketing is the ability to target your audience. Each commercial online service has demographics on its average user so that you can see the differences between the services. Also, thanks to forums, bulletin boards, newsgroups and mailing lists that cover every imaginable interest known to humankind, online services attract people with varied interests and tastes. Your job is to determine which consumers need your product and find the appropriate medium to reach them.

The Internet

Executive Summary

With more than 25 million members worldwide, the Internet offers a vast, worldwide audience for marketers. Even the commercial online services are hooking into the Internet, offering a rich new source of potential buyers. The Internet offers the best multimedia tools for presenting information, through the World Wide Web, a hypermedia environment (in other words, a place where marketers can present their information with pictures, animation, sound and text). Because of the simple tools needed to create a Web home page, or virtual storefront, any business can create an online presence for a modest investment to showcase their products and take orders. As with other systems, advertising is prohibited on the USENET newsgroups and mailing lists.

The Internet is difficult to use. This should change in 1995 as vendors introduce software programs.

The Internet has a unique culture that must be respected. The feeling among users is that the system is a big democracy, in which governing principles come from the grass roots, not from a central authority. Information and software are exchanged freely. Among old–timers there is an antibusiness sentiment for companies that abuse system resources by "spamming" the network (placing the same message in many different newsgroups) or placing ads in improper locations. Companies that give resources back to the Internauts are welcomed. Therefore, marketing must be conducted in a new, noninvasive, nonthreatening style that is full of information: two–way interactive dialogue.

Overview

Founded in 1968 as a Defense Department project to develop a worldwide communications system, ARPANET (the original name) connected computers located in seven universities. Today there are more than 2 million host machines linking more than 25 million people in 154 countries. The Internet is growing rapidly, with some estimates reaching one million new users a month. However, this is difficult to prove. Further, the commercial online systems CompuServe, America Online and Prodigy are creating accessways for their members to use the Internet and growth should continue to explode. Microsoft boasts that its Windows 95 operating system includes all the tools a person needs to navigate the Internet.

The Internet is a network of networks. It has no central authority, no governing body and no official policies on anything. It is as free–form as an amoeba. Customers can create anything they want, such as a virtual store on the World Wide Web or a private mailing list—provided they have the technical ability. Some have called the Internet the "Wild West" because there is no law and order—anything goes. Well, almost anything. Its main core of users come from the science and education fields and have used the service as an electronic library and meeting hall for years. In the past two years, this nucleus has been overrun with newcomers called "newbies," who must learn the "netiquette" (the etiquette of the Internet) to participate without having their heads handed to them in "flame" (outright insulting messages, often containing profanity and a comment about the person's lack of intelligence or manhood).

Audience at a Glance

Computer professionals, scientists and college students.

Demographics

Although statistics are hard to come by and are easily debated, recent reports claim there are 25 million people on the Internet, with another million signing up every month. Matrix Information and Directory Services conducts ongoing investigations about the size, shape and other characteristics of the Internet, estimates there are 27.5 million people who exchange e–mail with others, while 13.5 million users of 3.5 million computers are equipped to use the interactive services of the World Wide Web, in either the graphic or text form, as of October 1994. For information, send e–mail to `mids@tic.com` or visit their site on the World Wide Web `http://www.tic.com`. Matrix also publishes two magazines, *Matrix News* and *Matrix Maps Quarterly*. Its editor, John S. Quarterman is quoted frequently in *The New York Times* for his surveys of the Internet.

In addition, users of CompuServe, America Online, Prodigy and smaller commercial online services have access to the Internet's e–mail, USENET newsgroups and mailing lists, which raises the potential audience by another 6–7 million. Commercial online users also will have access to the World Wide Web in 1995, according to company announcements. This growth is staggering and has led to hockey stick–like lines on graphs. However, no one keeps detailed reports on who these users are; therefore, precise demographics are not available. The commercial online services keep audited demographics, which are detailed later in this chapter. If there aren't any auditors of Internet statistics, you might wonder how they are compiled and projected. These widely published figures come from estimates on the number of companies, governmental organizations and institutions that have access to the Internet. There were roughly 20,000 commercial accounts and 24,000 educational and governmental accounts as of mid–1994. From those accurate numbers, people have extrapolated the higher figures based on the number of people at each site who could use the Internet. In other words, if Really Big Company gets an Internet account, it is counted once in the master list of sites. RBC then provides accounts for each of its 1,000 employees, some of whom surf the Net, while others use it only for e–mail. For recent statistics, send e–mail to info@internetinfo.com.

Still, it is safe to make some assumptions about the purchasing decisions of the people who use the Internet. Because most colleges and universities in the United States are on the Internet and give free accounts to their students, faculty and staff, you can accurately project that these markets are strong demographic components of the Internet. Commercial vendors should note that these groups purchase entertainment services, music CDs, jeans, clothing, health and beauty aids, fast food, beer and other consumer products.

Scientists and researchers at these institutions also have free accounts. Through anecdotal research, these group members strongly dislike commercial activity on the Internet. They feel they have "important work to do" and prefer to use the system to send e–mail to colleagues around the world. Increased traffic from the dreaded newbies slows the delivery of their mail. Hence, they have an animosity toward newcomers and a fear that commercial activity will increase the popularity of their once–exclusive club.

Another key point to remember is that these people hate intrusive advertising. You must cater to them by inducing them to seek out information about your company. Direct mail is equal to direct disaster on the Internet.

Marketers also can assume users must be fairly sophisticated computer users because they must master arcane commands to navigate the Internet. Even setting up an account to use the popular Mosaic software requires a person who has the ability to understand sophisticated computer operations. This will change as Microsoft's Windows 95 operating system becomes widely distributed. If all the estimated 60 million people already using Microsoft operating systems buy the new software and go online, the nature of the Internet could change almost overnight in terms of numbers of users, income, interests, computing ability and attitude toward commercial operations.

Since late 1994, commercial interest from business consumers has grown considerably. As more businesses go online, the composition of the Internet will change dramatically. The most important note is that commercial activities will be welcomed, not dreaded, by those new members who are attracted to the Internet because of commercial opportunities.

Resources

- E–mail and mailbots (automatic response e–mail, similar to fax–back systems).
- Conferencing through IRC Chat and software services from private companies.
- More than 8,000 USENET newsgroups, which are bulletin boards where people with similar interests discuss topics of interest. Business areas include commerce, entrepreneurs, investments and multilevel marketing, investments. Noncommercial topics range the gamut from Tibetan folklore to physics to sex to the *Melrose Place* TV show. New topics are added almost every day and virtually anyone can create one. Messages on newsgroups are called "articles" or "posts." This is important to note, because other systems use different terms for the exact same functions. Thousands of private mailing lists also exist. These are like newsgroups in that people with similar interests can exchange notes with one another, but people must subscribe to these groups. Some mailing lists automatically accept new members, while others approve or deny subscriptions. Another difference is that people must go to the newsgroup to read messages. On mailing lists, every message is sent to every subscriber's personal e–mail box. In other words, newsgroup members must actively seek their messages, while mailing list members passively receive their messages. That means, if you post an article to a newsgroup, a member must go to that area to read it. If you post an article to a mailing list, it is sent to the subscriber's mailbox, where he or she is sure to see it.
- Reference databases include government sources and hundreds of colleges and universities.
- News from the Associated Press delivered through ClariNet and the *San Francisco Examiner*.
- Financial information from Dow Jones News Service and stock quotes.
- Travel services.
- Entertainment.

Opportunities for Marketers

The Internet offers many tools for marketing: The World Wide Web home pages, Gopher sites and FTP sites are basically libraries where companies can place files of information about products and services that customers can read at their leisure 24 hours a day from anywhere in the world. Web home pages are the coolest of the lot—and the easiest to use. Web home pages are multimedia and interactivity in action. It is just what the futurist ordered! In this system, the business structures and posts its files as hypertext links that allow customers to browse to their heart's content. Consumers can click on a main subject area such as toasters and then see pictures of every toaster in stock, followed by short descriptions. If they want more information, they can click on the term and find more and more detail. Whatever the business puts online, the customer can read. Marketers can add pictures, text and sound to their Web home page. It is way cool. For marketers, the Web has become the place to post brochures, data sheets and information about their businesses. Examples of Web home pages are provided in Chapter 7.

Here's how they differ. Gopher sites don't have multimedia capabilities. However, they do have the same ability to transfer files to consumers or allow the files to be read online. Information on a Gopher site is constructed as a series of menus. Consumers must drill down from menu to menu to find information. An FTP site is strictly a file transfer system. It works, but it isn't cool and is difficult to use.

E–mail and mailbots (automated mail systems, similar to fax–back systems) can also help marketers get the word out).

USENET newsgroups and mailing lists can be used by marketers to find out what people are talking about in more than 8,000 topics. Company officials can use these message areas to answer consumer's questions but are not allowed to advertise or promote their products or companies.

Management's Attitudes Toward Business and Marketing

Since there is no official central authority, there is no one in high places to say boo to online marketing. Many companies are beginning to explore the concept of online marketing, from advertising and publicity to sales and market share.

Consumers' Attitudes Toward Business and Marketing

Long–term members take a dim view of shameless self–promotion in USENET newsgroups and mailing lists. They are firm believers in netiquette—the etiquette of networks—described in Chapter 4. However, this attitude is changing rapidly as more and more people join the Internet. It is safe to say that people who don't jump for joy when they get direct mail at home will threaten to kill you if you send them direct mail online. Don't take their threats seriously, but don't sleep with both eyes closed either. Message areas, like Newsgroups and mailing lists can be used to create relationships using public relations techniques described in Chapter 9, Building Relationships with E–mail, and Chapter 12, Public Relations. Online marketers can make amends by giving back a valuable resource— information, not commercial hype—to the community. Examples are software, reports and surveys. The Internet is a friendly place if you practice reciprocity.

Online marketers won't suffer the slings and arrows of outraged Internauts if the marketers post their information and interactive advertisements on the designated shopping areas of the Internet, namely, the World Wide Web and Gopher sites. That's because people seek out information. That's okay. People object when advertising is thrust upon them. As the Internet grows in popularity and more mainstream people come online, commercial services will be a valued and accepted part of the system. Marketers should look to the World Wide Web as the most likely place to sell and advertise products.

Navigation

Although people talk about cruising the digital highway, you wouldn't want to set your computer on cruise control on the Net. You'd crash. The Internet is difficult to navigate and doesn't have a main menu system as the commercial online services do. There are several directories that list commercial sites. New companies come aboard so quickly that printed directories can be out of date as soon as they are published. New software from many vendors will make the system easier to steer. However, you should expect to devote serious time to learning to use the system and to promoting your World Wide Web home page. As far as putting material online, don't try this at home, kiddies. You will need a consultant to prepare your materials and load them to the server for all to see.

America Online

America Online
8619 Westwood Center Drive
Vienna, VA 22182–2285
703–448–8700
800–827–6364

Executive Summary

The fastest–growing commercial online service, America Online (AOL), with 2 million subscribers as of early 1995, claims to be the most active with 750,000 sessions held each day. Only recently AOL announced plans to offer products for sale. Its 2Market section will feature products from 25 well–known catalogs and companies. Kmart also announced that it would operate a sales center within AOL. America Online has been actively adding forums run by some of the country's largest and most respected magazines, which are exploring new frontiers of electronic interactive communications. The forums, run by newspapers, magazines, software publishers and other companies, are also profit centers for these businesses, which receive a portion of the connect charges of customers time spent online, as well as a bounty for each subscriber the forum introduces to the service. America Online is also home to ABC and NBC, which operate forums that display information about their shows and allow consumers to talk to them. A new graphical interface design was introduced in 1994 to make the system easier to use. The company is actively offering links to the Internet, including e–mail, Gopher and Web services.

Overview

Founded in 1985, the corporate mission of America Online (Fig. 3–1) is to create electronic communities. When the service was launched, it called its customers "members" when other services referred to their patrons as "users."

Figure 3–1. America Online opening screen. (Courtesy of America Online)

America Online focuses on interactive communities and provides a wide variety of features, including electronic mail, news and magazine, weather, sports, stock quotes, software files, computing support online classes and forums to discuss lifestyles and sports.

"America Online is highly regarded for its proprietary, easy–to–use graphical interfaces. The company has developed a flexible, scaleable architecture that enables us to rapidly embrace new opportunities—and to operate services at a relatively low cost," an AOL spokesman says. "As we move closer to the mass market and into more traditional consumer devices such as television, demand for a more graphical, enriching online experience will grow, and we are well positioned to play a leadership role."

America Online has been praised for its interface and technology. It has won awards from *PC Magazine* as a service that does things right.

America Online is participating in a number of new technologies, such as using cable TV as the conduit into PCs, and has announced support for TCP/IP and wireless.

Resources

America Online offers subscribers a wide variety of services including:

- E–mail.
- Conferences.
- 25 newspapers and magazines including the online versions of *Time, The New York Times* and the *Chicago Tribune.*
- Financial information, such as company reports and stock quotes.
- 300 forums run by companies to provide customer support, including Apple, IBM, Microsoft, Novell, Lotus and Tandy.
- 50 forums designed to appeal to lifestyles and hobbies, such as health, cooking, wine and sports.
- Travel services, including Eaasy Sabre from American Airlines, which allows consumers to buy tickets online.
- 60 information databases ranging from the Bible to the Internet (and its vast databases of information) to the Library of Congress.
- Entertainment areas, such as Hollywood Online and NBC Online.
- Opportunities for software publishers to operate forums to provide customer support, demonstrations, new products, press releases, shareware, updates and patches.
- Internet access for e–mail, USENET newsgroups, mailing lists, Gopher, FTP and World Wide Web.

Audience at a Glance

The young and cool.

Demographics

The company would not release detailed demographics on its users. America Online announced that it expects to have 3 million subscribers by the end of 1995.

The average age of a member is 39, the majority are college graduates (no exact figure is given) and 65–70% are male. The average household income is between $40–$50,000. They use AOL primarily for personal use, entertainment and work.

"Although the majority of AOL subscribers are men, women increasingly are signing on to our service," a spokesman said. "Most of our subscribers are college educated." Income figures were not revealed, but labeled as well to do.

Management's Attitude Toward Business and Marketing

America Online is aggressively pursuing relationships with information providers. The company has established strategic alliances with dozens of companies, including Time Warner, ABC, NBC, MTV, Knight–Ridder, Tribune, Hachette, IBM and Apple.

In late 1994, AOL announced strategic initiatives designed to take greater advantage of emerging market opportunities and to strengthen the company's position in the worldwide market for interactive services. "The focus of the AOL Services Company is on propelling the America Online brand into the lead as the Number One consumer online service and then solidifying a sustainable leadership position by enhancing the content and presentation of the service, developing new revenue streams from interactive advertising and transactions and strengthening ties with strategic partners," says AOL President Steve Case. "By continuing to expand the diversity and quality of the content and by making the content more useful and engaging through innovations in navigation, personalization and multimedia presentation, we believe we can move the AOL brand into the lead as the Number One consumer online service in the United States. We will then be well positioned to develop 'electronic markets' that marry information, communications and transactional capabilities. These electronic markets will be valued by our subscribers, as they will help them make better decisions more conveniently and they will be valued by our partners, as they will be the source of new revenue streams that can increase their profits."

"Now that AOL has reached more than 1 million subscribers, we are beginning to explore new ways to serve our customers by creating 'electronic markets,' " an AOL spokesman says. "Companies interested in advertising on AOL would find that the service combines the most useful information about a particular product, including discussion forums among other potential buyers, and information centers for additional information about the product(s). In other words, the information would be tailored to specific audiences in an engaging, non–intrusive fashion that provides the customer with the information he/she wants when he/she wants it. While AOL is not ready to offer its predictions about the future of online advertising, we welcome discussions with any potential advertisers."

America Online initiated AOL Greenhouse, a program designed for entrepreneurs to create unique online content and new interactive services. America Online will select a handful of creative, entrepreneurial online crusaders to offer new services tailored specifically to America Online and the Internet. In exchange, America Online will provide Greenhouse participants with access to its members, online promotion, participation in the America Online Web site and other Internet initiatives, production support and seed equity funding.

"The magic of this new medium is the ability for entrepreneurs to create compelling new content and help build an interactive community. We are looking forward to working with a new breed of content and service providers to provide fun, creative and, most of all, compelling content to our member community," says Ted Leonsis, president of AOL Services Company.

Opportunities for Marketers

America Online began offering its first shopping services in late 1994 with 2Market, a company that provides interactive shopping services for CD–ROM and online. Some 25 companies are offering products online including Lands' End, 800–Flowers, Crutchfield, Hammacher Schlemmer, the Metropolitan

Museum of Art, the Museum of Modern Art, Sony Music, Windham Hill Records, Sharper Image and Spiegel.

Classified advertising is available in a company–sponsored area, as well as with several of its online newspapers, including the *Chicago Tribune* and *San Jose Mercury News.*

While there hasn't been a large commercial presence on AOL until recently, there have been pockets of sales opportunities, which customers apparently have enjoyed. The Komando Forum has been selling software products for years with great success. Online travel services have also been available.

America Online forums and clubs do not permit advertising.

Companies can create their own forums which can include advertising, information, customer support and other materials to build relationships with customers.

America Online does not discuss growth figures, revenues, dollars spent, and so forth, a company spokesman says, nor does it speculate on the future of this market, the costs of operating an online "store" or shopper demographics (the last because of privacy concerns).

Customers' Attitudes Toward Business and Marketing

America Online has not had a comprehensive shopping mall or advertising services until recently, and so it is not known how consumers will react to these marketing methods. Since AOL does not permit advertising in forums, there won't be a loud outcry against advertisers, as there is with misguided marketers on the Internet. Since subscribers must actively seek out commercial storefronts, it can be assumed that these people won't be offended by marketers. Those subscribers who aren't interested won't go to a store.

Navigation

Navigation is easy, thanks to a graphical interface, keyword searching and online help system. New members can practice and get answer to their questions free in the Members to Members area.

CompuServe Information Services

CompuServe Information Services
5000 Arlington Centre Boulevard
Columbus, OH 43220
614–457–8600
800–848–8199

Executive Summary

The oldest commercial online service with more than 1.5 million subscribers, CompuServe (CIS) (Fig. 3–2) has pioneered virtual retailing with The Electronic Mall, which features catalogs and ordering from more than 100 companies, including J.C. Penny and Lands' End. CompuServe introduced a CD–ROM add–on that will help merchants present multimedia catalogs to potential customers. A new graphical interface was introduced in 1994 to help consumers use the service more easily. CompuServe offers forums as a profit center for information providers like CNN and *U.S. News & World Report*. Support forums are featured from nearly every major, and many small, computer hardware manufacturers and software publishers. CompuServe also maintains a classified advertisement section. CompuServe reaches a worldwide audience and has announced plans for a direct mail advertising campaign to triple European memberships to 450,000 by April 1996.

Overview

Founded in 1969 as a computer time–sharing service, CompuServe is a leading global provider of computer–based information and communications services to businesses and personal computer owners. Its goal has been to develop problem solving computer services that provide companies and individuals with reliable, cost–effective access to host server and data communications services.

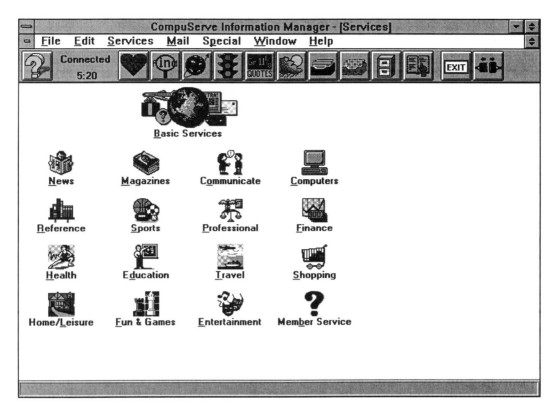

Figure 3–2. CompuServe opening screen. (Compliments of CompuServe)

A wholly–owned subsidiary of H&R Block, Inc., CIS has the large financial resources and support of the parent company to continue to be an aggressive, growth–oriented company. Revenues for the fiscal year ending April 30, 1994, were $429 million.

CompuServe sees advances in technology, including cable and personal digital assistants, as potential new vehicles for communicating information to a broader audience more quickly, less expensively and in richer form. "We are engaged in research and discussions in several of these areas and are developing strategies based on judgment of which technologies will be successful," a spokeswoman says, "The ultimate goal is to expand CompuServe's presence and success in the ever–growing market for information services."

Resources

CompuServe offers a rich menu of services, including:

- E–mail.
- Conferencing.
- More than 600 forums. These forums are used for three main purposes:
  - Companies provide customer support and product updates. Most major computer and software companies use these forums for online support and for building rapport with customers. Such companies include Microsoft, Novell, Lotus, Borland and Symantec.
  - Professional organizations to encourage the exchange of information among members. Typical groups include marketers, investors and entrepreneurs
  - Lifestyle topics that enrich the lives of its members, including heath, recreation, sexuality and entertainment.
- More than 50 newspapers are online, including the *Boston Globe*, *Chicago Tribune*, *Detroit Free Press* and *Washington Post*. Full–text, searchable articles are available from more than 500 publications.
- Financial news and information services, including investment analysis, news, financial forums, earnings projections and economic outlook, company information from Citibank, Standard & Poor's, D&B Dun's Market Identifiers, TRW Business Credit Profiles and interfaces to computer software programs and stock quotes.
- Travel services, Eaasy Sabre and Worldspan Travelshopper, which allow subscribers to find flight information and book flights, Golf Course Directory, Zagat's Restaurant Survey and the Bed and Breakfast Directory and ABC Worldwide Hotel Guide.
- Entertainment, including movie reviews, movie clips with full motion video and stereo audio, syndicated columnist Marilyn Beck, and Entertainment Drive, which puts consumers, moguls and Hollywood actors in touch with each other.

- Internet access including e–mail, USENET newsgroups, mailing lists and World Wide Web.

Audience at a Glance

Business people.

Demographics

CompuServe has more than 1.5 million members in the United States and 2.2 million worldwide in 138 countries. The service has grown rapidly: 1,200 in 1979 to 548,000 in 1989 to 1.5 million in 1993. An independent survey of its users conducted by Erdos & Morgan/MPG indicates that, they tend to be well–educated professionals with a relatively high household income. Other interesting results:

- 92% are male.
- Median age: 41.7 years. 60% are between the ages of 25 and 44; 36% are over 45.
- 69% have completed at least a four–year college degree program; 26% have earned a master's degree or doctorate.
- 72% are married; 19% have never married.
- 60% have no children under 18 in the household; 32% have one or two children.
- Average household income is $92,200; 59% have household incomes of $60,000 or more.
- 91% are employed in a business or profession; 28% hold the position of executive or officer; 46% are in professional or technical positions.
- 39% have a home–based business.

CompuServe provides a worldwide market, including 500,000 subscribers in Japan and 140,000 in Europe: CIS has subscribers in more than 140 countries.

Opportunities for Marketers

CompuServe's The Electronic Mall allows customers to browse and order products from 125 merchants, ranging from Lands' End and J.C. Penny to specialty stores selling gourmet food, consumer electronics and pharmaceuticals.

"During a recession–plagued economy the past few years, the Mall has continued to show steady, substantial growth in sales. Through June, 1994, the number of accesses increased by 90% over 1993, the number of orders placed rose by 57% and sales were up 50%," a spokesman says. The average sale was $71.04.

Companies can use video, sound, graphics or multimedia to promote their products with CompuServe CD, the multimedia enhancement to the information service. Electronic Mall merchants such as computer retailers and flower delivery operations are reaching members using audio and video. A hotlink from the CD to the information service also allows them to log on and make a purchase.

Advertisers in the Mall receive exposure in the monthly CompuServe magazine, which is distributed to all members. New services and promotions are featured in "What's New," which appears to all members when they log on to the service.

Companies can also create and foster relationships with customers by creating forums.

CompuServe has a classified advertising section for members. These ads can range from personal computer equipment for sale to a time–share in a chateau in France.

The newest form of advertising information can be found in *U.S. News & World Report* Forum. Subscribers who have WinCIM 1.3 will see an icon at the lower right–hand corner of the screen called "Promotions." This area gives advertisers in *U.S. News'* print publication a chance to reach those same readers but in an electronic environment. Advertisers include SAAB. This advertising is information–based and includes items like background on the manufacturer, photos of the new models, and the location of the nearest dealer.

The price to participate as a merchant is conducted on a case–by–case basis. On average, the annual investment, complete with advertising in the *CompuServe Magazine*, runs between $20,000 and $80,000, plus a 2% commission payable on each sale, according to CIS spokesman Keith Arnold.

Management's Attitude Toward Business and Marketing

CompuServe is pro–advertising in the right places—in The Electronic Mall, in Classifieds and in forums maintained by commercial vendors and information providers. CompuServe does not condone intrusive advertising.

Consumers Attitudes Toward Business and Marketing

Members seem to like online shopping, with the number of visits, orders and size of orders increasing steadily. Because sysops strike commercial messages from forums, subscribers are not exposed to intrusive advertising in any way, shape or form.

Navigation

Navigating CompuServe is easy, thanks to a graphical user interface, keyword searches, help and manuals. People can find what they are looking for with relative ease. Subscribers can search an index to find out about available services and merchants. When subscribers sign on each time, the What's New feature automatically tells of interesting new places to visit, while the monthly *CompuServe Magazine* provides additional exposure to the system, its services and its merchants. New members can practice navigating the system free in a special area, so they can overcome their anxieties and learn how to use the system without worrying about ringing up large bills.

Prodigy

Prodigy Service Company
445 Hamilton Avenue
White Plains, NY 10601
800–776–3449

Executive Summary

Without a doubt, Prodigy (Fig. 3–3) is the most advertiser–friendly service available. From its earliest days, Prodigy's screens displayed advertisements from the moment members signed on. A smoothly integrated system entices readers from a "leader" ad or teaser to more detailed information. Because of subscribers' distaste for intrusive advertising, Prodigy decided to eliminate this tactic from message areas, called BBSes, or bulletin boards, in 1994—four years after the company pursued this strategy as a birthright. The leader ads still appear in other areas. Prodigy also uses many static ads, including a new service that features ads resembling card deck advertising. This strategy flies in the face of the perceived belief that online ads must be interactive. The strategy must be working because advertisers are flocking to Prodigy. There are many opportunities to present ads in a glowing environment. Sound, pictures and graphics can illustrate ads and present a very inviting multimedia communication event. Prodigy remains a pro–business environment and claims to be one of the largest sellers of airline tickets, flowers and stock brokerage services.

Overview

Prodigy was founded in 1990 as a joint venture between IBM and Sears. Its charter was to create an interactive advertising and sales medium. From its earliest days, everything about Prodigy says *buy, buy, buy.* Even the screen is displayed with a constant stream of advertising messages. Advertising sponsors include financial services companies, car manufacturers, florists and software publishers.

According to company literature, the PC Financial Network, which operates on Prodigy, is the nation's largest online discount broker, with more than 100,000 accounts and $1 billion in assets. Prodigy says it books more airline tickets than all other PC–based booking services combined.

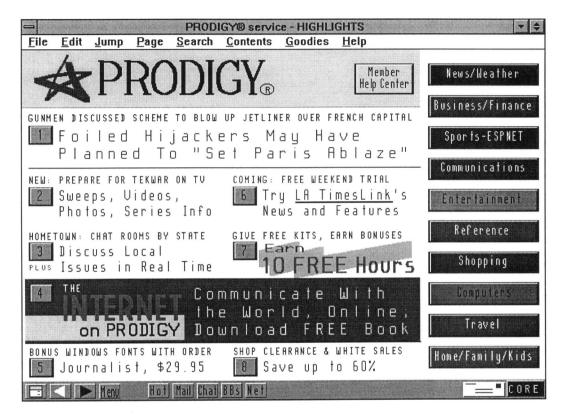

Figure 3–3. Prodigy opening screen. (Courtesy of Prodigy)

Resources

Prodigy offers a wide variety of services, including:

- E–mail with text, picture and sound.
- Conferencing.
- More than 850 bulletin board topics on lifestyles, health, sports and games, with subjects ranging from archaeology to zoology.

Guests such as Jay Leno and Jerry Seinfeld have visited the boards to talk to members.

- Prodigy has more than 700 informational and interactive features including news and weather, sports, kids' features, education and games and program highlights for 30 cable networks.
- Reference databases include *Consumer Reports*.
- Nearly a dozen newspapers, including *Newsday*, *Atlanta Journal and Constitution* and *Los Angeles Times*.
- Financial news from Dow Jones News Service and stock quotes.
- Travel services, including Eaasy Sabre, Zagat's Restaurant Reviews, and Mobil Travel Guide.
- Entertainment.
- Internet access includes e–mail, USENET newsgroups and World Wide Web.

Audience at a Glance

Families and children.

Demographics

Prodigy has more than 2.2 million members, the largest of any commercial online service. Unlike other commercial online services, Prodigy counts each family member separately, instead of as one subscriber. The ratio of men to women is the most balanced of all online systems: 60% men, 40% women. More than 300,000 children use Prodigy. Another interesting fact is that 300,000 Prodigy members are entrepreneurs who run businesses with 10 or fewer people. Prodigy is available only in the United States. Other statistics:

- Median age is 36 but 15% are 18 or younger.
- Median income is $60,529.
- 41% are parents.
- 75% have attended college; 43% graduated college.

Opportunities for Marketers

Advertisements on Prodigy cost between $20,000 and $40,000 per month. Prices vary depending on a variety of factors, including the length of the message. Companies can buy "leader" ads that run at the bottom of the screen or a leader ad that "toggles" to additional screens of information. For example, Coors placed a beer ad with a football theme for five screens.

Any company can advertise—from a "two–man flower shop to a nationally known company like Kraft Foods," says Carol Wallace, program manager, communications, for Prodigy.

Prodigy maintains several areas for members to buy classified advertising. Prodigy has its own section as well as those from daily newspapers, including *Atlanta Constitution and Journal*, *New York Newsday* and *Los Angeles Times*.

Companies can create forums on Prodigy. These forums allow for nationally known businesses to display information about their products and build rapport with subscribers by answering messages. Such companies include Toyota, Saturn, AAA of Southern California and Fidelity Investments.

Prodigy also has an online shopping service. Merchants includes J.C. Penny, Lands' End, Spiegel and Patagonia, as well as dozens of specialty shops like PC Flowers.

Prodigy also has facilities for companies to display graphics of their products. However, graphics should not be confused with pictures. Graphics are line art drawings that look nice and inviting but lack the rich detail seen in pictures. Transmission time is adequate at 9600 baud. Prodigy can send audio clips to users. So far, this feature is available in the news services, but not in shopping areas. News also can present pictures and display them in a reasonable time period. We can assume that, since the technology is available online, it is only a matter of time before these enhancements come to shopping as well. Windows users can see picture ads.

Management's Attitude Toward Business and Marketing

Prodigy couldn't be more conducive to online retailing and advertising. The system was designed for this purpose. Management is taking strong steps to integrate multimedia into advertising and shopping services.

Consumers' Attitudes Toward Business and Marketing

Customers expect advertising and apparently react well to it, as they buy lots of products and services.

Navigation

Navigation is easy with the graphical user interface, index, keywords and online help.

New Commercial Online Services

Several new online services began operating in late 1994 and early 1995, too late, for our purposes, to gather statistics on users in a meaningful way. Here is an overview of these services.

Apple Computer's eWorld

eWorld
Apple Computer Inc.
20525 Mariani Avenue
Cupertino, CA 95014
408–996–1010

eWorld, an online service created by Apple Computers in 1994, has a very small community of approximately 40,000 subscribers, all of whom use Macintosh or Newton computers, a very targeted audience. Apple announced that the service will grow its subscriber base by bundling the service with all Macintoshes. Also planned for expansion is the ability of PC computer users to subscribe to the service in 1995. Apple is marketing the service worldwide, which presents opportunities for companies to market products to a worldwide audience.

eWorld for Macintosh is "an online town square," according to Apple, which provides a global electronic mail system, together with news, information and other services from approximately 100 partners such as Reuters America Inc., Tribune Media Services, ZiffNet/Mac and *Inc*. Magazine Online.

The eWorld community consists of an electronic neighborhood of buildings, each representing a specific area of interest. Each building contains a series of online publications from well–known publishers, containing valuable information along with interactive conferences and discussion boards. For example, people starting small businesses can browse through the latest issue of magazines such as *Inc*. and *Upside* for ideas, then explore an online publication called *Working Solo* — a publication designed for people working in small businesses — and join in online discussions with other eWorld subscribers with similar interests to share thoughts and ideas.

eWorld is the best place for Apple customers to get the most out of their Macintosh, Newton or Workgroup Server. Many software and hardware vendors offer support and information forums, including Claris Corporation, Supermac Technology, CE Software and Global Village.

In the start–up phase, it is too soon to tell anything about its demographics or the customers' views on commerce. Management indicated that it is interested in offering sales opportunities to companies. Navigation is easy with the graphical user interface, index, keywords and online help.

Microsoft Network

> Microsoft Network
> One Microsoft Way
> Redmond, WA 98052–6399
> 206–882–8080

The Microsoft Network is designed to provide easy, affordable access to the rapidly expanding world of electronic information and communication for users of the Windows 95 operating system.

"The Microsoft Network's technology and business model is designed to help content and service providers fully realize the potential of the online market," according to Microsoft literature. "The Microsoft Network uses a platform model in which content and service providers will have maximum flexibility in creating products and pricing their services. Microsoft anticipates that providers will offer various pricing options, such as subscriptions, online transactions and ticketed events. Other services will be supported by advertising and commerce."

Unlike other commercial online services, content and service providers will have control over the look of their services. To enable the easy creation of rich multimedia content and services, Microsoft plans to provide a complete tool set and sponsor developer and design conferences to educate providers on how to make best use of the online medium.

"The Microsoft Network will offer interactive online communities built around ideas, people, products and brands," the company says. It is designed to bring customers affordable and easy–to–use access to electronic mail, bulletin boards and chat rooms on a variety of topics, file libraries, and Internet newsgroups. Members will be able to access online tips, add–ons, tools, product information and technical support directly from the Microsoft area of the service.

The Microsoft Network will be accessible in more than 35 countries and its client application will be localized in 20 languages.

AT&T Interchange Online Network

> AT&T Interchange Online Network
> 25 First Street
> Cambridge, MA 02141
> 617–252–5000

AT&T Interchange Online Network is a next–generation publishing platform that hosts a collection of special–interest online services that make it easy to access and use electronic information. The service will be commercially available in the middle of 1995, according to company documents.

As a next–generation publishing platform, Interchange provides publishers with an advanced architecture and editorial tools that enable them to build attractive, profitable franchises and to control every aspect of online publishing—including presentation of their brand identity, layout of their content, pricing and advertising. Pilot publishing partners who have announced plans to develop special–interest services on Interchange include Ziff–Davis Interactive—publishers of learning magazines about computing including *PC* magazine, *PC Computing* and others—the *Washington Post*, the Minneapolis–based *Star Tribune* and *Cowles Business Media*.

Interchange makes it easy for members to find and use information on the service and to participate in active communities drawn together by special interests. Interchange's graphical environment, hypertext links and powerful searching capabilities come together to give members the most engaging, informative online experience possible.

Originally a division of Ziff Communications Company, Interchange was purchased in late 1994 by AT&T Corp. Interchange complements and advances AT&T's strategy of providing open and intelligent "hosting" networks in which publishers, software companies, information providers and others can offer their products and services to their customers.

Marketplace MCI

Marketplace MCI offers an electronic shopping mall that it claims is safe for credit card transactions, toll–free nationwide access to the Internet and consulting and development services for businesses. MCI charges small businesses $2,000 a month to be connected as retailers to its electronic shopping mall on the Internet. Larger companies pay more. "Our goal is simple. When people think Internet, we want them to think MCI," says Vinton Cerf, MCI senior vice president of data architecture and codeveloper of the Internet.

Other Online Services

Numerous specialized online bulletin boards serve the needs of niche markets. The Women's Wire, for example, offers information and chat services on a range of issues relating to women. Because major online services are so male–oriented, this service stands out as a means of reaching an audience of women.

Genie, Delphi, Echo and the Well are respected, long–standing commercial online services that have devoted followings but small market share.

Thousands of privately owned and operated bulletin boards reach audiences with specific interests, such as science fiction, investing, sex, specific software programs, computer games, the environment and right– and left–wing politics. Many BBSes and smaller commercial online services offer e–mail access to the Internet. *Boardwatch* has information on the most popular BBSes and issues of the day `subscriptions@boardwatch.com, 1–800–933–6038`.

Summary

The Internet and commercial online services can offer a rich supply of tools to reach and influence targeted demographic groups. Each service has its strengths, weaknesses and audiences. By understanding these differences, online marketers can find the right markets for their products.

CHAPTER 4

Netiquette: Rules and Restrictions for Online Marketing

The rules of the road for online marketers are summed up in a single word—netiquette—the etiquette of networks. You would no sooner venture onto the Information Superhighway without practicing netiquette than you would drive a car in a foreign country without first checking to see if you should drive on the left side of the road or the right. A book on online marketing that does not point out the importance of the netiquette would be remiss indeed. For without netiquette, an online marketer would wind up as roadkill along the Information Superhighway.

Before you yawn and skip this chapter, be forewarned: This isn't your grandmother's etiquette. We're not talking about which fork to use with which course. We are talking about the rules of the road of online services. Violate them at your own risk—all the good work you planned will go up in smoke!

In this chapter, you will learn:

- What netiquette is and why it is important.
- Netiquette for online marketers.
- The rules of netiquette.
- How to put emotion into your messages with smileys.
- How you can market without fear of flaming.

The Information Superhighway holds vast promise for marketers who want to sell and advertise products online—but only for those who master the rules of the road. Online marketers must know which systems permit commercial activity and where. Violate these rules and you will be kicked off the system or your ads will be intercepted by administrators. Also, you need to understand the culture of the community of online systems, which seems to live for the opportunity to "flame" offenders of netiquette. A flame is a nasty note, filled with curses, threats, bad words and irrational rantings sent with hate and spite. Flagrant offenders of netiquette have been threatened with bodily harm. No one knows if anyone really would carry out those threats, but why bother to raise the ire of such people?

While you and I can agree that this behavior is rude, immature and unnecessary, that doesn't change the fact that flames exist. It is better to learn not to irritate your prospects than try to convert them against their will.

Why is there a need for netiquette? Like etiquette in the analog world, netiquette keeps social order and justice in the digital world. The Internet and commercial online services tolerate advertising in its proper place. They vehemently oppose advertising on its message boards. Most forum administrators on the commercial online services will kill offending messages before they reach the public or shortly thereafter. Violators are subject to ejection from the system. Since there is no central authority on the Internet, the users themselves have taken to policing their message boards. In fact, many rules are written by the subscribers and members. A netiquette of correct behavior is fast evolving on every major online service.

Here are the basic rules of netiquette. Follow them and you will be rewarded with lasting relationships. Ignore them and you'll stand alone.

Netiquette in a Nutshell

The Golden Rule of netiquette can be summed up in five words: *Don't advertise in inappropriate areas.* That seems pretty simple, but to drive the point, home here are a few definitions about what constitutes advertising and examples:

- Blatant promotion for products

  ```
  Hi. I sell sea shells by the seashore and online.
  Does anyone want to buy sea shells? I can make you a
  good offer. Please send me e-mail and I'll respond
  quickly, or call this number, 800-555-5555.
  ```

- Blatant self-promotion for consultants

  ```
  Hi, I prepare taxes for small businesses. If you are
  a small business, I'll do your taxes.
  ```

- Inappropriate messages for the group.

  ```
  I know this group is for people who play bagpipes,
  but you must be concerned with health. I sell a power
  drink that increases stamina while you play bagpipes.
  ```

- Get-rich-quick schemes.

  ```
  You can make a fortune selling my product. Call me
  and I'll tell you how.
  ```

Those messages would probably be killed by the system administrators on the commercial networks before they reached the public. So, if you tried to send the messages, you would be wasting your time. If you tried to send those messages to USENET newsgroups, they would be posted and read by people who have an inherent distaste for advertising. You probably would incur the wrath of hundreds of members, who would flame you with hate mail filled with profanity.

Netiquette and Online Marketers

Advertising is permitted in certain areas for which the advertiser pays the online service provider a fee, just as in newspapers, magazines, TV and radio. Marketers can place classified ads on CompuServe, America Online and Prodigy. They can also create virtual storefronts on the Internet's World Wide Web. They just can't cross the bridge into the discussion areas. Advertising is taboo on the discussion areas, such as the USENET newsgroups and mailing lists on the Internet, forums on CompuServe and America Online and bulletin boards on Prodigy.

Online services have many valid reasons to prohibit advertising in message areas. Here are a few reasons:

- They want to keep the message areas focused on the topic at hand to keep their customers happy.
- They want to make money on selling ads to make investors happy.
- They can't police the claims of unscrupulous advertisers, which would make the Federal Trade Commission (FTC) and the Securities and Exchanges Commission (SEC) unhappy.

Keep the Member Happy

The purpose of the message area is to allow members to meet other people and discuss issues of mutual concern—not to read ads. An occasional ad or note of self-promotion might sneak through, but not many. Violators are reminded of the system policy politely in a private message. Repeat offenders can be banned from online systems or particular forums.

This happened to a pair of lawyers who sent a message to thousands of USENET newsgroups to inform people of their services in helping to obtain green cards for immigrants. The online community calls this "spamming." People took offense at their mailboxes becoming cluttered and message boards filled with the oft-repeated message. They rebelled. They sent hate mail full of threats and curses. Thousands of irate members sent flames to the lawyers' Internet provider. They demanded that the lawyers be kicked off the system so that they couldn't flood the Internet with more advertisements. The Internet provider terminated their subscriptions.

Advertisements in messages are banned because system providers feel that their readers are busy people whose time is at a premium. They can't afford to waste time reading mail that isn't germane to the subject area. Also, on some systems, subscribers pay by the amount of time they are online or for every message they receive. These unwanted messages, therefore, cost readers money! No wonder they don't welcome an intrusive ad—especially one disguised as a message. Nothing can irritate a member more than wasting time scrolling through a seemingly endless list of get-rich-quick messages in his mailbox. Also, since some systems limit the number of messages that can be stored in a mailbox, junk messages could conceivably erase a long-awaited e-mail from a colleague.

Keep the Investors Happy

The Internet, as well as the commercial online services, is seeing a massive growth in commercial applications, shopping malls, catalogs and interactive advertising. These services can make money by charging for advertising space, just as newspapers, television and other media do. They want to control advertising in the proper areas so that they can make money while distributing an editorial and entertainment product that attracts subscribers.

Keep the FTC and SEC Happy

Online marketers are subject to the same laws as other marketers. A federal court has ordered a promotion on the Internet halted in response to a Federal Trade Commission false-advertising complaint.

"As these computer networks continue to grow, we will not tolerate the use of deceptive practices here any more than we have tolerated them on other recently emerged technologies for marketing," FTC Chairman Janet D. Steiger said in announcing the verdict in which the FTC charged a Sacramento, California, company with making false claims in promoting a credit-repair program. The company actually suggested illegal steps, the commission charged.

Online shysters have probably been on online systems since the first computerized bulletin board opened for business. While neophyte consumers might have first thought the best of everyone and never for a second considered the sender's ulterior motives, today's consumers are more wary. Alerted by newspaper accounts of the electronic versions of chain letters and pyramid schemes, today's consumers have been hardened by these following accounts:

- Misleading investment advice. Nearly every online system has an investment forum in which people can post questions or write messages. Many people post honest questions and answers relating to evaluations of the future direction of the market and stocks. However, some unscrupulous people have tried to manipulate prices of stocks by touting favorites on these forums. The Securities and Exchange Commission has warned employees and relatives of employees from several companies about giving stock tips online to boost the price of their stock.
- Get-rich-quick schemes. Scam artists try to post messages offering business deals that sound too good be true.
- Operators of network marketing and multilevel marketing programs seem to think the Internet is paved with prospects. It isn't. They are wasting their time and that of the Internauts.

Special Considerations for Online Publicity

The effective online marketer respects the rules of the commercial online services and the netiquette of the Internet. Like Karate masters, they learn to use the power of the force instead of fighting it. Three considerations should be added for online marketers:

1. Message length.
2. Appropriateness of topic.
3. Spamming.

Message Length

Since electronic mail is the main form of communication between parties on an online system, members get many pieces of mail each day. Message length becomes an issue. To get their attention, messages should be short, not longer than 24 lines, which is about the size of a computer monitor. This works out to about 240 words, which is almost the same amount as a double-spaced piece of regular typing paper. These messages should provide the gist of the material to be covered and ask readers if they want more information. Once permission is given, the follow-up message can be as long as needed to tell the story properly. If you follow this procedure, you will not be a victim of the kill file.

Appropriateness of Topic

When you visit a discussion group, you will see a subject line indicating the topic at hand. It could be anything from "need advice" to "looking for a job" to "new and need help." What these messages have in common is that people are looking for answers to specific questions. It is considered rude to jump into a conversation with a topic that doesn't match the one in the subject line. If you want to discuss something, send a private note, or start a new message with a new subject.

Spamming

Spamming is a technique of posting your messages to many discussion groups. You might think that multiple messages are a good way of blanketing your target audience. However, if you do this, you will invite wrath. People don't want to spend their time reading the same message over and over, or waste time and money killing duplicate messages. The rule is: Send your message once. If you forget this rule, however, some members will remind you—and not so nicely.

E-mail Netiquette for Online Marketers

The primary form of communication online is conducted through e-mail sent to electronic bulletin boards and forums or directly to people's e-mail boxes. Here are guidelines for writing and posting effective e-mail.

    1. ***Be commercial in the right places:*** Advertising is not allowed on most message boards. If you have a commercial announcement, place it only in message areas designed for that purpose, such as an Internet USENET newsgroup devoted to listing classified advertisements of computers for sale. It is possible to announce products or services in the few forums and newsgroups that specifically allow classified advertising. If in doubt, check first. Read the FAQs (frequently asked questions) and "lurk," or read messages for a few days or weeks, before posting an article.

    2. ***Be politically correct:*** Don't insult people by making disparaging remarks about anyone's age, sex, marital status, race, religion or sexual orientation.

    3. ***Be polite:*** E-mail almost always sounds harsher than it's meant. Your comments can appear caustic and jokes might be read as criticism because the reader can't see your facial expressions or vocal intonations. Therefore, be exceedingly polite. Err on the side of good taste. Assume that anything that could be seen as negative will be taken as such.

    4. ***Be brief:*** Online communication tends to be short. Many formalities of letter writing are not used, such as headings, greetings, salutations and closings. Short sentences, action verbs and messages of one screen length are desirable.

5. ***Be grammatical and accurate:*** Nothing looks worse than a typo. Check your spelling and grammar.

6. ***Be case-sensitive:*** DON'T TYPE IN UPPER CASE. It looks like you are shouting.

7. ***Be specific:*** Headlines will attract readers to your message or drive them away. "Need help with creating ads" is better than "Help wanted."

8. ***Be focused:*** Stay on the subject topic. If the topic is "coffee," don't reply with a message about your favorite restaurant. Save that for a new topic.

9. ***Be redundant:*** If you are responding to a message, summarize part of the message to which you are replying. Because people get so much mail, this will help remind the sender of the information and bring other people up to speed. However, don't include the entire message, just a relevant excerpt or a paraphrase. Use arrows to indicate that this is text from an earlier message. For example:

```
>>On March 15, Dan Janal wrote:
>>Where's the best place to get a cappuccino in Danville?

The best place is Susan's Kitchen Cafe.
```

Many new versions of software automatically insert the previous message and arrows if you select the "forward" or "reply" options.

10. ***Be a giver:*** Contribute to the community. Answer people's questions and calls for help. If you do, you will be a welcome part of the group. This will help you build credibility in the group, which can help you promote your own business in a noninvasive manner.

11. ***Be "singular:"*** Don't post the same message twice on the same forum. There are personal and technical reasons for this. People don't like wading through repetitive messages, especially when they are paying for each minute they are online or paying for each message received. The technical reason is that message boards have limited space. Once the queue is filled, older messages roll off the board and are replaced by new ones. If you waste space, you will knock off messages that might actually help people.

12. ***Be quiet:*** If you answer "Thanks" and "I agree" to every message, you will inadvertently force other people's responses off the board. When appropriate, send private mail, or use the term "TIA" for "Thanks in advance." The same is true for online conferences. Don't announce your comings and goings, and don't respond with "Hi" and Bye." If there are a dozen people in the conference and all of them send greetings, the conversation grinds to a halt. Don't spam or send copies of letters to several forums or newsgroups. People get upset if they see the

same note posted; additionally, the act of posting takes away from system resources and mailbox space that could be put to better use.

13. ***Be legal:*** Obey the forum's rules on advertising, self-promotion and etiquette. Scams, pyramid schemes and stock fraud are as illegal online as they are in other media.

14. ***Be yourself:*** Use your real name, not a CB handle or nickname. People deserve to know who they are talking to. That means using your real name, business and gender. It is difficult to conduct a serious conversation with someone named "Hot Pants." A member of a commercial online services might be known as John73141, so that people won't know who he is. If you want to be respected, use your real name.

15. ***Be informative:*** People like to read information, not ads, online.

16. ***Be informed:*** Read messages for a while to get a feel for the discussion before jumping in. Read help files or FAQs (Frequently Asked Questions) to learn how the system operates and what is allowed.

A Few Words About Flaming

Be flameproof. Flaming, or sending irate mail to people who violate netiquette, is a gross waste of time—for the sender as well as the innocent recipients, who must plow through the flames to get to the bottom of their mailboxes. Sending flames also slows down the responsiveness of the entire system, as the one message must be transmitted to each participant in the mailing list—which could number in the hundreds or even thousands. Flaming is childish and unproductive. Don't do it!

Commercial services won't permit vulgar language or threats against its members. It is a violation of their subscriber agreement. Flaming can get you kicked off the system permanently.

Therefore, flaming is limited to the Internet, which has no central authority. Flaming probably began on the Internet because people were anonymous—they could send messages and never be found out. They could act without consequences. Many have flamed and will continue to do so. As a marketer, you won't increase your credibility if you flame anyone.

If you use proper netiquette, you will show that you are a member of the community who understands and respects its traditions.

Putting Emotion into Messages with Smileys

E-mail messages generally sound harsher than you intend because it does not convey the voice inflections and body language that make spoken communication an efficient means of conveying information. Online members have developed a special symbolic language that allows writers to show a kinder, gentler side. The language is called "emoticons," short for emotion and icons called "smileys." An emoticon is a combination of keyboard symbols that look like stick figures. When viewed by tilting your head sideways, these characters appear to be faces that smile, wink or grimace. These emoticons are used by the sender to add an emotional tone to the message that might otherwise be lost in the emotionless world of terse e-mail messages. There are dozens of emoticons that convey different subtle messages. Here are a few examples (tilt your head to the left for best results):

     :-) smile
     ;-) wink
     :- > very happy
     :- < disappointed
     :-D laughing

E-Mail Shorthand

A variation on emoticons involves using specialized constructions of letters to convey emotions. For example, a writer can avoid being misinterpreted as having written a sarcastic message by adding a grin, <g>, to indicate he is only kidding.

To write messages faster and avoid repetitions an e-mail shorthand has developed that involves using abbreviations for often-repeated phrases. Here are several popular conventions and examples in average sentences:

     • IMHO: in my humble opinion
        `IMHO, the 49ers will win the Super Bowl.`

- LOL: laughing out loud
  ```
  Did you see Seinfeld last night! I was LOL!
  ```
- ROFL: rolling on the floor laughing
  ```
  You think that was funny? How about Kramer and the
  cigar? I was ROFL!
  ```
- INAL: I'm not a lawyer (usually followed by legal advice)
  ```
  INAL but I think you should sue for back wages.
  ```
- TIA: thanks in advance
  ```
  TIA for your help in finding those files for me.
  ```
- BTW: by the way
  ```
  BTW, the price is $49.95, not $99.95
  ```
- PMFJI: pardon me for jumping in (when a new person enters a conversation)
  ```
  PMFJI, but I have experience in this area and thought
  you would like to know.
  ```

For example, a note might read:

```
BTW, I read in today's paper that the lawyers will use the
insanity defense. INAL, but IMHO, this is ridiculous! I'm ROFL.
What do you think? TIA.
```

If you use these e-mail expressions, you will show that you are a member of the community who understands its mores. Using symbolic language will help you get your messages across. One minor warning: Some people hate smileys because they are too cute.

Summary

Marketing on the Information Superhighway can be done if you follow the rules of the road. Your online neighbors are quick to give friendship, impart advice and ask for help. However, they are as skeptical as any consumer who hears of a get-rich-quick scheme. A system of etiquette, named "netiquette," has developed on each system and in each forum. Obey the rules and carefully observe the customs or you will be ostracized from the community and your message will be lost. If you master these rules of netiquette and adopt the mindset of the consumer, you can reap the rich rewards of the online consumer.

CHAPTER 5

Market Research

A well-orchestrated marketing program begins with solid research. The very foundation of the marketing plan is accurate, up-to-date information about the consumer and the marketplace. Good market research enables the company to create effective product and company positioning, marketing messages and pricing strategies. A depth of information will guide the marketer in brainstorming and creating effective advertisements, publicity and promotions. In fact, if the marketing research is conducted properly, selling becomes almost superfluous because the company has created a product the market needs and wants.

In this chapter, you will learn:

- How market research can help you sell products.
- What kinds of information is available online.
- Where to find marketing-related information online.

Without information, companies can't honestly know what the market really thinks and wants. Without proper research, company leaders might make mistakes that could have been easily prevented. Without looking at demographic figures, companies might not realize that better markets exist for their products—or that their original target market doesn't need the service offered. Even worse than not doing any research is using old research. For example, changes in government regulations can affect your ability to market a product. Since this information probably won't be the lead story on the six o'clock news, you need to be able to develop reliable sources of information that are accurate and timely.

A good business plan tries to answer these questions and many others: Who would buy this product or service? What demographic characteristics do they have? Where do they live? What do they read? Who are the competitors? What are their financial statements?

The Internet and commercial online services have the answers.

The Online Library

There is no better place to find the answers to these questions than the research services that are available on the Internet and commercial online services. The Information Superhighway is a vast electronic library that can be searched 24 hours a day with a computer and modem. You don't have to worry about this library being closed on weekends, fight for a parking spot or find that another library patron is reading the one copy of the report you absolutely must have to make your deadline. Online research centers have several other advantages over the local library. They offer complete databases of information that are easily searched and continuously updated. While marketers have long worried about whether information was current, online services are more likely to have material that is hot off the presses—even before the data has gone to the printing plant! For instance, the *Commerce Business Daily*, which prints notices of government bids, is available online before it is mailed to subscribers.

Thousands of databases are available for the online marketer. Virtually every magazine, newspaper government publication and census abstract is online. Intrepid researchers can find data from the historical archives of *The New York Times* to tiny trade journals, from unpublished college Ph.D. dissertations to citations from the Library of Congress. Another advantage of online research is that you can save the information to your computer, insert it into reports and print it. You save the time of taking notes and typing them into the computer. Of course, copyright laws require you to note sources and comply with regulations.

Researchers are beginning to find more information available online than in many newspapers. A recent trend among daily newspapers is to maintain electronic versions of the papers on the online services. In addition to the stories the print subscriber reads, the online versions have additional material not found in the dailies. This should come as a welcome relief to the serious researcher, who knows that printed newspapers must trim a story to fit the available space in the newspaper. Online newspapers have no limit on the amount of space they can use. Therefore, the online researcher has access to every article written by such major news-gathering organizations as the Associated Press, United Press International and Reuters. Since many of these articles aren't printed in the daily paper because of the lack of room, the online researcher can find information not generally known to the public at large.

Also, researchers have access to companies' press releases—original source material in the form that the company wished to present. You can read quotes, figures and background material that the paper either omitted, reworded or, perhaps, garbled. These press releases are invaluable sources of original business information. Since newspapers don't have the space to print each press release, even information from large, publicly traded companies will never be seen by the general public. However, the online researcher can find this information and make more informed decisions because of that data. Two companies, Business Wire and PR Newswire, print such press releases online for a fee. To learn how to put your press releases online, please refer to Chapter 12, Public Relations.

In addition to printed publications, online services also have access to demographic information collected by the United States Census Bureau and from private sources. By using these databases, you could find, for example, how many restaurants with liquor licenses are operating in any zip code in the U.S. Or you could find the complete analysis of the household incomes, educational levels and housing statistics of any county in the country. Information can be captured to your disk for use in reports, spreadsheets and presentations.

You can find information fairly easily. Searching online reference materials has several gigantic advantages over print. By taking an electronic trip to the library, you can save time by searching thousands of publications for specific information in a matter of seconds. This can be done so quickly because every major word in every publication is indexed into an electronic concordance. Technologists call these indexed words "keywords." For example, when you ask the computer to find information, you can request that it find a keyword, such as "Apple." Because that keyword might find articles about fruit as well as computers, you can narrow the search by adding keywords, such as "Apple" and "Computer." To further limit your search, you can specify the dates of the publications, such as "after 1989." You can also make the search more specific by linking keywords, dates and publications, such as "Apple" and "Computer" and "Macintosh" between 1990 and 1992 in *The New York Times*, written by Peter Lewis. That's how exact a search can be. Best yet, you'll have the sources in a matter of seconds. In the time it takes to search through one copy of a newspaper for the name of a company, an online search could find every reference to a company in thousands of publications going back a hundred years!

Because of the power of the online research tools and the breadth of their information databases, you might even find information from publications you didn't know existed. With more than 10,000 publications online, you couldn't possibly be familiar with them all. Thanks to online research tools, you only need to know how to ask the right questions to find the right answers.

In addition to providing a library full of documents and statistics, online services also allow the marketer to spot new trends. By reading bulletin boards, forums, newgroups and the like, marketers can get the pulse of the community. With more than 10,000 topics available on the Internet and commercial online services, marketers of anything from tennis shoes to bookstores to paint ball parlors can find out what new trends are developing and which ones are fading away. You can bet something is hot when a new USENET newsgroups springs up on the Internet to discuss it. If you want to find out about the Mighty Morphin Power Rangers, you can do so online. It is also a well-known fact that enterprising newspaper reporters read bulletin boards to find out what's hot and what people are talking about. Then they write stories about those topics. Just as radio talk shows can present a snapshot of what interests America at a given point, bulletin boards can present a true picture of what's hot and what's not. It is the ultimate man-in-the-street interview!

All this information can help the marketer accurately analyze the market, its competition and its potential as a bases for writing a successful business plan.

Online Resources

This section will show you descriptions and access codes for selected databases that can help marketers. You will find thumbnail sketches of the services, along with the name of the online service and the index words that will take you to the reference material. Because services change prices frequently, we have not included the fees, although they generally range from free to $50 for reports or are metered by the amount of time you spend online. Each service displays the prices prominently, so you will always know in advance how much the data will cost before you order. In some cases, you will be able to see sample reports so that you can determine if the service meets your needs. Topics covered in this section are:

- General and specialized newspapers and periodicals.
- Today's news.
- News and business magazines.
- Historical research.

- Demographics.
- Investing, finance and company information.
- Other useful resources.

To reach these services, type in the appropriate shortcut word. For the sake of style, the shortcut word is integrated into the text. For consistency, the style is:

CompuServe	`CompuServe: Go WORD`
America Online	`AOL: Keyword WORD`
Prodigy	`Prodigy: Jump WORD`
Internet—World Wide Web	`http://address`
Internet—FTP	`ftp.address`
Internet—Gopher	`Gopher.address`
Internet—Telnet	`telnet.address`

Of course you will replace "word" or "address" with the appropriate material.

General and Specialized Newspapers and Periodicals

Marketers need to keep up-to-date with facts. Information that is old—even by a few days—can cause tremendous waste of time and money. Keeping abreast of the news helps marketers in many ways, according to Brad Templeton, publisher and chairman of ClariNet Communications Corp., of San Jose, California, the major news provider to the Internet, companies, schools and organizations. Monitoring the news on a daily basis can help build strong marketing programs by providing information that will help you:

- Keep up with the competition. News can be searched any number of times each day to find news on any company or industry.
- See what new government regulations are being considered or adopted.
- Stay in touch with changes in politics, locally, nationally and internationally. Changes in political climates in other nations could affect your ability to sell there or to purchase raw goods.
- Track stock prices and volumes. If your competitor's stock price and volume are moving rapidly, you know something is going on.

Many leading newspapers print online versions the same day as the print edition. So marketers in Chicago can read about trends in the *Los Angeles Times* Prodigy: Jump LATIMES, while consultants in Seattle can check out the headlines from the *Washington Post* Interchange: DIGITAL INK. Computer executives in Boston can read the latest developments in Silicon Valley from the *San Jose Mercury News* AOL: Keyword MERCURY, while people in New York don't even have to run down to the newsstand to buy a copy of *The New York Times* AOL: Keyword @TIMES (which contains only the entertainment parts of the paper). Information from these services can be saved to disk and printed (provided you obey copyright regulations). Here is a review of current periodicals that are available online.

Today's News

CompuServe offers current articles from many sources through the Executive News Service CompuServe: Go ENS, a powerful news clipping service which gives you access to the Associated Press, United Press International, Reuters Reports, the *Washington Post*, Deutsche Presse-Agentur and OTC NewsAlert. ENS helps you manage this vast flow of information (as many as 10,000 stories a day) in several ways: You can review current news whenever you like and see headlines for every article, just as a daily newspaper editor would. You can also have ENS search the newswires for articles of particular interest to you. The articles will be saved in folders that you can read whenever you like (Fig. 5-1). Business Wire and PR Newswire are available CompuServe: Go TBW, Go ENS.

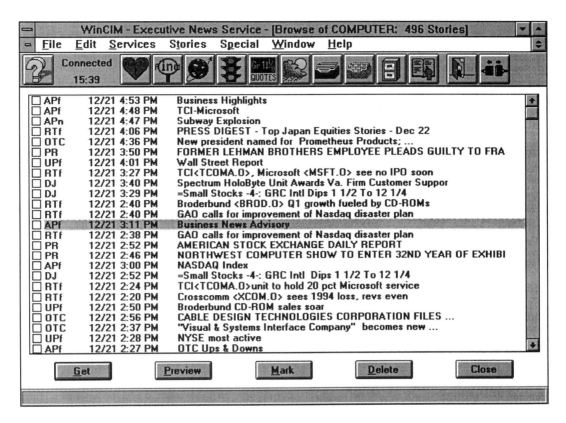

Figure 5-1. CompuServe's Executive News Service displays headlines of articles.
(Compliments of CompuServe)

Prodigy's Journalist `Prodigy: Jump JOURNALIST` is a news-gathering vehicle that presents the news displayed as a daily newspaper, complete with headlines, pictures and text. You tell it which keywords to search for and the system does the rest (Fig. 5-2). Prodigy also lets you hear sound, just like you would on the car radio. Journalist is available in computer stores and is published by PED Software Company of San Jose, California (408) 253-0894. Prodigy has several newspapers online including the *Atlanta Constitution*, `Prodigy: Jump ACCESS ATLANTA`, *Milwaukee Journal*, `Prodigy: Jump MILWAUKEE`, *New York Newsday*, `Prodigy: Jump NEWSDAY DIRECT`, and the *Los Angeles Times*, `PRODIGY: Jump TIMESLINK`.

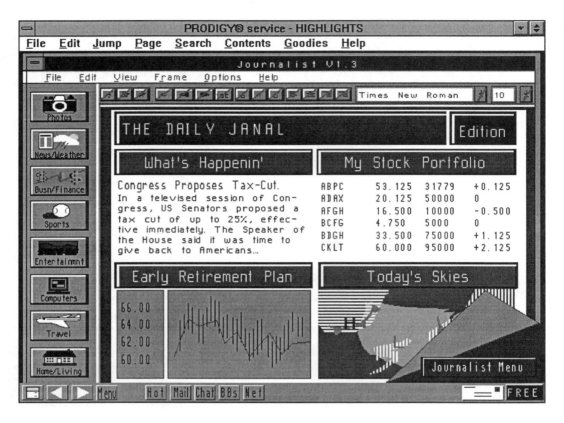

Figure 5-2. The Journalist on Prodigy prints a personalized newspapers.
(Courtesy of Prodigy)

America Online contains full text of more than a dozen newspapers and magazines including: *Time* magazine AOL: Keyword TIME, *Investor's Business Daily* AOL: Keyword: IBD, *The Atlantic Monthly* AOL: Keyword ATLANTIC, *Chicago Tribune* AOL: Keyword CHICAGO, *San Jose Mercury News* AOL: Keyword MERCURY, CNN Newsroom Online AOL: Keyword CNN, and CSPAN Online AOL: Keyword CSPAN. PR Newswire is available through the Business News section AOL: Keyword BUSINESS.

America Online offers two methods for subscribers to find information. The News Hound is an automatic text search system which works only with the Mercury News Center's stories and ads. AOL's text search icon culls the entire contents of the news section to find matching articles (Fig. 5-3). To use this service, type in the Keyword: BUSINESS for news and select the text search icon.

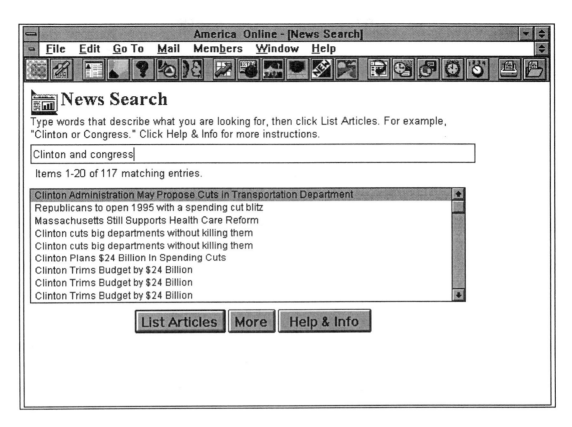

Figure 5-3. America Online subscribers can find news with a manual keyword search. (Courtesy of America Online)

The Nightly Business Report AOL: Keyword NBR the country's most-watched daily business news program, maintains a forum containing transcripts of its reports on business, financial and economic news.

Internet's ClariNet e.News service provides 1,000 news stories in 300 categories and pictures each day from the Associated Press and Reuters. It sends the information to subscribers in a format compatible with USENET newsgroups. News can be read on a daily basis or can be archived for 30 days. There is no keyword search capability. However you can order the news articles downloaded into your system, where your own system tools can locate keywords or articles of interest. News is categorized by more than 300 topics ranging from international to local, technology to financial. Some of the more interesting topics for marketers are:

Group	What you'll find
CLARI.BIZ.MERGERS	Mergers
CLARI.BIZ.PRODUCTS	New products and services
CLARI.BIZ.URGENT	Breaking news
CLARI.BIZ.INVEST	News for investors
CLARI.BIZ.FEATURES	Business news features
CLARI.NEWS.CONSUMER	Consumer news
CLARI.BIZ.ENTERTAIN	Entertainment industry news
CLARI.BIZ.INDUSTRY.***	Industry specific news, such as retailing, health, print media and many others. Substitute the industry you want to monitor for ***

Information services will continue to improve. The company is also planning to add press releases from a major service. They plan to double the content in 1995. The ability to deliver sound and moving pictures are in the works, says Brad Templeton, chairman and publisher for ClariNet Communications Corp., of San Jose, California., a privately held company founded in 1988 http://www.clarinet.com. "It's the electronic newspaper of the future," he says. "Modem–based services are way too slow and newspapers print only some of the news a day after it happens. ClariNet e.News is the best of both worlds. You get the speed of broadcast news along with the in-depth coverage of newspapers. You get the ability to do computer searching because it's in machine readable form, and it's all available via the machine on your desk."

Interchange will offer the *Washington Post* and *Minneapolis Star Tribune*.

News and Business Magazines

Business Week, the world's largest business magazine, is available on America Online AOL: Keyword BUSINESS WEEK. *Business Week* Online includes the entire weekly North America story lineup plus stories that are exclusive to *Business Week's* international editions published outside the United States.

America Online subscribers receive the current issue online in advance of the magazine's newsstand or subscription delivery. Also planned are online conferences with newsmakers, live forums with *Business Week* editors and reporters, message boards, and talk sessions on subjects of timely interest to business executives nationwide. The service includes searchable archives of back issues and new online products to be developed from established *Business Week* features. Copies are also available on the Electronic Newsstand on the Internet `http://enews.com`.

Newsweek `Prodigy: Jump Newsweek` allows readers to "jump into the next generation of digital journalism with *Newsweek* Interactive. The first truly multimedia news magazine integrating photos, sound, graphics, text," that "captures *Newsweek's* substance, style, personality," according to company literature. The current issue of *Newsweek* is available online each Sunday afternoon — a day before the print version hits the newsstands.

Time magazine `AOL: Keyword TIME` provides all the stories in the print edition to online readers by Sunday afternoon before the magazine hits the newsstands. *Time* also prints a daily news update, and back issues can be searched by keywords.

U.S. News & World Report `CompuServe: Go USN` also offers the complete text of the current issue plus searchable historical issues.

Historical Research

News of the recent past and the past few years can help marketers get a perspective on events and discover the history of their competitors as well as see how the field has advanced. Here is a list of sources arranged by online service.

CompuServe

CompuServe `CompuServe: Go NEWSARCHIVE` offers more than 50 daily newspapers online, including the *Boston Globe, Washington Post, Detroit Free Press, Florida Today, Akron Beacon Journal, Buffalo News* and *Baltimore Sun.*

Computer Database Plus `CompuServe: Go COMPDB` lets you retrieve computer-related articles from more than 230 magazines, newspapers and journals. You'll find news, reviews, and product introductions in areas such as hardware, software, electronics, engineering, communications and the application of technology. Comprehensive coverage includes popular, trade and professional titles. Full-text publications include *PC Week, PC Magazine, Macweek, InfoWorld* and the Newsbytes news service. You can find a complete list of publications in Computer Database Plus, in the Ziff Support Forum, CompuServe: Go ZIFFHELP. Download the file cdppub.txt from the ComputerDB Plus library 9.

Business Database Plus CompuServe: Go BUSDB lets you retrieve full-text articles from more than 1,000 business magazines, trade journals, newsletters and regional business newspapers. You can find a complete list of publications in Business Database Plus in the Ziff Support Forum, CompuServe: Go ZIFFHELP. Download the file bdppub.txt from the BusinessDB Plus library 8.

Magazine Database Plus CompuServe: Go MAGDB lets you retrieve full-text articles from more than 140 general-interest magazines, journals and reports. The database contains a wealth of diverse publications, from *Time* to *The Atlantic Monthly, Forbes* to *Kiplinger's Personal Finance* magazine, the *New Republic* to *National Review, Good Housekeeping* to *Cosmopolitan*. A complete list of publications is in Magazine Database Plus, in the Ziff Support Forum, CompuServe: Go ZIFFHELP. Download the file mdppub.txt from the MagazineDB Plus library 11.

Health Database Plus CompuServe: Go HDB lets you retrieve articles from consumer and professional publications on health care, disease prevention and treatment, fitness and nutrition, children and the elderly, substance abuse and smoking and just about any health-related topic. The core of Health Database Plus is a collection of publications with coverage oriented to nonprofessional readers. Core publications range from newsstand titles such as *Men's Health, Parents Magazine, Prevention and Runner's World* to more specialized reports and journals such as *AIDS Weekly* from the Centers for Disease Control, *Morbidity and Mortality Weekly Report, Patient Care* and *RN*. The collection also includes a number of pamphlets issued by organizations such as the American Lung Association. Augmenting this coverage is a collection of technical and professional journals such as *Journal of the American Medical Association, Lancet,* and the *New England Journal of Medicine*. A list of the core publications is in the Ziff Support Forum, CompuServe: Go ZIFFHELP. Download the file hdppub.txt from the HealthDB Plus library 10.

IQUEST CompuServe: Go IQUEST provides access to over 800 databases spanning the worlds of business, government, research, news—even popular entertainment and sports

KNOWLEDGE INDEX `CompuServe: Go KI` gives you access to over 50,000 journals and reference works, including *Books in Print*, PR Newswire and *Standard & Poor's News*.

America Online

America Online contains full-text versions and bulletin boards for more than 25 consumer publications including: *Bicycling* magazine `AOL: Keyword BIKE`, *National Geographic* `AOL: Keyword NGS`, *Omni* `AOL: Keyword OMNI`, Popular *Photography* `AOL: Keyword PHOTOS`, *Saturday Review* `AOL: Keyword SRO`, *Scientific America* `AOL: Keyword SCIAM`, *The New Republic* `AOL: Keyword TNR`, *Road and Track* `AOL: Keyword ROAD AND TRACK`, and *Car and Driver* `AOL: Keyword CAR AND DRIVER`. Additional publications come online frequently. Check the Newsstand Section for the latest titles; AOL has begun an aggressive pursuit of periodicals. Bulletin boards let you discuss current trends with members.

The Cowles/SIMBA Media Information Network `AOL: Keyword SIMBA` lets you search through back issues of newsletters, user contributions and a message board that covers virtually every area of media and information.

Demographics

Demographics can tell you where your customers live and which markets are emerging. The Internet and CompuServe has a wealth of information.

Internet

Census Bureau news releases, tip sheets and other statistics and information are available on the Internet at:

```
Gopher.census.gov
Gopher.lib.umich.edu
http://www.census.gov/
```

CompuServe

Business Demographics Reports CompuServe: Go BUSDEM are designed to help businesses analyze their markets. The reports are based on information from the U.S. Census Bureau. Two types of reports are available. The Business to Business Report includes information on all broad Standard Industrial Classification (SIC) categories. Each report provides the total number of employees in each category for a designated geographical area. The Advertisers' Service Report includes data on businesses that constitute the SICs for Retail Trade. Each report breaks down the total number of businesses for each specified geographical unit in relation to company size. Reports of either type can be requested by zip code, county, state, metropolitan area, ADI (Arbitron TV Markets), DMA (Nielsen TV Markets), or the entire United States. Sample reports are available online.

SUPERSITE CompuServe: Go SUPERSITE enables you to produce a variety of demographic and sales potential reports for the entire United States, any state, county, zip code, SMSA (Metropolitan Area), ADI (Arbitron TV Market), DMA (Nielsen TV Market), Place, Census Tract, MCD (Minor Civil Division) or aggregation of these.

ACORN Target Marketing CompuServe: Go SUPERSITE provides information on these industries: apparel, investments, appliances, leisure activities, automotive, media, baby products, mail order, beverages, personal products, cameras, shoes and footwear, sports, credit cards, restaurants, electronics, tools, furniture and furnishings, toys, garden and lawn, travel, grocery, insurance and home improvement.

Investing/Finance/Company Information

Marketers can find stock quotes for the current day and historical quotes on every system. In a rare show of unity, CompuServe, AOL and Prodigy each use the same access word: QUOTES. Internet has a private service that sells stock pricing information, called Quote.Com. Here are other resources for finding out what story the money tells.

CompuServe

Disclosure CompuServe: Go SEC,SELECT DISCLOSURE lists financial reports, including income, balance sheet and ratio reports on more than 10,500 companies. Standard & Poor's CompuServe: Go S&P provides capsule summaries and financial digests of companies. TRW Business Profiles CompuServe: Go TRW can help marketers conduct reference checks.

Dun's Market Identifiers CompuServe: Go DUNS contains directory information on over 7.8 million U.S. businesses. You'll find the company address and telephone number, sales figures, number of employees, net worth, date and state of incorporation, corporate family relationships and chief executive name.

America Online

Commerce Business Daily AOL: Keyword CBD lists notices of proposed government procurement actions, contract awards, sales of government property and other procurement information. A new edition of the CBD is issued by the Government Printing Office every business day. Federal Information & News Dispatch, Inc., provides the CBD in electronic format the day before the publication is printed and mailed by the Government Printing Office.

Profiles of more than 1,100 of the largest, most influential and fastest growing public and private companies in the United States and the world are listed in Hoover's Company Profiles database AOL: Keyword HOOVER.

Internet

The Economic Bulletin Board from the Department of Commerce, `TELNET.EBB.STAT-USA.GOV/ PASSWORD:TEST OR GUEST` contains data on economic conditions, economic indicators, employment, foreign trade, monetary matters and more in 20 general subject areas. The EBB contains press releases and statistical information from the Bureau of Economic Analysis, the Bureau of the Census, the Federal Reserve Board, the Bureau of Labor Statistics, the Department of Treasury and other agencies.

FedWorld, which is from the National Technical Information Service `telnet.fedworld.gov` system, provides access to more than 100 U.S. government computer bulletin boards that contain U.S. government publications and statistical files.

The Food and Drug Administration Bulletin Board System contains FDA news releases, enforcement reports, import alerts, drug and product approval lists, Federal Register summaries, informational publications, articles from FDA Consumer and more `telnet.fdabbs.fda.gov login.bbs`.

EDGAR lets you see 1994 public Securities and Exchange Commission findings `http://www.town.hall.org` or `Gopher.town.hall.org`.

Other Useful Resources

Here are listings of other useful information sources for marketers.

Intelligent Agents

If you want to find out what people are saying on the Internet's USENET newsgroups about your company and its products, or about your competitors, you should use the Stanford NetNews Filtering Service. This free service will scour each of the 8,000 Newsgroups and search for the terms you specify. For example, you can ask it to look for references to Ford, Chrysler, General Motors, Toyota, Honda and the car industry. Messages will be sent to your e-mail box every day.

To create an account, follow these steps:

1. Send e-mail to `netnews@db.stanford.edu`
2. Leave the subject blank. As the body of the message, type `subscribe` and the search terms, for example:
   `subscribe food recipe not fish`
3. You can use this service even if you don't have an account on the Internet. All you need is an account on CompuServe, AOL or Prodigy that can send and receive Internet e-mail.

For more information on this service, check out the service's World Wide Web home page. The address is, `http://woodstock.stanford.edu:2000/`

- Farcast, an agent-based news and information service, lets you browse and search its collection of news, industry press releases, reference material and stock quotes 24 hours a day. Farcast can also automatically send you articles of interest. For information, send e-mail with the word "hello" in the subject line to: `Info@farcast.com`.

Encyclopedias

The Academic American Encyclopedia `CompuServe: Go AAE; Prodigy: JUMP: ENCYCLOPEDIA`, published by Grolier Electronic Publishing, contains the full text of the print classic, including over 10 million words in over 33,000 articles. It is updated quarterly, making it the most current encyclopedia available. A general-interest, short-entry encyclopedia, the AAE is an indispensable source of information for marketers.

America Online members can use Compton's Encyclopedia `AOL: Keyword COMPTON or AOL: Keyword ENCYCLOPEDIA`, which consists of more than 9 million words, 5,274 long articles and 29,322 concise articles.

Small Business

Microsoft Small Business Center `AOL: Keyword SMALL BUSINESS` contains information for small business owners (or people considering starting a small business). You'll find articles on subjects like exporting, finance and marketing from organizations like the U.S. Small Business Administration, the U.S. Chamber of Commerce, the National Federation of Independent Business, Dun & Bradstreet, *Inc.* magazine and many others. Typical articles teach you how to find financing and write a press release. The center also contains business software templates and programs. You can get personalized help for your small business from the Service Corps of Retired Executives. Finally, you can post messages to the Small Business Center message boards to see what other small business owners are talking about or to raise your own issues for discussion.

Miscellaneous

The U.S. Patent Archives from 1970 to 1993 are available on the University of North Carolina's computers, which are accessible from the Internet `http://sunsite.unc.edu/patents/intropat.html`.

Phone*File CompuServe: Go PHONES is an electronic name, address and telephone book of over 83 million U.S. households compiled from publicly available sources.

Biz*File CompuServe: Go BIZFILE provides access to listings for approximately 92 million businesses in the United States and 1.6 million in Canada. All businesses listed in the 5,300 Yellow Pages directories in the United States and Canada are included, with the exception of 800 numbers.

Marquis Who's Who CompuServe: Go BIOGRAPHY lists the accomplishments of noteworthy people.

Library of Congress INTERNET: gopher.marvel.loc.gov hopes to have 5 million images digitized by the year 2000, its bicentennial. The collections will be made available in "plain vanilla electronic form" online at no charge.

Several business schools are online and offer files of interest to marketers. To see a master list on the Internet's World Wide Web, type the address:

`http://www.dartmouth.edu/Pages/Tuck/bschools.html`

Economics and financial topics are covered in the University of Texas Web home page `http://riskweb.bus.utexas.edu/finweb.htm`.

The Computer Industry Almanac eWorld: shortcut CIA provides marketers with a huge database of names, addresses and phone numbers of 3,000 companies, 1,000 magazines, 250 market research firms, 280 public relations and marketing communications agencies, and 9,500 leaders of the computer industry. These contacts can be invaluable for software and hardware companies hoping to create strategic alliances, gain distribution and market and publicize their products.

Grant-Getter's Guide to the Internet `gopher.uidaho.edu` points to the Federal Register, Fedworld and other sites, as well as listing a bibliography of grant resources on the Internet.

Document Center provides information on industry standards and specifications `http://www.service.com/doccenter/home.html`.

Summary

Great marketing starts with great research. Online services provide virtual online libraries of up-to-date information that can help you find information quickly about the industry, competitors and trends. In many ways, online research is better than printed materials because the information is revised more often, is distributed faster and is easy to integrate into reports. If you conduct online research, your marketing plan will be much more solid.

CHAPTER 6

Becoming a More Effective Marketer

If you think you know it all, think again. There are ideas, visions and dreams you have yet to experience. Fortunately for you, your online peers are ready, willing and able to serve as mentors, advisors, colleagues and reality testers.

In this chapter, you will learn:

- How you will benefit by joining professional forums online.
- Where to find professional forums online and how to reach them.

The playing field in online marketing changes dramatically from one day to the next. Yesterday's truisms might not apply to today's problems. New players enter the game and new technologies take hold to change life as you know it. You need to keep up with the changes and to learn from others' successes and failures or you will waste a great deal of time and money.

The best places to keep in touch with the changes in marketing strategies are in online marketing forums, bulletin boards, newgroups and mailing lists. The Internet and commercial online services have forums devoted to helping marketing professionals working at large companies, associations and local businesses, as well as work-at-home professionals and service providers. These areas are great places to learn about the new dimensions of online marketing by posting questions to noncompetitive and helpful peers. After all, who can teach you about the online community and its mores better than the people who actually use the systems?

These repositories also hold vast libraries of reference material that can teach you just about everything from how to fund your company to how to prepare a disaster plan for crises resulting from product tampering. Most files are preceded by dialogue boxes that describe the material in the file. See (Fig. 6-1). By viewing this box, you can see if the material in the file is really what you want to read before investing the time to download or view the entire file.

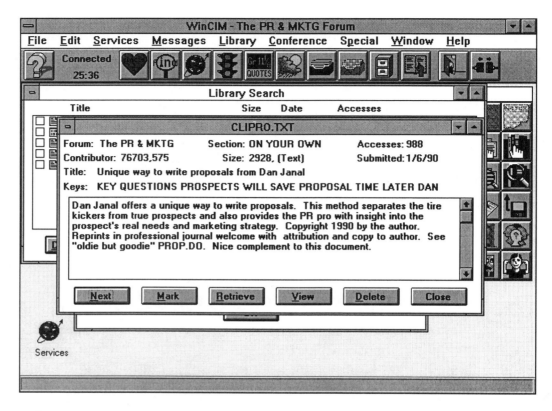

Figure 6-1. A preview box shows a description of a file on the Public Relations and Marketing Forum library on CompuServe. (Compliments of CompuServe)

These bulletin boards are staffed by helpful system administrators who go by different names on each system. Internet's USENET newsgroups are staffed by moderators, mailing lists are run by owners and Web home pages are run by webmasters. CompuServe's forums are headed by forum administrators and sysops, for system operators. America Online has hosts. Prodigy features board leaders. Some forums are hosted by one person, others by a dozen. Each person lends his or her expertise and time to help newcomers. The commercial online services tend to be friendlier to newcomers and dispense advice about how to use the tools effectively. The Internet's USENET newsgroups and mailing lists tend to be a bit grumpier in welcoming newcomers, who are expected to "lurk" or read messages for a few days or weeks to get the flow of the conversations, and also to read FAQs (files containing Frequently Asked Questions) to learn the culture of the area.

Forum operators hope that each person not only asks questions, but also contributes his or her knowledge to others who raise questions and joins in the general discussions. These hosts do their part for the love of helping others; few get paid and those that do take salaries that couldn't fund a full-time job.

Information is unbiased and free from commercial advocacy. In fact, strict warnings are posted that prohibit advertising and self-promotion (except to say what kind of work you do, so the host can make points relevant to your industry).

As a result of these online networking sessions, strong personal friendships can form between people who have never met face to face. One group, the Public Relations Special Interest Group meets once a year at the annual meeting of the Public Relations Society of America and has planned dinners and special outings.

The areas also let you learn from your customers and prospects.

"You can learn from the online community," says Christina O'Connell, president of O'Connell and Associates, an online public relations consultant coco@pcnet.com. "Simply reading newsgroups and forums can be the most effective market research around. Monitor the comments of your target market to learn what features matter and what causes folks to love or hate a product."

Finally, by participating in conversations with opinion leaders, industry sages and VIPs who frequent these areas, you can develop lasting relationships with them.

Netiquette

The rules of netiquette apply to these forums. That means no advertising or solicitation of members. There are slight variations on the rules for self-promotion in that people can describe what they do as a means of introducing themselves to the community. This topic is discussed in detail in Chapter 4.

Case Study: Schaeffer & Goldentyer

Not only can professional forums help marketers find information, they can help find just about anything.

"During the summer, I was working on three videos on technology and communication: they focused on the cellular telephone, the Internet, and fax machines," says Debra Goldentyer, of Schaeffer & Goldentyer, which produces video and multimedia programs for employee training, education, and public relations in Oakland, California. "I needed information, 'real people' actors, and props, including: an old fax machine; translations into Japanese and Chinese of a fake ad I'd written; eight people of various ethnicities, sexes, and ages; a radio scanner; a dial telephone; a page from the New York City phone book; a packet of info on the Internet; and a bunch of other odd items."

She used CompuServe to find these items by posting notices on the Public Relations and Marketing Forum and WORK Forum and sending e-mail to people who responded to her queries.

"I got a dial telephone (remember those?) from a woman who lives about 150 miles from here. I got a scanner from a guy who lives about two blocks from here. I got four actors. I got translations from a guy in Hong Kong and from a woman in New York City who's not on CompuServe, but whose parents are and they were so proud of her calligraphy, they hooked us up. I got Internet materials from a copyright lawyer in Philadelphia (who, incidentally, is an old boss of mine; we stumbled onto each other right here). I got a page from a New York City phone book in exchange for two pages from the San Francisco phone book (seriously)," she says. "The videos came out terrific and I got to keep the dial phone!"

Marketing Forums and Mailing Lists

Here are forums, descriptions and access codes for bulletin boards for marketers.

CompuServe

The Public Relations and Marketing Forum `CompuServe: Go PRSIG`, provides a message board and libraries of files on the following topics: general help, creative matters, desktop publishing, technology, education, marketing, advertising, direct mail, research, media relations and crisis communications. A complete index of files and short descriptions can be found in the library file called `INDEX.TXT`.

Entrepreneurs Small Business Forum `CompuServe: Go SMALLBIZ` provides information, communications and contacts for entrepreneurs and wannabees. The forum provides information ranging from ways to raise investment capital to management advice.

Working from Home Forum `CompuServe: Go WORK` provides information for people who are running small businesses from their homes—or want to. Moderated by Paul and Sarah Edwards, who have written several best-selling books about working at home, the forum offers messages and files on more than 20 topics, including management consulting, auditing businesses, international business and training and human resources. A list of all files in the forum libraries can be found in Library 1 in the files `MASTER.DIR, MASTER.EXE` or `MASTER.ZIP`.

America Online

Microsoft Small Business Center `AOL: Keyword SMALL BUSINESS` contains information for small business owners (or people considering starting a small business). You can also get personalized help for your small business from the Service Corps of Retired Executives. Finally, you can post messages to the Small Business Center message boards to see what other small business owners are talking about or to raise your own issues for discussion.

Photography Forum `AOL: Keyword PHOTOGRAPHY` helps professional photographers trade notes on such topics as royalties, licensing and copyright.

Prodigy

The Business Bulletin Board `Prodigy: JUMP BUSINESS` allows members to post questions on a wide variety of topics and read articles from home-based business magazines.

Advertising Age `Prodigy: Jump ADAGE; eWorld: Go to Business and Financial Plaza, click on Business Resources, look for the Ad Age/Creativity icon` lets you post questions for the moderators and columnists. You'll find reprints of some but not all of its articles on Prodigy. On eWorld, you'll get a daily briefing of marketing and advertising news, including new campaigns, reviews, guest critics and a bulletin board.

eWorld

Marketing Guru Regis McKenna operates an eWorld forum called Real-Time Marketing in which marketers can talk to one another and read marketing information and resources.

Terri Lonier, author of the *Working Solo* book, hosts the Working Solo Online Business Forum, `eWorld:WS or go to the Business & Finance Plaza: Business Resources:Working Solo`. Subscribers can network with other entrepreneurs, browse extensive databases or download files from small business libraries and find valuable information specifically designed to assist entrepreneurs. Monthly online conferences bring leading entrepreneurs to the forum for lively "real-time" discussions on marketing, technology, management, news, and other issues of interest to independent entrepreneurs.

Internet

The Internet is the host of several mailing lists devoted to marketing and advertising. You don't have to be on the Internet to subscribe to a mailing list. CompuServe, America Online and Prodigy members can join these mailing lists as well through gateways on their systems.

Here is a list of marketing mailing lists you might find useful. New ones are being added all the time, so be on the lookout for references to other mailing lists. To get the most current list, send e-mail to `lists@bayne.com`. The list is maintained by Kim Bayne, president of wolfBayne Communications.

INET-MARKETING lets marketers discuss current issues of marketing and advertising on the Internet. Recent topics included the accuracy of demographics and the changing nature of the Internet user in the face of access from other online services.

To subscribe, send the message:
`SUBSCRIBE INET-MARKETING Your Name`
to the e-mail address
`LISTPROC@EINET.NET`

A digest version is available. After you have received a confirmation message that you have been added to the list:

To get a digest, send the message
`SET INET-MARKETING MAIL DIGEST`
to the e-mail address
`LISTPROC@EINET.NET`

FREE-MARKET discusses Internet marketing.
To subscribe, send the message
`SUB FREE-MARKET Your Name`
to the e-mail address
`LISTSERV@AR.COM`

Internet advertising issues are discussed in CNI-ADVERTISE.
To subscribe, send the message
`SUBSCRIBE CNI-ADVERTISE Your Name`
to the e-mail address
`LISTPROC@CNI.ORG`

HTMARCOM discusses high-tech marketing issues.
To subscribe, send the message
`SUBSCRIBE HTMARCOM Your Name`
to the e-mail address
`LISTSERV@RMII.COM`

HEP2-L is devoted to marketing on the Internet.
To subscribe, send the message
`SUBSCRIBE PRFORUM Your Name`
to the e-mail address
`LISTSERV@INDYCMS.IUPUI.EDU`

GINLIST, the Global Interact Network, brings together business educators and practitioners with an interest in international business/marketing issues.
To subscribe, send the message
`SUBSCRIBE GINLIST Your Name`
to the e-mail address
`LISTSERV@msu.edu`

RITIM-L, the Telecommunications and Information Marketing List, is a forum for scholars and managers to exchange ideas and experiences on such topics as technology in the household, the future of cyberspace and home shopping. The list is sponsored by the Research Institute for Telecommunications and Information Marketing (RITIM).
To subscribe, send the message
`SUBSCRIBE RITIM-L Your Name`
to the e-mail address
`LISTSERV@uriacc.uri.edu`

MARKET-L, offers marketing practitioners, students and educators a place to discuss such topics as pricing tactics, distribution, promotion and advertising, segmentation, surveys, service quality, marketing planning for non-profits, positioning, exporting, market models, product design, marketing information systems and decision support, channel structure, relationship marketing, database marketing, marketing ethics, branding and sales force compensation.
To subscribe, send the message
`SUBSCRIBE MARKET-L Your Name`
to the e-mail address
`LISTSERV@NERVM.NERDC.UFL.EDU`

NEWPROD discusses new product development for products and service industries. Practitioners, academics and consultants trade messages on marketing, market research, management science, R & D, quality and organization behavior.

To subscribe, send the message
```
SUBSCRIBE NEWPROD Your Name
```
to the e-mail address
```
majordomo@world.std.com
```

The Product_Dev list is for discussing new product development.
To subscribe, send the message
```
SUBSCRIBE PRODUCT_DEV Your Name
```
to the e-mail address
```
product_dev-request@msoe.edu
```

Tips on Joining Mailing Lists

To join a mailing list, you must send an e-mail note to the list operator with the message `Subscribe LISTNAME YOUR NAME`. That's it. Don't type anything else, like "Please add me to this list. I hear it is great!!!" This note will confuse the software and result in your receiving an error message instead of a subscription. When your subscription has been accepted, you will receive a confirming note and information about the list, which includes instructions for unsubscribing. If the list has been discontinued, which happens frequently, you'll receive a note in your mailbox saying the mail can't be delivered.

Members of the commercial online services can join mailing lists as well. These instructions should work. However, since these systems are continually refining their software, please read the instructions on each system to make sure.

Managing Your Mail

Unlike the other systems, in which members must actively go to the forum to read messages, on the Internet, mailing list messages are sent directly to the e-mail box of every subscriber. This means you can expect a flood of messages on a daily basis if you subscribe to several lists. You will quickly develop a sense of being overwhelmed by the volume of mail. Therefore, be selective about joining lists. If a list does not meet your expectations, you should unsubscribe. You can also manage your mail more productively if the list has a digest format. That means the moderator takes everyone's messages and lumps them into one big e-mail message instead of 50 smaller ones. This option is also better than individual messages because you can follow conversations more easily.

To separate urgent messages from mailing lists articles, you might consider creating two mailboxes: one for personal and business mail that has a high priority; the other a catchall mailbox for messages from mailing lists. Several software programs announced that they would begin supporting intelligent sorting systems that would place private e-mail and mailing list messages in different folders so you can sort through them more easily.

Multilevel Marketing

Multilevel marketers (MLMs) can find camaraderie in the Internet USENET Newsgroup `alt.business.multi-level`. To join, follow the steps to subscribe to newsgroups as noted by your Internet software. MLMs can also find information on the CompuServe's Work at Home Forum, `CompuServe: Go WORK`. One note of caution: These forums exist to help MLMs converse with one another and are not places to post information about joining new MLM programs.

Summary

By joining professional groups on the Internet and commercial online services, online marketers can hone their skills and learn new strategies. To get the most out of these forums, you have to do more than just join—you must participate. You can exchange war stories, stay abreast of new trends, test ideas, get advice and impart wisdom. Chances are, the more you contribute, the more benefit you will receive.

SECTION 2

Making the Sale

There are many ways to make money on the Internet and commercial online services. This section will show you how companies are using these services to set up stores and sell products online. You'll also learn how to sell information online and how to create long-lasting relationships with customers.

CHAPTER 7

Online Shopping

The exciting promise of online marketing is the ability to make the sale. The Internet and commercial online services can deliver this today! Whether it be a trip to the virtual mall or browsing an online catalog, marketers can use online services to make money.

"You are never going to get more attention from any customer than when they are online. Both their hands are on the keyboard and both their eyes are on the monitor," says Carol Wallace, program manager, communications, for Prodigy. "You are interacting with them. They have pre–selected you. They want to see you. This is a very intimate selling situation."

In this chapter, you will learn:

- Why you should consider selling products online.
- How to sell products online.
- Security issues.
- Tools you can use to sell products.
- How to create your own World Wide Web home page on the Internet.
- Examples of Web home pages.
- Case histories of companies on the Web.
- How to participate in electronic shopping centers on CompuServe, Prodigy and America Online.
- Other opportunities available for online shopping.
- Differences between print catalogs and online catalogs.

When online shopping first began in 1984, customers were suspicious. They didn't like the idea of not being able to see and touch products. They weren't sure about sending their credit card information over the computer line. While they might have appreciated the time they saved on shopping, there wasn't a large supply of products to select from.

All that has changed. Hundreds of merchants offer products online—from clothing to books to vacations. Big names like B. Dalton, Land's End and J.C. Penney offer online shopping. Small companies selling T–shirts, self–published mystery novels or computer software also offer their wares online. Technology is improving to the point where people can see pictures of products and read or hear descriptions. Data encryption is developing to the point where it can reliably protect sensitive information such as customer credit card information.

These improvements are having an impact. In 1994, sales of products from the commercial online services ranged from $50 million to $200 million, according to SIMBA Information, Inc., of Wilton, Connecticut. Because the commercial online services don't reveal sales figures, precise numbers are unavailable. The Internet does not gather statistics on worldwide sales.

Online shopping offers several advantages over shopping in person. Comparison shopping is quick and easy. Consumers can order directly from the comfort of their home or office, 24 hours a day from anywhere in the world. The store never closes. There are no traffic jams, no parking places to fight over and no waste of time.

Shopping has never been easier for consumers. They can order products directly from the merchant by using a computer and a modem. Shoppers also can browse at their own pace and can't be hassled by pushy salespeople. Orders are paid for by credit card, which merchants can verify before processing the order. If customers prefer, many companies offer toll–free order services via 800 numbers. Delivery varies by merchant, but it is usually made by a recognized carrier such as Federal Express or UPS so that companies can track receipts. Consumers usually get their products within 72 hours.

Online information can be delivered immediately to consumers via e–mail. They don't have to wait three weeks for a catalog to reach them by mail. They can view the information and make a buying decision immediately. In this way, online services help fulfill demand.

Merchants benefit as well. They gain an additional distribution channel for their products. Online shoppers tend to have more disposable income than the average consumer. Online marketers can keep track of their best customers and alert them to sales and special promotions. Vendors can build relationships with customers through online sales, support and service. The flexible publishing platforms of the Internet and commercial online services offer the marketer the chance to build relationships by publishing unlimited amounts of information for consumers to devour at their own pace.

The Internet and online commercial services offer different concepts in selling. They range from a totally interactive medium on Internet's World Wide Web, complete with multimedia presentations, to graphics and colorful drawings on Prodigy, America Online and CompuServe. The ability to sell with the tools of sound and motion picture presentations is in the works on all the commercial online services. One day, the computer could achieve television's ability to deliver commercials complete with sound and synchronized pictures. The commercial online services also are exploring sales opportunities involving CD–ROM. These storage devices could contain audio and video files that would otherwise take too long to transmit over the phone lines.

Key to the success of an online store is interactivity.

"Online marketers need to make their information informative, engaging and nonintrusive. Because the services, products, etc., are interactive, shoppers must want to surf these areas. If the information does not engage them, they won't scan the area. It's as simple as that," an America Online company spokesman says.

The Online Catalog

Online data can be seen as an electronic version of the company catalog— complete with pictures that entice the eye, words that inspire the imagination and a price that doesn't make consumers think twice. Plus, electronic information is less expensive to deliver than catalogs: there aren't any printing or postage costs. Online marketers with wry senses of humor are fond of saying they don't like to spend money mailing "dead trees" to customers.

The lowered cost of doing business online means that some merchants can enjoy a larger profit margin, while others pass the savings along to consumers in the form of extra low prices. Still others view the online systems as another distribution channel that features the same pricing structure as catalogs or direct mail.

Merchants can change information, product lineups and pricing immediately to take advantage of market trends, price tests and the like. Some companies, of course, would like to move quickly but can't because of internal operations, though at least the promise is available.

Print isn't outdated yet. Hard copy catalogs can display color more attractively than computers. Print catalogs can be read on the bus or in the bathroom. Also, consumers can flip through pages more easily and see several pieces of information at once. This is handy when, say, they are looking at the order form and then need to flip back to page 20 to find the product number for the kite they wanted to buy. Yet online consumers can find information quickly by linking from one page to the next and can order directly from the page.

Regardless, the elements of proper advertising must be present for online marketing to work effectively. "Companies are living in a fantasy if they think people will buy online if they provide bad copy, bad pictures and no reason to buy," says Marc Fleischmann, president, Internet Distribution Services, Inc. of Palo Alto, California, a marketing design technology company that helps companies market their services on the Internet.

Case Study: Hello Direct

"As direct marketers, we can't be one–trick ponies anymore. We can't produce one catalog and send it to everyone. We have to adapt the message to the media and the target audience," says Chuck Volwiler, vice president of marketing for Hello Direct, a $30 million, San Jose–California–based developer and marketer of telecommunication products for business. The company created a World Wide Web version of its four–color, 72–page catalog featuring 275 products, which is sent to 11.5 million prospects, `http://www.hello-direct.com/hd/`. The home page includes the table of contents and pictures of several products. Product pages follow, which include product descriptions, pictures, prices and ordering information.

The Web allows his company to reach new markets with targeted messages and graphics that show the company's telephones, headsets and accessories. "We don't want to mail one more catalog than we have to. And we don't want to send a catalog to someone who doesn't want one."

Hello Direct, which has 85 employees and has grown 50%–80% since its inception in 1987, has achieved its goals by creating a Web home page.

"There is much less waste—and misdirected messages—with the Web. There are no problems with the wrong message or an inappropriate message. You can tailor the message because people select what they need."

The hypertext aspects of the Web allow Hello Direct to present varying levels of information to meet the needs of its users who require different amounts of information.

"The whole area is very exciting to me because of the kind of products we sell. Some customers need to read a paragraph and others need to read about the entire product category in depth. Some products require a tremendous amount of information to sell. This is not cost–effective in a print catalog. With the Internet, we can create a teaser ad that draws the customer in and lets them follow the path to find the information they need. There is much more depth and interactivity online than in print."

The company looked at all the online services before choosing the Internet.

"We chose the Internet because many of our customers were online or had access to the Net. It would be a good way to acquire new customers and to provide current customers with e–mail support. That is our goal," he says. "With Mosaic software capabilities, we felt we could get better reproduction of our graphics."

Hello Direct sees its Web home page as the first in a series of evolving information products. "Right now we want to present our products and offer an 800 number to call for orders," Volwiler says. "The next step is online ordering followed by online support."

The company is so pleased with its first venture into interactivity on the Web that it is budgeting for the future.

"Our creative costs will rise as we focus on creating user–friendly environments to customers," he says. But he adds that the investment must be worth the effort. "We can't afford to dump money into a channel that takes years to see a return. We need to get a short–term return."

Faceless Transactions: Benefit or Hindrance?

The computer offers the opportunity for sales to be conducted completely without a human operator at the sales center. This is great for companies that want to cut personnel costs. Also, some customers simply don't like aggressive salespeople and so they prefer ordering online.

However, faceless and voiceless transactions might cost some companies more in the long run.

"Vendors don't want faceless transactions. Customer service operators build customer rapport, add–on sales and sell service," says Marc Fleischmann, of IDS.

Finally, other groups of consumers actually do want to talk to a person, even if it is over the phone, so they can have pertinent questions answered.

These are reasons to reinforce the belief that online marketing is but one part of the marketing mix and another channel of distribution—not the only one.

Security for Online Ordering

Taking the order online is easy. Ensuring the confidentiality of the data might not be—at least not yet.

Customers can easily order products several ways. They can pick up the phone and call your order center, send an e–mail note, complete an online order form, or print out your order form and send it to you via fax or phone.

Questions of security arise for both consumer and merchant. The consumer wonders if her credit card information is secure on a network. Can hackers steal credit card numbers? The merchant wonders if he can be protected against fraud. Is the person ordering the legal owner of the card or a thief ?

The specter of fraud exists for the merchant as well. He might receive calls from thieves who are placing orders with stolen credit cards. Good business practice calls for merchants to call the credit card authorization center to make sure the card is valid. However, fast thieves can place many orders online before the card's original owner realizes the card is missing and calls in to report the disappearance. By that time, many merchants could be liable for a lot of money.

Just as in any credit card transaction, there are certain risks. Proponents of online shopping say security of credit card numbers is just as reliable—or unreliable—as in any other transaction. After all, thieves can steal credit card numbers from carbons tossed into the garbage in a restaurant or store. Unscrupulous employees can steal credit card numbers given to them over the phone or sent in via mail order. All businesses have risks.

The commercial online services assert that they have secure systems that cannot be violated by hackers trying to steal credit card information. The Internet does not make such claims.

Companies are developing data encryption software that will make all information—including credit cards—more secure. The threat of stolen credit card numbers might be a thing of the past very rapidly as companies create encryption programs. Microsoft and VISA announced that they had developed a secure system, as did Netscape Communications Corp., of San Jose, California, a leading publisher of Internet software, which formed an alliance with First Data, a credit card processor, based in Hackensack, New Jersey. Other players in the market include CyberCash of Vienna, Virginia, and Open Market, Inc., of Cambridge, Massachusetts.

Because of these potential risks, banks also are wary about online transactions and have established stiffer than usual requirements for new merchants who sell products online. They are taking a hard–nosed approach to granting credit card processing terminals to companies that do business on online services.

"Banks are afraid of mail order and online businesses. They don't want to take the risk of being vulnerable," says Bob Schechner of Northwest Bank Services of Phoenix (602) 948-3102, which arranges for online businesses to obtain credit card processing services, a process that takes about two weeks. He urges companies to take these steps to protect themselves from fraud and returns:

- Send the product by a carrier that gets a signed record of delivery. Customers can't claim they never received the product. If they honestly didn't receive the product, the shipper's records can be traced.
- Call the credit card authorization center to verify the credit card number before shipping the product.
- Ship the product quickly. People change their minds and then claim they never ordered the product.
- Ask for the customer's address for verification purposes. This is especially important for online orders of information products or other products that are transmitted to the customer over the online system, like a newsletter, software, research or consulting service. In those cases, the merchant or consultant probably wouldn't have thought to make a record of the address because he isn't mailing or shipping anything over a normal shipping route to the customer.
- Ship the package COD (Cash on Delivery).
- Request payment in advance.

Online marketers can employ other strategies to fight fraud. A method that seems to work is the membership program. In this method, you would permit access to the shopping ordering area to members. To become a member, the customer would have to submit her address and credit card information in advance to the merchant, who would ascertain the validity of the information. The new member would receive a membership number and password that she must use to place an order. Since it is unlikely that anyone could get both password and number, the system is safe.

Third–party companies also are brokering this service so that each consumer doesn't have to register with each merchant.

Security issues are discussed in the USENET newsgroups `alt.security.pgp` and `sci.crypt`.

Digital Audit Trails

Ensuring the validity of materials sent over the Internet is now possible with The Digital Notary System from Surety Technologies, of Chatham, New Jersey, a spin–off of Bellcore. The system lets users irrefutably freeze the contents of documents in time by affixing a secure digital time stamp without revealing the contents to a third party. The new system creates the digital equivalent of a paper audit trail for businesses' records.

"A digital time bomb is ticking away within the halls of corporate America. Electronic records, unverifiable and easily tampered with, can explode into staggering liabilities that undermine electronic commerce itself," says Dr. W. Scott Stornetta, Surety's chairman. "The Digital Notary System defuses this threat once and for all by giving businesses the ability to safeguard and validate these records."

The system can verify that a specific order was received at a specific time. It cannot conclusively verify *who* sent it but it will verify *when* it was sent and *what* the order contained.

A personal version of the system is available from `http://www.surety.com` or `ftp.surety.com`. Information about corporate licenses can be obtained by sending e–mail to `steve@surety.com`.

Organizing Your Online Presence for Sales Success

The Web home page can be an instrumental tool in building sales, according to Kristin Zhivago editor of *Marketing Technology* in Menlo Park, California, (415) 328-6000, kristin@zhivago.com. Here are her views on how online activities affect marketing and how to coordinate online presences to build sales:

Online marketing is not just going to *fit into* the marketing mix. It is going to *drive* the marketing effort. If you think of the selling process from the customer's viewpoint, it is a *buying process*. Online marketing has the potential to remove the barriers a customer normally encounters while trying to buy something.

The customer sees the buying process in three distinct phases: recognizing a need, searching for the solution, and making a purchase. Using traditional buying methods, the search for the solution can be time–consuming and frustrating. There is a lot of back–and–forth with vendors.

Throughout the buying process, the customer is seeking answers to specific questions, in a particular order. The vendors provide their answers through salespeople, tech support, literature, videos, demos, and other promotional pieces. Once the questions are answered satisfactorily, the customer will make a buying decision.

If your Web site is well–designed, customers can quickly get answers to their questions. While the need is still fresh in their minds, they will be transformed from someone with a problem to someone who has identified, and wants to purchase, a particular solution. This compresses the buying cycle and will have a profound effect on marketing practices.

Your Web site will be a successful marketing tool only if you organize it to conveniently answer all of the customer's questions. That may seem obvious, but considering how poorly standard marketing materials have provided answers in the past, we are not expecting Web sites to be any better. Organizing the presentation of the information so that it matches the customer's question sequence is particularly important with online marketing, because it is an interactive medium. It puts the customer in the driver's seat. The last thing you want to do is make your customer drive all over Cyberspace waiting for downloads, and getting lost, locked out, and ticked off.

As you start to organize your Web site, don't assume that you already know how your customers ask questions, or that your salespeople will be able to tell you. Salespeople usually talk to customers who are already partway through their buying process. Your site needs to start at the beginning of the process, and progress unobtrusively as your customers work their way towards a purchase.

Call customers and ask them about their buying process. Tell them you are designing your Web site and you want it to make sense to them. Listen carefully. By the tenth phone call, the proper structure should be obvious. There will be clear, identifiable patterns. Use this information to design your Web site, and you will be rewarded with sales from grateful customers. You will have removed the frustration and confusion from their buying process.

Talking to customers will also make you confident that you are doing the right thing. I guarantee that the customer's view of the buying process is different from your company's view of the selling process. You will have to fight for the customer's interests in internal meetings.

If you do not know your customers well, you will not be able to make the logical, fact–based arguments needed to win. The company–centric view will prevail, and customers will be frustrated when they visit your site. If you have spoken with customers, you will not only know what to do, but you will be able to use real–world examples when the arguments start. Anecdotes have an incredibly powerful effect on co–workers, many of whom are holding tightly to cherished, but incorrect ideas about who the customers are and how the customers buy.

Online marketing has the potential to become your most profitable marketing vehicle, because it shortens the buying cycle and can provide detailed sales–tracking data (which has been lacking with other marketing vehicles). But it also requires a substantial investment. Because it is interactive, and online, customers expect it to be kept up to date, and refreshed substantially every few weeks. You will need a Webmaster to do that.

You will also need a Netmonitor, who will constantly watch the various bulletin boards, sites, and discussion lists for questions on your types of products. When appropriate, your Netmonitor should be able to jump in and answer those questions, using pre–approved copy and/or ideas.

So, you will need at least two more people in your marketing department, devoted exclusively to your online marketing efforts. And you can't afford to stop using your standard broadcasting vehicles, which will bring customers to your Net site. Since all of your traditional marketing communications work will need to continue, your total marketing budget will have to be increased.

However, online marketing will decrease the amount of time the salespeople and technical people spend answering questions. This should reduce the total amount of money and resources your company devotes to making the sale.

Where Do We Go from Here?

Now that you have an overview of the benefits and parameters of online sales, let's explore the opportunities for sales on the Internet's World Wide Web and the commercial online services.

World Wide Web: Interactive Selling at Its Best

In this section, you will learn:

- What a Web home page is.
- What kinds of companies have home pages.
- Interesting and well–designed home pages.
- How to plan the interface, design and content of a home page.
- How to market your Web home page.
- Software and commands to create the home page.
- How to hire a consultant to create a Web home page and what prices to expect.
- Costs associated with creating a home page.
- The benefits of shared marketing: malls and shared space.

Clearly, the most exciting interactive sales and marketing tool to date is the Internet's World Wide Web, also known as the Web and WWW. The Web lets you create a virtual shopping experience through the use of hypermedia—a combination of text, pictures and sound that consumers can access to learn more about your company and its products and place an order. A home page, which is really a series of pages and files containing text, pictures and sound, can be compared to a catalog or to a store because customers can read about products, see them in action and place an order. A home page will usually include an overview of the company as well as point–and–click access to product or service information, access to online catalogs, product order forms and other literature.

The Web can help you create a truly interactive sales presentation for a prospect because he selects the information he is interested in. The customer can pick and choose the product he wants to see, read as much information as he wants and ask questions (and find answers) at any time of the day or night—and place an order from anywhere in the world. Consumers can do this by pointing and clicking on designated words and graphics in a document to read information located on a computer miles, or countries, away.

Because of the high degree of interactivity, companies can have the luxury of creating sales presentations that are tailored to each customer's individual needs. Also, marketers can create multiple selling propositions—a different reason to buy for each customer. In this manner, everyone who visits the Web can get personal treatment. At its best, the Web creates a personal selling experience. Customers can see a demonstration of the product in full color. They can hear a step–by–step explanation of how to use your products to cook a better meal, listen to the eggs cracking and watch a happy family eating the food.

Best yet, creating a Web site and the supporting pages doesn't cost an arm and a leg. With the right tools and training, anyone can design a page and have it loaded onto a computer server for the whole world (literally) to see. The Web is truly every person's printing press.

Proper use of this technology can help you create online messages that are the best of the major online systems. While the ads won't give television a run for its money, they do a good job of presenting reams of catalog information.

That is the reality of the Web and the promise of the Web. While all these features are possible, today's technology is too slow to be totally enjoyable for many potential customers. Today's consumer wants instant access to information. Unfortunately, computers take a great deal of time to transfer files, draw pictures and play audio files on a customer's screen. As people get faster modems and information providers lease faster telephone lines, the promise of online multimedia will become a reality. The phone companies and cable operators are exploring methods of making faster transfers affordable. These comments shouldn't be taken as negative, merely as guidelines in designing the home page to take advantage of today's technology—and prepare for the future.

Measurement

Two ways to determine whether marketing is successful are to find out how many people have seen your message and to identify who they are. You can find out how many people visited the home page and each individual page. This can be a

boon to marketers who are testing messages and features. They can see which information was requested and how often. They can determine which sales pitches work more effectively.

However, the Web does not identify customers. It only records the name of the machine from which the user is making a request. Consumers must give you that information directly. You can urge them to do so by requesting they sign a register book or send e–mail. You can entice them to send their names and addresses by granting them access to other areas of the home page or by offering free software or products.

Navigating the Web

To read a Web home page, consumers must use a software program generically called a browser. There are text browsers and graphical browsers. A text browser, such as Lynx, displays only the text information of a file, but not the pictures, sound or video. Graphical browsers, such as NCSA Mosaic, Netscape and Netcom's NetCruiser make surfing the Net fun and easy. These relatively new programs are helping to overcome the problem of Internet access, which has been, slow, difficult and confusing. Consumers simply point and click on icons and highlighted text to be able to read more information and see pictures.

These software programs are becoming more popular and their usage will increase dramatically. Mosaic is a free software program created by the University of Illinois. Commercial versions are being sold by many companies and are widely available. The major commercial online services (CompuServe, America Online and Prodigy) will offer access to the Internet with their own software. IBM's OS/2 Warp includes Internet access and a built–in browser. Microsoft's Windows 95 operating system will include a browser.

This all points to a huge increase in people's ability to access the Web and its commercial sites. Where the Internet was once a difficult place to navigate, these browsers will help people find what they need.

To go to a home page, users must type a command string that begins with the `http://` which stands for hypertext transfer protocol. The next string is the address, which is known as the URL, or uniform resource locator. For example, to reach my home page, you would type:

`http://www.janal-communications.com/janal.html`

This statement tells the browser to go to an specific address and retrieve the information. When it does, you will see that home page displayed on your screen.

Companies on the Web

More than 7,000 businesses have home pages—including 30% of the Fortune 500 —and hundreds more seem to be going online every week, according to Marc Fleischmann of Internet Distribution Services. They range from large companies, like GE Plastics, General Motors, Intel, Proctor & Gamble, Mr. Coffee, and Morgan Stanley to small businesses—like mine. People are even putting their resumes online to find jobs in the high–tech industries. How's that for advertising!

Companies are using the Web to reach consumers, such as:

- Hello Direct, phone accessories
  `http://www.hello-direct.com/hd/`
- Embassy Suites, hotels reservations.
  `http://www.promus.com/embassy.html`
- Rolling Stones, music
  `http://www.stones.com.`
- Sugarloaf, Maine, a ski resort
  `http://www.sugarloaf.com/biz/sugarloaf/`

Business–to–business selling is a reason for these companies to be on the Web:

- IndustryNet `http://www.industry.net`
- Alldata Corp., car recall and repair information
  `http://www.alldata.tsb.com`
- Taligent, a computer company, `http://www.taligent.com`

High–tech companies are also posting job listings online.

In a move that shows the benefits of integrated marketing, MCI's Gramercy Press, a hit commercial series, created a home page so that its fans can learn more about the service. In the first eight hours, 100,000 people viewed the area, according to a company spokesman.

An entire industry—travel—is adopting the Web. Hotels, motels, restaurants, airlines and other companies in the travel industry can make money on the Internet by creating Web home pages that show pictures of the rooms, restaurants and other relevant products. By using online ordering or toll–free telephone lines, readers can place reservations.

Anyone who wonders if the Internet is a mass market, a niche market or a business–to–business market need only look at the Web to see that all three markets are amply represented.

Shopping on Web Home Pages: The Great Leveler

Ironically, one of the more interesting benefits of online shopping and catalogs is that small companies can compete effectively against big ones.

"Small companies with a well–designed home page can look every bit as professional and credible as a large, multinational company. Small companies can build instant credibility with a Web home page," says Wendie Bernstein Lash, president of the Internet Roundtable Society, an Internet presence provider based in San Mateo, California. "People can't tell if you do business from a 90–story office building or a two–room rented suite. Web home pages level the playing field for small companies."

The Internet holds the greatest leverage for small companies because the costs of getting online are low—basically the cost of negotiating a "lease" with an online service provider and paying an Internet presence provider to create the pages—generally less than $1,000. The commercial online services charge in much the same way as TV stations and magazines—by the tens of thousands of dollars. They might even take a percentage of sales. The Net is a bargain!

Guided Tours: Web Home Pages

The best way to truly understand the World Wide Web and its implications for shopping and to begin thinking about organizing your home page is to visit several home pages. This section will take you on a guided tour of several home pages that clearly illustrate how to make shopping interesting, fun and interactive. The examples come from a variety of categories that show that the Web can be home to many different products, from mass markets, like film and hot sauce, to business markets, such as real estate, software and consulting.

Touring a Home Page: Seattle FilmWorks

To get a good understanding of a Web home page, it is best to take a tour of a site that does it right. Let's look at Seattle FilmWorks, whose Internet address is `http://solutionsrc.com/PHOTOWORKS`. This site was selected because it has the following important elements:

- It entices viewers with a visually stunning interface, in this case, photographs.
- It promotes interactivity by sponsoring contests and free offers. By offering two free rolls of film, the company has received hundreds of orders, from as far away as Czechoslovakia and Switzerland. The contest changes every month, so new people can enter and win prizes.
- The company gathers names and addresses of its readers by using the interactive features.
- It encourages repeat visits by containing a library of information on photography. This is a natural since everyone who visits this site is interested in taking better pictures.

If your home page is designed correctly, your customers will be able to see an attractive and inviting catalog of the products and services that you offer. Let's look at various elements.

Each home page could be compared to a table of contents from a well–designed magazine or brochure. There are no set rules or formats for designing a Web home page. You have complete artistic control over the design, look and feel of the page.

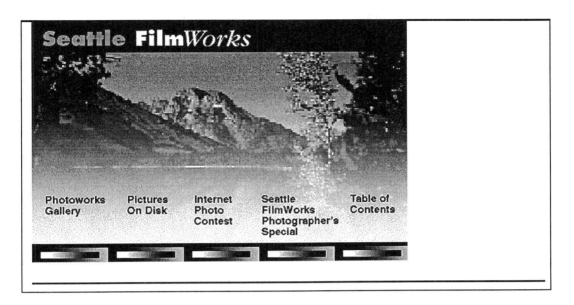

Figure 7–1. Beautiful graphics invite readers to see Seattle FilmWorks.
(Courtesy of Seattle FilmWorks)

In this example (Fig. 7–1), you will see the Seattle FilmWorks logo at the top of the screen. This logo is carried through on each page to present a unified look to the entire presentation. The colors are bold and the typeface easy to read.

Many Web home pages have the following elements: a company logo at the top of the screen, titles that explain what information can be found and pictures that show various products. The page is about the size of a computer screen. The full range of colors are available as well as an unlimited amount of space to print text.

Let's look at the opening graphic. Notice how it contains buttons for the "Gallery," "Picture," "Contest," "Special" and "Table of Contents." A consumer who clicks on the appropriate button will be whisked to the corresponding pages containing the specific information.

For now, let's stay on this page, because there is more than meets the eye.

One interesting design consideration is that the page can extend deeper than the screen, though not wider. This means that you actually have a great deal of room to work with beyond the depth of the user's screen. You must make a decision about to what the user first sees on the screen, and what he can see when he scrolls down the page—if you want him to scroll down the page.

In this example, the home page does indeed contain more information than can fit onto a screen. You'll notice that the top of the film graphic appears near the bottom of the screen. The elevator bars at the far right of the screen show computer–literate readers that they can navigate downward to see more of the page. Less computer–literate readers will see that there is more art and, hopefully, realize that they can see this material by scrolling. Unfortunately, there are no computer manuals on a home page. Readers must be given explicit instructions if you want them to interact with your site. As the reader scrolls further down the page, he reads about the highlights of the site.

Do you want to continue to view Photoworks with graphics or <u>without?</u>

PhotoWorks Gallery

PhotoWorks reveals three never-before-published photos of Marilyn Monroe.

Pictures On Disk

Seattle FilmWorks introduces an easy, low-cost way to get your own photos on a floppy disk.

Internet Photo Contest

See previous winners. Your photo could soon win you $250.

Seattle FilmWorks Photographer's Special

Get up to 24 of your images digitized free with your first film developing order.

Figure 7–2. To save time, give readers a choice to see a text–only home page.
(Courtesy of Seattle FilmWorks)

The home page asks readers if they prefer to have the page delivered without pictures (Fig. 7–2). It also provides a table of contents for the rest of the information at this site. Even though this home page relies heavily on photos to make its impression—after all, people who come to this site are interested in taking pictures—it is important for every Web home page to offer this feature. Because pictures can take a long time to display on the reader's screen, they might not want to kill an hour waiting for the page to display on the screen. Remember that people have short attention spans—even shorter when they are paying online and telephone charges! In the case of this site, the opening page took nearly 10 minutes to transfer on a 14.4–kilobaud modem in the middle of the day. Other pictures and graphics took equally long periods of time. When you design your pages, you must consider whether people are willing to trade time for value. In this case, many people are interested in seeing good photographs and will probably wait for them to transmit. Will they do so in your home page? Are the pictures valuable additions to the information–gathering and distribution process? Do they enhance the interactive experience? Or are they cute, visually interesting place holders that don't really add a whole lot? You need to decide (or test the page with others and act on the results).

One work–around solution to the problem of large art files and slow transmission is to use small, thumbnail–sized art and give the reader the opportunity to click on it to see a full–screen version.

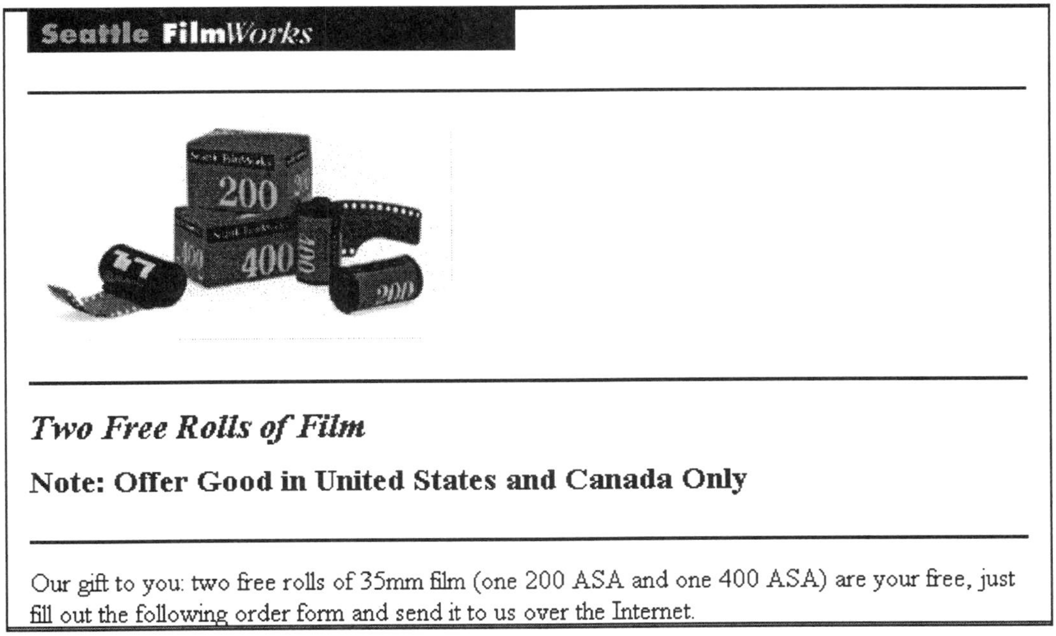

Figure 7–3. Offering free samples is a great way to attract people.
(Courtesy of Seattle FilmWorks)

The special offer (Fig. 7–3) is located on a page offering two free rolls of film. Notice how the company banner unifies the page to the home page and enforces the uniform look. It also helps to build logo and brand identity.

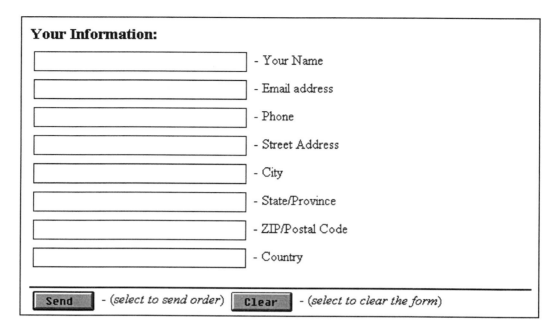

Figure 7–4 Order forms should be uncluttered. (Courtesy of Seattle FilmWorks)

The order form (Fig. 7–4) is sweet and simple. Anyone can understand it. There is no legal gobbledygook. If you want the film, you fill out the coupon. The form asks for the reader's name, postal address and e–mail address.

The designers realized that people will fill out a simple form but might hesitate if it begins to take too long or asks a lot of questions. Two push buttons at the bottom of the screen allow the user to send the request or stop the process. In either case consumers are sent back to the home page, where they can make more choices. This screen fulfills one of the most important functions in marketing: It captures the reader's name and contact information. The Web has no provision for identifying readers. So, if you want to know who has visited your site, you must ask them.

"What's really important is capturing information from people who visit the site," says Dan Fine of Fine Communications in Seattle, a database marketer who created the site.

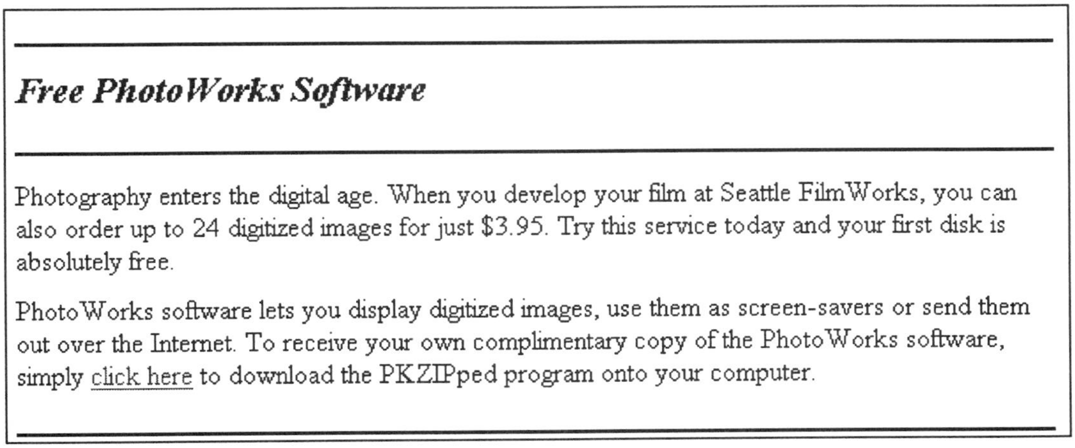

Free PhotoWorks Software

Photography enters the digital age. When you develop your film at Seattle FilmWorks, you can also order up to 24 digitized images for just $3.95. Try this service today and your first disk is absolutely free.

PhotoWorks software lets you display digitized images, use them as screen-savers or send them out over the Internet. To receive your own complimentary copy of the PhotoWorks software, simply click here to download the PKZIPped program onto your computer.

Figure 7–5. Free software is sure to draw people to your home page.
(Courtesy of Seattle FilmWorks)

The home page offers readers free software (Fig. 7–5) to turn their photos into screen savers—a naturally great idea for this audience. To receive the software, readers were told to "click here" after reading a description of the program. Behind the scenes, the computer did the rest. Downloading the software was easy.

One note: The file took more than 30 minutes to download. There was no indication to the reader how large the file was or how long to expect the transfer to last. Even when the file was being transmitted, the screen displays only the size of the file transmitted to that point, not the total file size, so the reader has no idea how long this will take. You don't want to risk upsetting your readers, so you would do well to tell them the size of the file and estimate how long the transfer will take over several modem speeds. People won't get upset over a long transmission if they can budget their time in advance.

One of the key points in designing a Web home page is to add value to the reader's experience. This area accomplishes this task in several ways. It offers:

- *A free, useful product:* Most people who visit this site will want the film because they shoot pictures. This is a great lure.
- *Interactivity:* By giving readers the chance to participate in a contest where they can submit their photos—or see winners. To make the contest current, prizes are given each month. This ensures that people will have something new to look at and have another chance to enter.

- ***Free information:*** Distributing free information is a cherished tradition on the Internet, so this tactic works well by dispensing information that has obvious value. In this case, the information answers questions about photography.
- ***Free software:*** If people like free information, they love free software. This tactic not only draws people to the home page, it ties in with the general theme of the page. This software is truly useful and reinforces the marketing message of letting this company develop your film so that you can use the images on your computer.

Touring a Home Page: Intelligent Market Analytics, Inc.

Intelligent Market Analytics http://www.marketmind.com/ is a publisher of software for investors. Its home page was selected as an example for software publishers who can use the Internet to sell and distribute software. After all, doesn't everyone on the Net have a computer?

This page makes good use of:

- Downloading software.
- Registering software.
- Fee information and manuals.
- Instant printing.
- Links to other home pages of interest to investors.

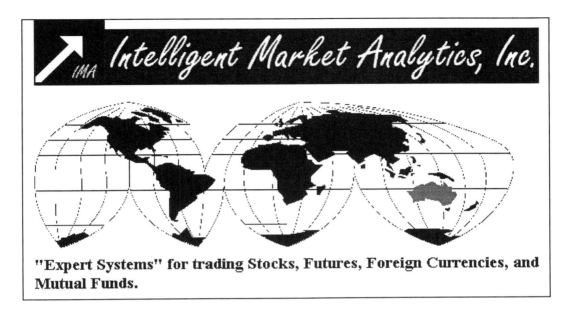

Figure 7–6. Nice graphic and clear positioning explain Intelligent Market Analytic's mission. (Courtesy of Intelligent Market Analytics, Inc.)

The first thing you notice when the page displays (Fig. 7–6) is the bright graphic in vibrant colors and the friendly, inviting typeface. You can read about what the company does and what the consumer can find on this page in the very first paragraph, so the customer's time is not wasted.

If you interested in a truly intelligent approach to the worlds financial markets we have the answer for you!

Complete Package and 30-day Trial $269

- Complete package includes SuperCharts 2.1 , MarketMind 3.0, and data on selected futures, stocks, and mutual funds.

30-day trial systems $88
- 30 day trial requires that you currently use SuperCharts 2.0 or higher or TradeStation3.0 or higher by Omega Research.

For immediate downloading:
set - Load to Disk - to ON, then
Click on your selection below:

Free demo

1)   Once you have down loaded file run "pkunzip Demo.zip"
2)   Then type demo at the DOS PROMPT.

Figure 7–7. You must explain how to do complicated procedures.
(Courtesy of Intelligent Market Analytics, Inc.)

In the section called the complete package (Fig. 7–7), the reader quickly finds the offer, the price and the terms—again, no wasted time. The word "trial" is good, as the reader knows there aren't any surprises about pricing.

This page links to a section that uses the word that Internet users most want to see: *Free* demo download. It should be noted that full instructions for downloading are given in the link, which also contains information on system requirements, installation procedures and, most importantly, uninstalling procedures. Because of the large size of the program and its intense system requirements, this step really is a must. The size of the files are given so that users can estimate the amount of time it will take to receive the files. Few things frustrate computer users as much as waiting for files.

To make life easy for readers, the company has afforded them the ability to print the instructions directly from the home page while staying online. All they have to do is follow the instructions printed on the screen.

If you were to read the installation instructions, you'd see that in order to use the demo, you must call the company. While this is an extra, unwelcome step for the consumer, the tactic was clearly designed to allow the company to capture the user's name and address so that it could create a relationship. To make life easier for the consumer, the best times to call are posted in this note. Notice that readers can download the manual. This is a nice touch, because people might want to read the manual of this sophisticated program to see all features.

Here are some links of interest to investors and market analysts:

GNN Personal Finance Center
Security APL Inc.
FINWeb Home Page
CTSNET Business & Finance Center
MIT AILab Sources of Finance Information
MIT AILab Experimental Stock Market Data

Figure 7–8. References to related areas provide a service to consumers.
(Courtesy of Intelligent Market Analytics, Inc.)

A list at the bottom of the home page (Fig. 7–8) lists other Web home pages that would interest people who stop here. Presumably, the other sites would list this one as well in the best tradition of "I'll scratch your back if you scratch mine." This tactic can be useful to promote your home page as well.

Software publishers should note the selling and licensing terms on the home page. People can use the software for 30 days as a free trial. To increase sales, a message to register comes on the screen each day after day 19. Prospects are told here that they must register by the 30th day and pay the full fee or arrange for a lease to become a registered user.

Another neat feature is a welcoming letter from the company president, Robert L. Kendall Jr. It's nice to know who's in charge. Online citizens like to make their feelings known, positive and negative. Now they know who to call.

Touring a Home Page: Hot! Hot! Hot!

Lobo Enterprises operates a World Wide Web home page that offers hot sauces for sale `http://www.hot.presence.com/hot/`. It is an excellent example of a catalog that features easy access to its contents through a menu, clear instructions and imaginative and fun artwork.

The home page hits you right between the eyes with vibrant artwork in hot colors (Fig. 7–9). The introduction tells you about the hot sauces available, like Bat's Brew, Nuclear Hell and Ring of Fire.

Welcome to Hot Hot Hot, the Net's coolest hot sauce shop!

(brought to you by Presence)

We want to welcome you to the Internet's first "Culinary Headshop!" Here you'll find fiery foodstuffs you never thought existed. Please come in and browse!

We have over 100 products of fire and the list is always growing. With names like Bats Brew, Nuclear Hell, and Ring of Fire, we're sure you'll find something you like.

Figure 7–9. Main menu for Hot! Hot! Hot! Catalog. (Courtesy of Presence)

If you're a first time user of the World Wide Web, you may want to take a look at:

- an introduction to the Web
- the NetCruiser user guide If you're a first time user of this catalog, you may be interested in taking a look at:

- catalog instructions or
- an introduction from the owners We try very hard to accommodate all user agent types (so, for example, we know that you're using NetCruiser), however, we're not always completely successful. If you see anything that doesn't look right, please send us mail describing the problem. Thank you very much.

Users with Graphic Browsers: We have tried to make all of the graphics small enough that it is not necessary to turn off image loading on your browser. If you do have image loading turned off, you should note that a number of important navigational links will not be available.

And now, To the Catalog!

Figure 7–10. Newbies can read instructions; old–timers can jump to the catalog.
(Courtesy of Presence)

Home pages can actually be longer than a screen, as is this one. If you scroll down (Fig. 7–10), you'll see a nice set of instructions to guide you through the system of pages. The narrative also tells you that the smart software has determined which client you are using and has adapted the layout to accommodate that screen, a very nice touch! The images, we are told, have been constructed to transmit quickly—a bonus. At the bottom of the screen, there is a hot link to the catalog.

The Net's Coolest Hot Shop

We have one of the largest collections of international hot sauces for you to discover; best of all it's here, online and always available.

Hot Hot Hot Holiday Specials!

Figure 7–11. Main menu for the catalog. (Courtesy of Presence)

The catalog's opening screen (Fig. 7–11) grabs attention immediately with its vibrant colors. Rather than use a simple table of contents like a printed catalog, the graphic is linked to each succeeding page, so that users can select hot sauces by heat level, origin, ingredients or name, with appropriate graphics to illustrate the themes.

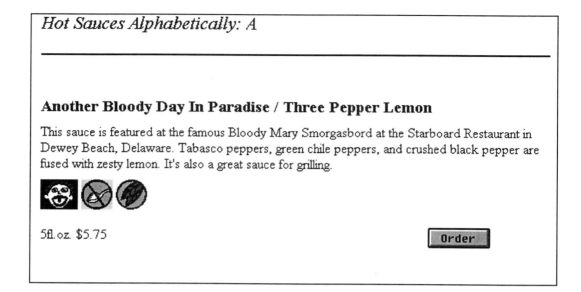

Figure 7–12. Product description links to an order form. (Courtesy of Presence)

The product description (Fig. 7–12) provides short overviews, with three icons that help readers see at a glance the various ratings for heat and other factors, a text description of the ingredients and the best cooking use for the product. Size and price are displayed so that readers can see them easily.

Notice the order button on the page. This page is not cluttered and gives readers the information they need quickly.

What's new at HotHotHot(TM)?

11/26/94: A huge special holiday section for all of your year-end shopping needs!

11/24/94: 16 NEW Sauces!

- Ay! Caramba
- Barbados Jack
- California Just Chili Co.
- Endorphin Rush
- Flavors of the Rainforest Papaya
- Gib's Bottled Hell
- Gib's Nuclear Hell
- Island Soy Sauce
- Melinda's Amarillo Hot Sauce
- Mongo Hot Sauce
- Montezuma Habanero Chipotle
- Oso Hot Sauce
- Papaya Curry

Figure 7–13. "What's new" tells people about offerings. (Courtesy of Presence)

The "What's new" page (Fig. 7–13) is dated so that people can see if the listings have changed since their last browse. Products are listed with text only, so the page displays quickly. Each title is a hot link that, when clicked, will lead the consumer to a description of the hot sauce. Traditional marketing shows its hand here with clever titles. Who can resist a hot sauce named "Endorphin Rush"?

Our featured sauce this month is Dave's Insanity Sauce, Private Reserve, a limited edition super-hot version of Dave's.

Be sure to check out our What's New page and our Comment of the Month.

To order a sauce, select [**Select**] --we'll keep track of your order for you!

Also, if you ever have any questions or comments, just select

Copyright (c) 1994 Presence and Lobo Enterprises

Figure 7–14. Merchants feature sale items, just as in a store. (Courtesy of Presence)

The online version of an end–cap display in a retail store is seen in the "featured product" (Fig. 7–14) that highlights an item the merchant wants to showcase. Consider doing this to your selected products.

Touring a Home Page: InfoPlace

InfoPlace is an Internet presence provider which means it creates Web home pages for companies and places them online. This very simple design (Fig. 7–15) was chosen because the company had one task: to show prospective clients what kinds of services the company provides. By clicking on the appropriate anchors, readers can find out about the services this company offers.

The address is `http://www.infoplace.com/infoplace/`.

The page is light on art, which means the page will draw quickly even on slow machines—a benefit. The prospect who wants to see examples of the company's work is directed to companies listed on the screen. Selecting those companies will take the prospect directly to the page.

To see the file that composed this page and the underlying commands, please see Table 7–1 later in this chapter.

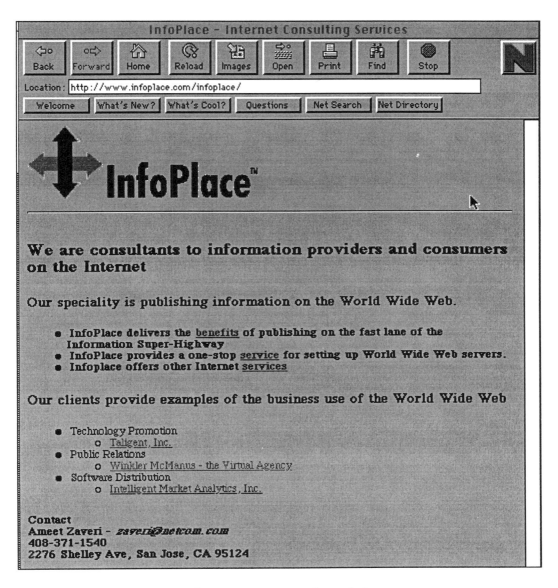

Figure 7–15. InfoPlace home page is simple and clean. (Courtesy of InfoPlace)

Touring a Home Page: Alldata

Alldata is the publisher of the world's largest database of vehicle repair and maintenance information. Currently over 10,000 auto repair facilities nationwide use Alldata's diagnostic and repair database to fix cars faster and more accurately. The Internet was a logical place for the company to be, says Bob Lash, executive president of the Internet Roundtable Society, an Internet presence provider that created the site. "The vast majority of Internet users own a car, and 10% of car owners do their own do–it–yourself repair work," he says. "They felt they had saturated their prime market, the auto service market. By providing information that is useful to many people, they could reach the consumer market."

ALLDATA Corporation is the leading publisher of electronic automotive repair information. Currently over 10,000 repair facilities nationwide use ALLDATA's diagnostic and repair database to fix cars faster and more accurately. Today you can have access through this server to crucial maintenance, safety, recall and repair information for your vehicle from ALLDATA's extensive database. In addition, you can download **ALLDATA - LINK software** (IBM compatibles) for full access to over 1,000,000 pages of vehicle repair and maintenance information on a **free trial basis.**

 See Recall Notice and Technical Service Bulletin (TSB) Titles for Your Car

- How TSBs can help you maintain your car
- What are Recall Notice Titles and how they benefit you

Figure 7–16. Artists can be creative, as Alldata's home page shows a car that appears to be in motion. (Copyright 1994. Internet Roundtable Society)

This page is selected as an example of an information–rich home page. The company is building its credibility as a Net–wise company. This can pay off as consumers go to dealers and ask if they use the Alldata repair database.

It is easy to see how the customers will benefit from the mountains of free and useful information—more than a million pages in all.

Let's look at the page (Fig. 7–16). An illustration at the top of the page identifies the company and presents an attractive visual welcome to readers. The leading paragraph clearly describes what the company does and what the reader will find in the home page: "crucial maintenance, safety, recall and repair information for your vehicle from Alldata's extensive database." It is important to let readers know up front what to expect. In this example, readers don't have to wait for large pictures to appear slowly on the screen before finding out whether they want to spend time at this site.

Alldata offers free software, always a powerful inducement to readers. The software permits readers to access more than a million pages of vehicle repair and maintenance information on a free trial basis.

The next section features icons of attractive tires that are drawn so well that they almost appear to be moving. This is a good use of art that relates to the subject matter.

Case Study: Homebuyer's Fair

ASK Real Estate Information Services, of Silver Spring, Maryland created The Homebuyer's Fair http://homefair.com "to bring revolutionary benefits to home buyers," says Arnold Kling. "We believe that the Internet can be used to enable you to access more information at a much lower cost. That in turn will empower you to keep more of your own money when you buy a home—to avoid the 'junk fees,' exorbitant commissions, and other large expenses that traditionally have been imposed on the home buyer."

Figure 7–17. Homebuyer's Fair's simple graphic presents an inviting atmosphere. (Courtesy of ASK Real Estate Information Services)

The home page consists of useful information and interactive exhibits, like a mortgage calculator and information on such topics as: 15–year vs. 30–year mortgages; interest rates; should you sell your house yourself?; using a buyer's broker; watching out for scams; lowering your down payment; FAQs about mortgage insurance and ARM Index History. Consumers can also hunt for houses and condominiums in the Washington, D.C. area.

Homebuyer's Fair hopes to make money on the page by charging information providers, such as lenders, builders, and other service providers who exhibit on the page.

"Fairs and expos usually charge some minimal admission to consumers as well as earning fees from companies that exhibit," says Kling. "It seems fairly implausible to us to charge consumers, so that we are concentrating on earning revenue from exhibitors."

Traffic at the fair was slow at its introduction, but has picked up speed.

"As a Fair, we faced the classic 'chicken–and–egg' challenge that you need interesting exhibits to draw traffic, and you need traffic in order to convince businesses to put up interesting exhibits," says Kling. "We started out with displays from two lenders, prototype house exhibits, and a fraction of the material that we now have in the information booth. Because there were so few commercial Web sites when we began, our site actually was relatively interesting. We were selected as 'Editor's Choice' for the month of July by the Internet Letter info@netweek.com. However, after our first week, traffic settled down to less than 2,000 home page accesses per month."

In response to low traffic, Kling put in place information to boost interest.

"By mid–August, we had created the 'Electronic Postcard' for mortgage lenders, and we had set up the Washington, D.C. New Homes Guide online. This gave us some real substance, and traffic began to rise. As of late November 1994, we were getting over 4,000 home page accesses per month, and this figure seems likely to increase rapidly from this point forward. The total number of hits, which other sites sometimes use as a measure of traffic, for us is over 10 times the number of home page accesses, meaning that the average individual visiting the fair looks at over 10 of our pages. Also, our current visitors appear to be more engaged in the home–buying process and therefore more willing to request services from our exhibitors," says Kling.

Partly because of the very nature of a brokering business—matching buyer and seller—real estate on the Internet has excellent potential. "We believe that the use of the Internet for real estate marketing is going to grow explosively. Simply maintaining our 'What's New' page could well be a full–time job within nine months," Kling says. "Here is a scenario that we believe is plausible: Within a few years the Internet will be the best source of house listings. The Multiple Listing Services (MLS) of the real estate boards will either be merged into the Internet or will have been overtaken by Internet listings. You will look for houses online, and then visit only those houses in which you have a strong interest."

The physical storage of real estate listings will be highly decentralized, with any one computer holding only a tiny percentage of listings. For a while, there will be centralized indexes of real estate listings that link to the individual advertisements, but eventually search engines will replace the indexes. In the future, Kling says, buyers may advertise as readily as sellers.

"We may see people describing their requirements for a home in an advertisement, and sellers responding to those ads," Kling says. "In the financing arena, home buyers may assemble their own loan application packages. You will collect your own documents, including a credit report that is signed digitally by the reporting agency. You may be able to get your loan underwritten and approved by an automated system before you even send it to a lender. Then you will direct your package to the lender that can best meet your needs."

Touring a Home Page: HomeBuyer's Fair

This page contains a wealth of information of interest to purchasers of homes. It opens with an inviting graphic representing a fair's information booth (Fig. 7–17).

What can I find at the Homebuyer's Fair?

In the information booth, you can find pamphlets and articles about topics of interest to people buying and selling homes You can get a glimpse of the future of home listings in the Houses for Sale booth. In the Obtain a Mortgage booth you can use calculators to compute monthly payments, find out the loan amount for which you qualify, check out displays from various lenders, and contact lenders directly.

We keep track of What's New in sites pertaining to real estate on the Net. We have a page that explains How to Exhibit. If you get "lost" and want to see an index, we have a map of the Fair, which on some pages is symbolized by a small graphic of a compass.

For those who are not ready to buy a home, we have apartment search services for several cities. Finally, we have a section to browse if you are interested in the subjects of business and commerce on the Web.

Figure 7–18. Overviews help readers see if this home page appeals to them.
(Courtesy of ASK Real Estate Information Services)

Scrolling further down this page reveals a section called "What Can I Find at the Homebuyer's Fair?" (Fig. 7–18), a great aid to an information–rich home page. By reading this information, consumers can find links to:

- What's new. This item is a must for home pages that expect to draw consumers back time after time. People need to be able to find out what's new and explore there. If they think the information doesn't change, they won't come back.
- Most popular exhibits. This item helps consumers see the highlights of the area. If they have limited time, this feature helps them hit the hot spots.
- Links to related home pages, with explanations. This area is not only a service to readers who want to find related information, it is a benefit to the information provider who can maintain a referral network with related home pages.

- What is *not* on the HomeBuyer's Fair. This unique category helps to set user expectations. By reading this information, consumers will know if they should be here at all.

Case Study: IndustryNet

Automation Network News, ANN, of Pittsburgh, is a database marketing and information firm focusing on engineers, professionals, buyers and specifiers within industry and manufacturing. Automation Network News promotes local commerce in 14 U.S. regions with database marketing programs, using regional print, database and seminar products. *Industry Report* is the largest controlled circulation publication for industry in the regions it serves. The *Locator* is the largest electronic Yellow Pages for industry in the nation. Automation Network News keeps in direct contact with its user base through teleresearch for its Continuing Education Seminar programs. It made over 100,000 telephone calls to its users in 1994, discussing their preferences, interests and industrial buying decisions.

The wealth of data supplied by these ongoing businesses fuels IndustryNET ANN's online service `http://www.industry.net`. IndustryNET, like all ANN products, is free, just as the print publishing model of controlled circulation.

IndustryNET is an online news and information system that also includes marketing information on the latest products and technologies, training schedules, demo disks, product catalogs and other information from the industry's leading manufacturers. The area will draw people for the news, but also entices them with shareware software, job postings, stock prices and sports news.

IndustryNET steps beyond the traditional publishing paradigm by having a service that will set up forums for companies. These forums are a medium to display promotional materials for new products, catalogs, seminars and training schedules, as well as to distribute software programs, updates and demos without incurring large costs for production and distribution. The forums support online ordering and requests for quotations.

"Your forum in IndustryNET generates prospects for a full year, yet only costs about the same as a one–time full–page ad in a typical monthly trade journal. The big difference is that your forum works every day throughout the year generating inquiries, supporting existing customers and providing invaluable feedback to your sales and marketing departments," the company says.

Using this, IndustryNET is publisher, mall manager and ad agency.

"You have to be all of them," says Ron Tozzie, manager of IndustryNET's Professional Organizations Group, Pittsburgh `ronald.tozzie@industry.net`.

Just having the technology to go onto the Internet is not enough, he asserts.

"We pride ourselves on content. We have industry–insiders, journalists, graphics and technical writers," he says. The services link industrial product information with local supplier information with news. "The Internet is only one medium we use to bring buyers and sellers together. We never lose sight of that."

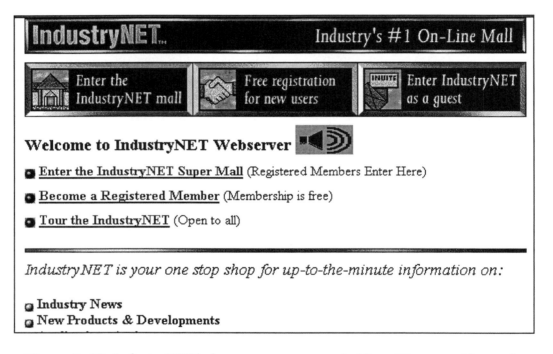

Figure 7–19. IndustryNET's home page presents bold, striking graphics and an easy–to–use push–button interface. (Source: IndustryNET)

Automation Network News integrates the Internet as one part of its overall marketing program.

"If we focused only on the Internet, it would be very difficult to maintain our high level of content," says Tozzie. "High levels of useful content, with a local orientation for the user is key."

Touring a Home Page: IndustryNET

The IndustryNET home page (Fig. 7–19) is attractive and easy to navigate. The IndustryNET banner is displayed on the top of the page along with its positioning statement "Industry's #1 On–Line Mall." Three active icons below allow people to enter the mall, register free or enter the mall as a guest with limited privileges. This model allows current members to bypass new–member information and lets prospects find out how to register. The word "free" tells people immediately that they have nothing to lose. If they select this option, they will see a registration form asking about addresses, job responsibilities and product interest.

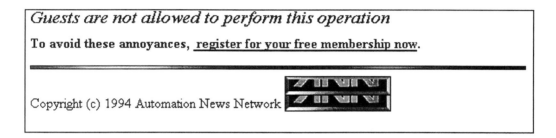

Figure 7–20. Blocking services might persuade guests to join the free service.
(Source: IndustryNET)

An interesting note is that, for guest visits, certain features are blocked off. For example, nonmembers can see the main listings for such categories as shareware and press releases, but can't actually access this information. Instead, they see (Fig. 7–20) "Guests are not allowed to perform this operation." This is politely worded and doesn't offend. Information about free registration follows. This is an important screen if you want to capture, for follow–up service, the names and addresses and vital information about the people who visit your site. This is especially true for ANN, which does a great deal of telemarketing of services such as training sessions.

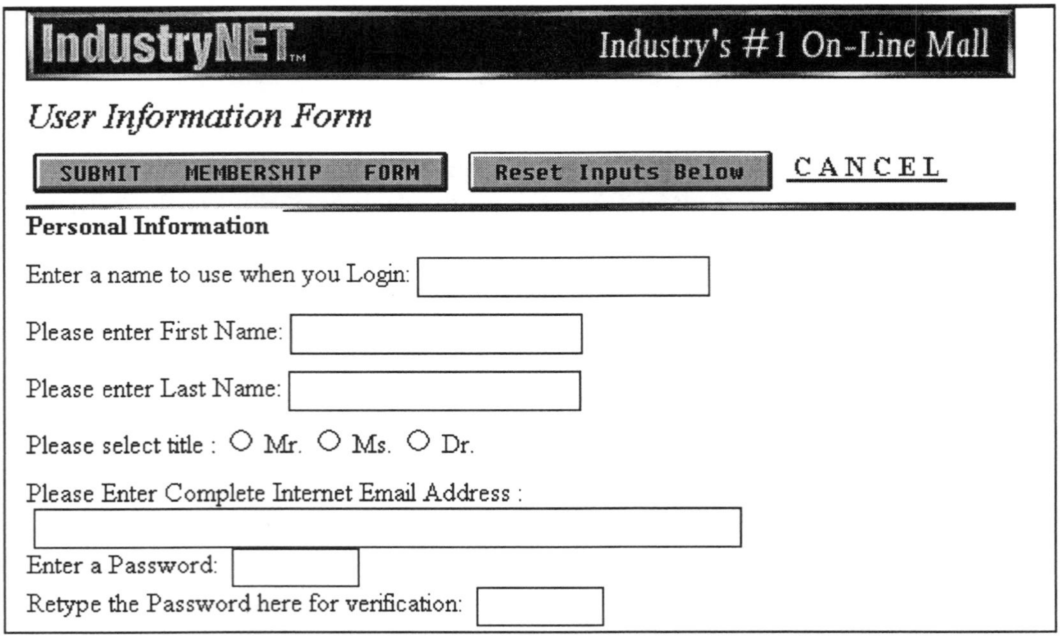

Figure 7–21. Registration forms must be easy to complete. (Source: IndustryNET)

The screen provides a direct link to a registration form, which is easy to fill out online (Fig. 7–21).

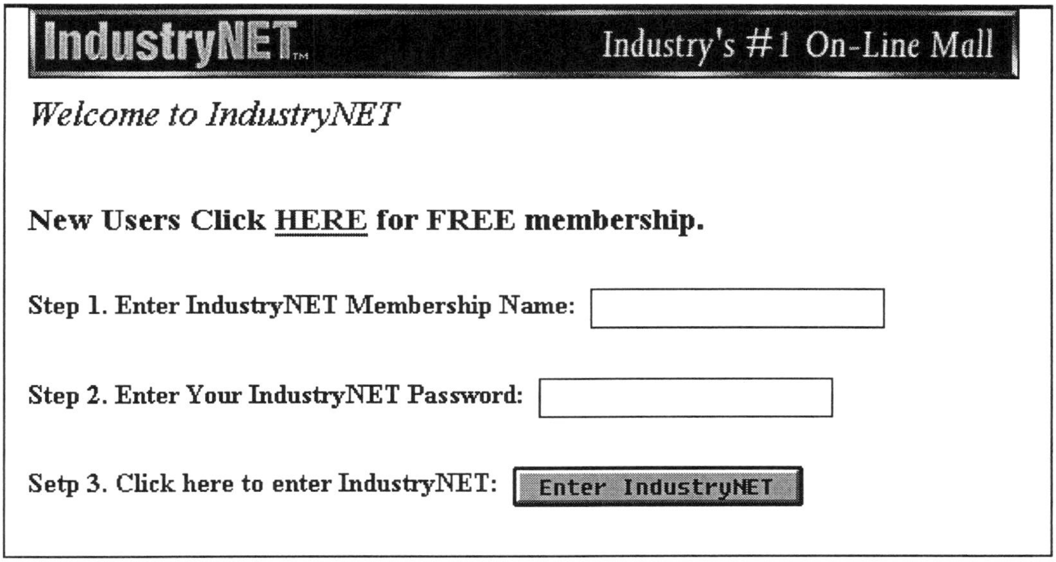

Figure 7–22. Members must identify themselves to use the service.
(Source: IndustryNET)

To enter the area, members must complete a form (Fig. 7–22). This procedure is used to ensure that only members can gain access to the service. Since there is no fee for this service, the requirement helps the company gather the name of the user and vital demographic information. Other companies that charge consumers to access the area might want to study this method.

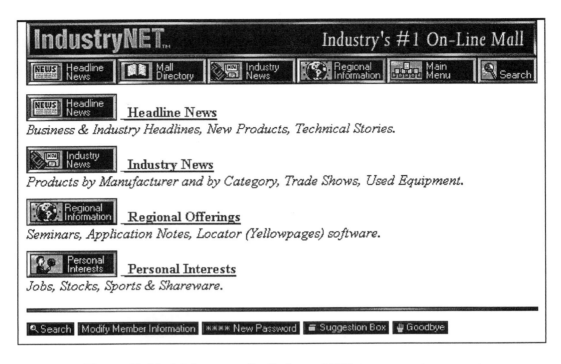

Figure 7–23. Main menu for IndustryNET. (Source: IndustryNET)

Members then see a main menu page (Fig. 7–23) that lists the available options, such as news and shareware. Notice that the look and feel of the main screen carries over to subsequent screens to maintain a unified presentation.

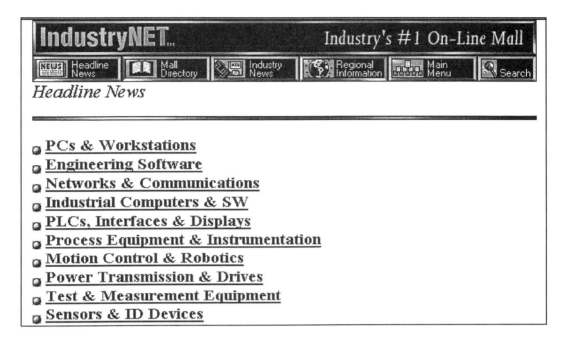

Figure 7–24. News menu. (Source: IndustryNET)

As a news service, IndustryNET provides a menulike system (Fig. 7–24) on the home page to find news of particular industries. Readers first select from a menu of industries and then see a menu of press releases in that industry. Clicking on the headline will reveal the press release.

Industrial Locator Software

The Industrial Locator is an incredibly simple to use PC based software program that's the #1 buying guide for engineering and purchasing professionals. It provides the user with direct access to suppliers and service providers in their area. (Make sure you download the Industrial Locator program as well as the Data for your region of the country.)

- **Industrial Locator Program**
- **Western PA/West Virginia Data**
- **Northern Ohio Data**
- **Southern Ohio/Kentucky Data**
- **Greater Delaware Valley Data**

*Figure 7–25. Menus lead people to needed information. (*Source: IndustryNET)

One of the main functions of ANN is to link buyer and seller. To do this, it created databases of products and companies located by region. The database can be searched with software that can be downloaded free (Fig. 7–25).

IndustryNET is also one of the only online services in the nation offering dial–up and telnet services (in VT100, ANSI and graphical interfaces) as well as World Wide Web server, all from the same database.

This is a carefully thought–out service that integrates well into the total marketing program.

Case Study: Quote.Com

Quote.Com, Inc. is a provider of financial information that helps investors on the Internet. It was chosen as an example of a company that is charging for access to its service on the World Wide Web. Most home pages offer free information in hopes of making money from advertisers who want to reach their readers, or by offering information that will build a relationship in which the reader becomes a customer. As business models take shape on the Internet, Quote.Com `http://www.quote.com` is one to study. Even the home page (Fig. 7–26) shows the products it offers and an inducement to subscribe.

Figure 7–26. Quote.Com's home page shows key features. (Courtesy of Quote.Com)

"One of the reasons I started Quote.Com was because I noticed that investors were becoming more actively involved in their investment decisions," says Chris Cooper, president of Quote.Com Inc. "I've tried to create a place on the Internet where investors can find all of the tools they need to be as informed as a broker on Wall Street. The Basic Plus service, at $33.95 per month, bundles professional tools at a price an individual investor can afford."

Members pay their fee and are given a password that allows them to use the services in Quote.Com.

Cooper studied the market and found that more people than ever before are investing their money in the stock market. "Returns on more traditional means of investing are simply not enough to keep up with inflation. Factor in large commissions from full–service brokers and there is not much money left. As a result, many people have taken control of their finances by using discount brokerage houses. To succeed in this scenario investors have to take an active role in their portfolios, including research, analysis, and awareness of breaking news," he says.

In response to these needs Quote.Com created several levels of service, called "packages," which include news services, Business Wire and PR Newswire, quotes, portfolio tracking, research tools, and one–year price histories for stocks, commodities and mutual funds, Hoover's Company Profiles and Standard & Poor's Marketscope. Packages can also include e–mail notification of news from portfolio items, price limits and end–of–the–day pricing. This is an excellent example of using technology to add value. Prices range from $9.95 to $39.95 per month.

The company has taken advantage of the fact that users have different methods of finding information on the Internet. Users can access Quote.Com through five different connection methods. Quote.Com's custom quote server is available through telnet access `telnet quote.com`, e–mail `infoquote.com`, direct Internet connection on a World Wide Web browser `http://www.quote.com/`, via File Transfer Protocol at `ftp.quote.com`, or through custom software provided by Quote.Com or its site licensees.

Like most successful home pages, Quote.Com offers a free service to turn prospects into customers. In this case, the company offers a complimentary membership in the Quote.Com financial market data service. When users register, they can retrieve five quotes a day from any of the U.S. exchanges, symbol searches and limited balance sheet data. In addition to the Basic Service subscription, users can choose from an á la carte menu of optional services and pay an additional fee by the month or by the individual one–time usage.

By following this strategy, the company neared the break–even point after four months of operation.

Touring a Home Page: Boardwatch Magazine

Figure 7–27. Boardwatch's *home page features a menu.* (Courtesy of Boardwatch)

Boardwatch Magazine is the leading monthly publication covering the computer bulletin board marketplace. Its home page shows an attractive logo and its positioning statement, "Guide to Electronic Bulletin Boards and the Internet" (Fig. 7–27). Four bulleted hyperlinks follow which allows readers to read the welcome message and articles, subscribe or send e–mail to the editors.

Subscribe to Boardwatch Magazine & Save 37% off of the cover price!

Here is how you can subscribe to Boardwatch Magazine:

By E-Mail: subscriptions@boardwatch.com

By Phone: 1-800-933-6038

By Fax: (303)-973-3731

By Bulletin Board: (303)-973-4222

By telnet: Telnet to Boardwatch Magazine. Note: You must configure you web browser to point to your telnet program.

⬤ *The information that we require to place your order include your Name, Address, City, State, and Zip.*

Figure 7–28. Subscribing to Boardwatch *is simple with so many options.*
(Courtesy of Boardwatch)

The subscription page (Fig. 7–28) begins with an attractive offer: "Save 37% off the cover price." It then lists ways to order for e–mail, phone, fax, BBS and telnet. This tactic takes advantage of every communications method, which is a good idea since different people might feel more comfortable calling instead of sending e–mail—or vice versa.

Touring a Home Page: Janal Communications

Janal Communications is a public relations agency specializing in software publishers and computer hardware manufacturers. In addition to promoting the author, this home page solves several interesting marketing objectives for consultants and authors.

Janal Communications Home Page

Welcome to the **Janal Communications** Home Page. We're a public relations agency that helps computer hardware and software companies sell more products by getting their products reviewed in the media. We also help publicize any company doing business on the Internet or commercial online services. You'll find information about our services, as well as our three products, *How to Publicize High Tech Products and Services, Publicity Builder Software,* and *The Online Marketing Handbook.*

Free Information

Learn how to position your products effectively when you read the **"The Foolproof Positioning**

Figure 7–29. Service providers can create a home page.
(Courtesy of Janal Communications)

The opening paragraph (Fig. 7–29) explains the purpose of the company and what can be found on the home page, including information about the company and two books and a software program written by Dan Janal. The hyperlinks will take readers to more information about these topics. Four pictures draw across the screen—one for Dan Janal, and another for the publicity book and software, as well as a photo of Ivan Levison, a direct mail copywriter. This is a visual menu, in which readers can find information by clicking on these photos.

Services Profile

Janal Communications provides expert, personal, hands-on, cost-efficient public relations, marketing and marketing communications services to hardware and software companies.

Janal Communications creates the relevant and motivating idea that helps a company establish a leadership position, and executes a public relations plan geared toward generating visibility and credibility to stimulate sales.

Capabilities include:

1) Application stories and case histories.
2) Business, product and service positioning.
3) Business, product and service introductions.
4) Collateral.
5) Customer, prospect and media audits, surveys.
6) Distributor and dealer support.
7) Employee communications.
8) Event marketing.

Figure 7–30. Service–oriented companies can list their offerings on the Web.
(Courtesy of Janal Communications)

Clicking on Janal's photo will display a fact sheet (Fig. 7–30) about the company with hyperlinks to the services the company provides. Selecting the book icon will lead the reader to a page (Fig. 7–31) that displays the book's cover, ordering information, overview, testimonials, table of contents and order form. The same information is available for the software program.

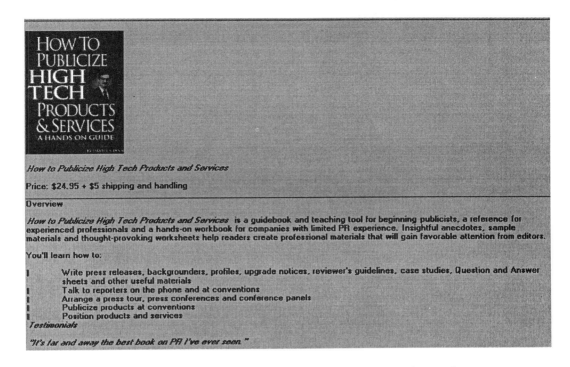

How to Publicize High Tech Products and Services

Price: $24.95 + $5 shipping and handling

Overview

How to Publicize High Tech Products and Services is a guidebook and teaching tool for beginning publicists, a reference for experienced professionals and a hands-on workbook for companies with limited PR experience. Insightful anecdotes, sample materials and thought-provoking worksheets help readers create professional materials that will gain favorable attention from editors.

You'll learn how to:

- Write press releases, backgrounders, profiles, upgrade notices, reviewer's guidelines, case studies, Question and Answer sheets and other useful materials
- Talk to reporters on the phone and at conventions
- Arrange a press tour, press conferences and conference panels
- Publicize products at conventions
- Position products and services

Testimonials

"It's far and away the best book on PR I've ever seen."

Figure 7–31. Authors can promote books on the Web.
(Courtesy of Janal Communications)

Consultants, speakers and trainers have written books and pamphlets. This page shows how they can present information that prospects generally want to read before ordering a book. Sample chapters can also be included. The home page includes a hot link to a free article on how companies can position their products.

Clicking on the Ivan Levison icon will link to information about his services and ten articles he has written about how to write better copy (Fig. 7–32). This data serves several purposes: It offers the reader useful information and it exposes each consultant's clients to the other's business.

Although I made space available to Ivan free so that I could offer his terrific articles to my readers, other companies might consider renting the space to complementary consultants and companies. Notice that the design of the page is simple and elegant, with a picture, company information and titles of the articles.

Ivan Levison

Ivan Levison is an award-winning freelance copywriter who specializes in writing high-impact direct response materials for software and hardware companies. He creates persuasive sales letters, motivating upgrade letters, complete mailing packages, response-oriented advertising, and more.

●   **See <u>articles</u> written by Ivan Levison**

Figure 7–32. Consultants can offer free information to add value to home pages.
(Courtesy of Janal Communications)

Just so people don't think this page was put into this book as an example of shameless self–promotion, let's look at a design flaw. The logo is a text display, not artwork. Any home page can have either but, as we have seen in the previous examples, stunning artwork can be created. I intend to change the logo. This also illustrates that many pages are "under construction" and constantly undergoing revisions as we learn which elements work and what looks good.

Tips for Designing Pages

A well–designed Web home page is essential to attract customers and guide them to making intelligent buying decisions. Designing Web home pages is partly subjective and partly formula. Let's look at several key areas:

- Content: What you want to say and strategies for getting people to return.
- Interface: How you present the information visually and how the user interacts with it. This is the organization, menu and icons.

Content

Time and space are two critical concerns for marketers—usually. When they buy advertising space on a TV show, time is very expensive. When they plan to print a brochure, space is expensive. When they plan a newspaper ad, every word and picture is at a premium. These elements don't matter on the Web, because space is unlimited.

Therefore, when creating the content for a home page, the marketer must ask many questions:

- What material will you place online? Do you place your entire catalog, or just the highlights? If your Internet service provider charges the going rate—which is inexpensive and getting more competitive all the time—you can afford to place every nut and screw in your inventory online. This is a boon to companies with large inventories, such as bookstores, music stores and technical components. However, the more products you offer, the harder it could be to find specific products. You can avoid this dilemma by using menus that allow consumers to find what they are looking for. For example a music lover could drill down through menus labeled: Records, Classical, Symphonies, Beethoven and then hear the opening strains of the Fifth Symphony. This can also be accomplished faster by providing search capabilities.
- How much information will you use to describe it? A single line, a paragraph or a full page? Again, with unlimited space, you can provide customers with the answers to every question they could think of. You can use short descriptions written for consumers and pages of technical specifications and schematic drawings for engineers. For example, a stereo speaker could be described with an appeal to emotion as in: "Impress your friends with the best sound available." It can also be sold to the audiophile who demands to know the technical specifications of each component.

- Pictures can sell a product in a way that text can't. Should you include pictures? How many? Should they be in color or black and white? Since transmission of pictures is slow, careful thought must be given to whether the benefit of seeing a picture will outweigh the possible impatience of consumers. One useful strategy is to keep a thumbnail–sized photograph and a full screen–sized version on file. Display the small picture, but give the consumer the option of seeing it displayed as large as the screen. Another tactic is to use fewer colors so the files are smaller and transmit faster.
- Will sound or video enhance the shopping experience? For an entertainment company or a training company, a video might do a better job of selling than any brochure could because the customer can see a clip from a movie or a training session in action.

Marketing Considerations

Consumers must actively go to a Web home page. Therefore, marketers need to attract consumers, keep them coming back and motivate them to tell their friends to visit the site. Here are several techniques:

- ***What's new:*** Every home page should have a "What's New" icon leading to a page that tells consumers about new information and features. Without this device, consumers probably won't find your latest updates. If you don't regularly add new features, people will stop making return visits.
- ***Changing information:*** Multiple impressions are a key to the success of any advertising campaign: The more often a person is exposed to your message, the more likely it is that he or she will buy. Therefore, you must create a reason for people to come back to your site. You can do this by adding new features, information and free samples, as described in Chapter 8.
- ***Other interesting places:*** At the bottom of a home page, you might consider listing related home pages that would interest your readers. This function will, with reciprocity from other marketers, lead to a valuable source of new prospects.

- ***Ordering information:*** Placing the order must be easy. Your home page should contain an icon that links to an ordering form or dispalys a phone number in case they worry about online ordering.
- ***Register and comments:*** Capturing names and addresses of readers is of paramount importance to create relationships. Inviting strategies to gather this information include asking the reader to sign a register and add comments about the home page.

Interface

An interface is the visual display of digital information. It is the way marketers communicate with consumers through the computer. If the interface is fun, exciting and pretty and if it leads the consumer to a highly interactive experience, the interface is a success. If consumers are confused, the interface is a failure.

A good user interface is critical to the success of a Web home page, as it is with all forms of sales communications on all the commercial online systems.

Bad interfaces, like bad clothes, that stand out and hide the person, detract from the message. Good interfaces, like good clothes, that are rarely seen and don't take attention away from the person, don't distract the reader from the message. A badly designed interface reminds people that they are dealing with a machine. A well–designed interface is so unobtrusive that people can concentrate on the information instead of the computer.

Fortunately, there are keys to good interface design. The best way to understand good design is to browse through home pages and play with them. Make notes on what you like and what you don't. This section will discuss several tips from Internet presence providers.

Organization

Organization is critically important when creating a home page. People need to see quickly what kinds of information and services you have and be able to reach those areas readily. If information is tossed up in a haphazard manner, you will probably lose your prospects.

Web home pages should look clean, neat, and professionally designed. A sloppy home page is a turnoff. You'll know it when you see it—and so will your customers. While a pretty home page won't assure sales, an ugly one won't help. What is beauty? True, art is in the eye of the beholder, but there are a few tried–and–true design elements that should be included in a home page:

- *Company logo:* Tells the customer whose store they're in.
- *Welcoming message:* Tells the prospect what the company does and what information is located on the page.
- *Index:* Lets readers know quickly what information is available. Indexes can be text–only or picture icons or a combination.
- *Pictures:* Present a professional image and add to the "wow" factor. However, they should be small pictures, as large ones take too long to appear on the screen—a turn off. If you use pictures, create large and small versions of the same pictures. However, display only the small picture. Let the reader know he can see the larger picture if he wants to by clicking on the small one.
- *Notes:* Explain where to get more information.
- *Access to easy ordering:* Create an icon or link to an order form so the consumer can place the order when he is hot.
- *Combination of text and graphics to tell your story:* For a photo processing company, pictures are the story. For a software publisher, pictures of screens can help translate complicated concepts. For a lawyer, accountant or copywriter, words might tell the story best.
- *Text/Picture options:* Allow the reader the ability to see your information with or without pictures. On some older software, pictures won't appear at all. You must design your pages to account for the text–only software programs that are still a big part of the market. Also, because pictures can take a long time to display, people might want to avoid them so that they can access the text faster. You should give them the option.
- *File size:* People can become frustrated if your page sends a large file because it is slow to appear on the screen. Part of this reaction can be circumvented if you let people know how large the file is and how long it will take to transmit. That way they can decide to retrieve it and wait patiently for it to appear.

- ***Easy access to information:*** While this seems obvious, all too many home pages make readers search endlessly for information. For example, one home page asks readers to press a button to see the table of contents. This information should be immediately available. Instead, readers are forced to wait for a slow transmission of the page, which includes a large picture file.
- ***Test the page with different browsers:*** Each software browser displays text, color and spacing slightly differently. You must test your page against the leading programs to ensure that the browser doesn't frustrate your artist's scheme by pushing text off the screen, bumping pieces of artwork into one another, or other unforeseen problems. Since different browsers print text in different colors, be sure not to confuse your readers by saying "If you click on the green text, you'll see the related information." The text might actually appear in red on some browsers. Instead, say "If you click on the highlighted text or italicized text."
- ***Colors:*** Use bright pictures or light colors to attract attention. Then build the rest of the interface and menu around that.

Icons

Because there are no instruction manuals on how to use each Web home page, icons should be used to help readers find information quickly.

"People recognize symbols rather than text," says Bill Linder, of Columbus PBX, a one–stop information resource center that creates Web home pages in Columbus, Indiana. "Imagine seeing a road sign from 100 feet away. You notice its size, shape and color. Is it a stop sign or perhaps a yield sign? You begin to act on that information. As you get closer to the sign, you see the word 'Stop' but you've already begun to apply the brakes.

"To complete the analogy, think of the international symbol set. Even without a word, you know that the picture icon means, for example, 'Skiing' or 'No parking.' The same is true with icons on the Web. Customers understand their meaning faster and make decisions faster with pictures."

You don't have to design a page from scratch. Numerous icons, buttons and backgrounds are available as shareware, which means you can test–drive the material and pay for it if you decide to continue using it.

Menus

Menus are an easy way for customers to find information. Successful strategies include creating an overall menu that leads customers to greater levels of information and depth. Each menu also should have information on ordering so that once the customer is convinced she should buy the product, she can do so without having to wade through additional materials.

When you design menus, put your best products at the beginning or the consumer might never see them. Remember that a page can be longer than a screen and that anything below the bottom of the screen will not be seen unless the reader scrolls to it or hits a hot link.

The best way to do this is to create a menu that has a short description of each major product area. For example, an appliance store could have menu listings for irons, toasters, blenders, coffee makers and can openers. Each item could then lead to another menu that lists the brand names of each of five models. So, if the customer selected blenders, she would see listings for five different models, complete with pictures of the units and a two–line description that includes the price. If she wanted more information, another menu could reveal such information as operating instructions, recipes and comparisons to other models.

Each menu should have information on how to purchase the item. This can be done as an online ordering form that can be completed and returned to the store either through e–mail, fax or snail mail. (e.g., to order, call 1–800–555–1212 or e–mail to orderform@estore.com).

Menus should also give users a link to return to the top of the page.

Test Drive/Usability

To ensure the greatest amount of usability, the Web home page should be tested before it goes online. A test drive by a typical user will show you whether the user understands the icons and can follow the scheme of things. For the best results, let a non–technical person try to use the system. Remember: The best system is the one that is most easily understood and used.

Publicizing the Web Home Page

Just because you have built a better mousetrap online doesn't mean anyone will beat a path to your door. You must let people know your catalog is online or you won't get any response. Finding information on the Internet can be difficult. It is like being in a big mall that has no directory. You might stumble onto four stores you never knew existed, but might not see the one store you specifically wanted to find. Unlike a shopping mall, you can't see a printed directory that is up–to–date and you don't discover new shops merely by strolling around the grand promenade near the food court.

"The whole problem with the Internet is that we know the information is out there, but how do we get to it?" says Temara DiGenero, a training specialist for Digital Express.

On the Internet, you need to create word of mouth to let other people know your home page exists. Unless you tell people that you have a home page and where it is, only a small fraction of your audience will ever stumble upon it. A question that online marketers must face is how to let their target market know they are online. You can—and must—publicize the Web home page's existence if you want people to find it. Here are several approved methods.

Strategy: Register the Home Page Address in a Directory

Benefit: People will find out about your home page and may decide to visit.
Discussion: Several organizations maintain directories of Web home pages and let you post your site free. Readers can search the database for free as well.

- CERN maintains a master World Wide Web Yellow Pages of academic and commercial Web sites. Viewers can browse by subject. This is a free service in which you can send one paragraph of information and a GIF file that could contain your company logo or a picture of the product. You can get a copy of the list to see what your posting should look like by typing the following URL *exactly* as follows. Pay attention to uppercase, lowercase and spacing:

```
http://info.cern.ch//hypertext/DataSources/by
Subject/Yellow/Overview.html/
```

To send your request for space, send e–mail to:

```
www-request@info.cern.ch
```

This page contains information about new or changed sites on the World Wide Web, updated three times a week. You can view the current listings in this document (previous seven days, most recent date first), view previous listings in the What's New Archives, or submit an entry.

- **Submit an Entry to What's New**
- **Search What's New Archives**
- **About the NCSA What's New Page**
- **Reader Comments:** See what your fellow Web travelers have to say about our new look page size, and commercial listings.

PICK OF THE WEEK: Mac Net Journal
Philadelphia, PA, US

Figure 7–33. "What's New" links to interesting home pages.
(The Global Network Navigator™, O'Reilly & Associates, Inc. © 1993, 1994, 1995)

- GNN (Global Network Navigator) maintains the "NCSA What's New" Page (Figures 7–33, 7–34) `http:/gnn.com/wn/whats-new.html` that was conceived by NCSA, which created Mosaic. It contains information about new or changed sites on the World Wide Web and is updated three times a week. Companies can submit their information free by going to the GNN home page and following the instructions for submitting an entry to: `http://gnn.com/wn/whats'new-form.html`

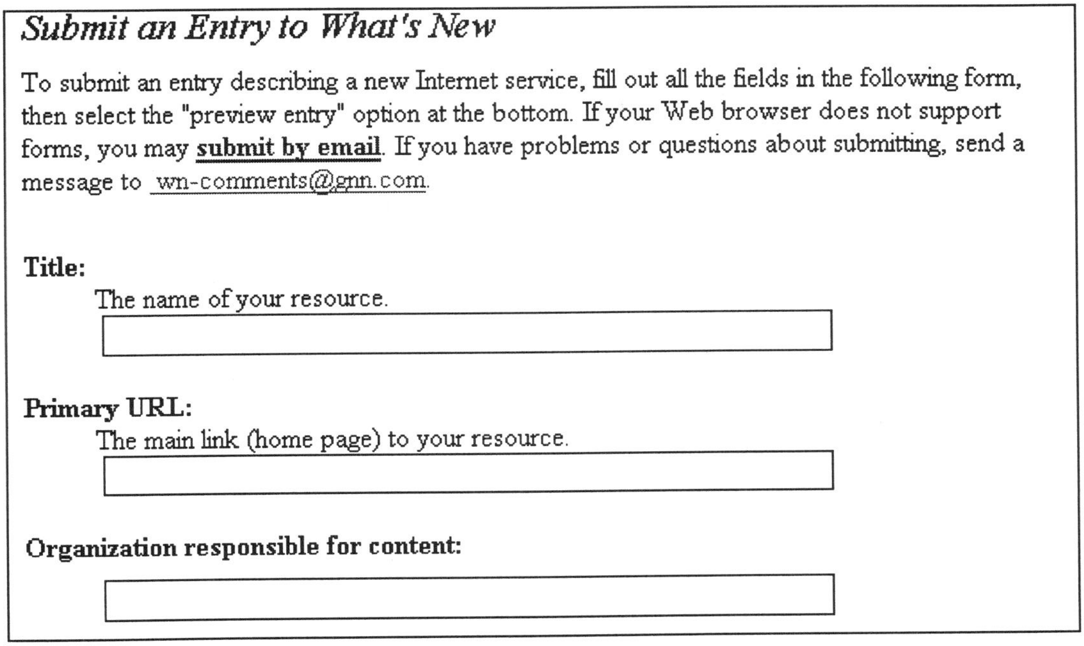

Submit an Entry to What's New

To submit an entry describing a new Internet service, fill out all the fields in the following form, then select the "preview entry" option at the bottom. If your Web browser does not support forms, you may **submit by email**. If you have problems or questions about submitting, send a message to wn-comments@gnn.com.

Title:

The name of your resource.

[   ]

Primary URL:

The main link (home page) to your resource.

[   ]

Organization responsible for content:

[   ]

Figure 7–34. Submitting your new home page listing is free and easy.
(The Global Network Navigator™, O'Reilly & Associates, Inc. © 1993, 1994, 1995)

- Companies can sponsor the opening page for a fee based on the number of times the page is read each day.
- The World Wide Web Worm lists home pages and provides references to people who search for information. To register your home page, type this address:

```
http://www.cs.colorado.edu/homes/mcbryan/public_html/
bb/instruction
```

- Carnegie Mellon University maintains a registry of Web home pages that can be searched free. To register your home page, type this address and follow the instructions. This address should be typed on one line:

```
http://www.fuzine.mt.cs.cmu.edu/mlm/lycos-
register.html
```

- Open Market maintains a free directory service for home pages. To register type the following address and follow the on–screen instructions:

  ```
  http://www.directory.net/dir/submit.cgi
  ```

- Business Web also maintains a free directory to register home pages. To register, type:

  ```
  http://www.bizweb.com/InfoForm/InfoForm.html
  ```

  Follow the on–screen instructions.

- WebCrawler also maintains a free directory service for Web home page. To register, type:

  ```
  http://www.biotech.washington.edu/WebCrawler/Submit
  ```

  Follow the on–screen instructions.

- Yahoo also allows companies to post their Web home pages and descriptions on their service. To register, type:

  ```
  http://akebono.stanford.edu/yahoo/bin/add
  ```

  Follow the on–screen instructions.

- EINet Galaxy provides a similar service. To register, type:

  ```
  http://einet.net
  ```

  Follow the on–screen instructions.

- The Internet Mall is a weekly online publication that lists commercial sites. "The vast majority of information I get from companies sending in blurbs about themselves," says Dave Taylor, of Intuitive Systems, an Internet business consultant and graduate student. To learn how to have your business added to the Mall, send e–mail to:

  `taylor@netcom.com` with subject `SEND ADDME`. To get a copy of the publication, send e–mail to: `taylor@netcom.com` with subject `SEND MALL`.

Strategy: List Your Home Page Address on Complementary Home Pages

Benefit: Increases exposure to your home page.

Discussion: You can publicize your home page by creating alliances with complementary home pages. Look for home pages that are in related areas and agree to create a mutual referral system. You'll add their site as a link to your home page, and they'll do the same. This is usually done by placing a category at the bottom of your Web home page that points to a "Hot List of Interesting Places to Visit."

To find complementary home pages, use these services:

- Open Market's Commercial Sites: `http://www.directory.net`
- Business Web: `http://www.bizweb.com`
- Harvest: `http://Harvest.cs.colorado.edu/brokers/www-home-pages/query.html`
- MIT's commerce area:
  `http://tns-www.lcs.mit.edu/commerce.html`
  "What's New" section lists updated information.

Strategy: Print the Home Page Address on Company Materials

Benefit: Increases exposure.

Discussion: Use traditional methods of advertising, such as printing the address on your business card and stationery, sending fliers and ads to prospective customers and placing the address in print ads.

Strategy: Post Messages on Newsgroups

Benefit: Increases exposure.

Discussion: Mailing lists and newsgroups in your subject area could be interested in your home page. As we've pointed out before, you cannot send advertisements to these groups, but you can join the discussion and, when appropriate, say "`By the way, you might be interested in the information I have at my Web home page. You can reach it by typing http://myhomepage.com.`"

Strategy: Print the Home Page Address in Advertisements

Benefit: Increases exposure.

Discussion: Refer to Web home page in your printed advertisements in newspapers and magazines, as well as in your printed catalogs, press releases, promotions, brochures and other materials.

Strategy: Tell Reporters About Your Home Page

Benefit: Increase exposure.

Discussion: Several publications print the addresses of cool Web pages free:

- *Houston Chronicle* reporter Dwight Silverman writes about interesting places on the Internet in his column, which is syndicated to about 10 other newspapers throughout Texas and Louisiana. To reach him, send e–mail to:
  `dwight.silverman@chron.com`
  Akron Beacon Journal columnist Glenn Gamboa writes about cool web sites in his column, which also appear on America Online. Send e–mail to:
  ggamboa@aol.com or *ggamboa@beaconjournal.com* (there isn't a period between "beacon" and "journal").
- *Advertising Age* prints a list of "Cool Internet Sites." Send e–mail to Interactive Media and Marketing at:
  `Sdonaton@eworld.com`
  `Dwilliamsn@eworld.com`
  `YWKJ04A@prodigy.com`
  `YNXB44A@prodigy.com.`
  An Internet e–mail address is not available.
- *Internet Yellow Pages* (Osborne/McGraw–Hill) is a delightful book about interesting places to visit on the Internet. Authors Harley Hahn and Rick Stout invite inquires sent to `catalog @rain.org`.

Also, call your local newspaper's business reporter. If you live in a small to medium–sized city, your home page might be news, particularly if it is the first in the area. At papers in larger cities, your story might not be unique, but you can offer to be a source to the reporter for information about the Internet, which is a hot story.

If you follow these examples, you will be able to build traffic to your Web home page.

Service Providers

If you are not comfortable with the technical and artistic aspects of creating a Web home page, don't worry. There are companies that can handle all these details.

A cottage industry for creating home pages is springing up. These companies offer complete creation of Web home pages and supporting materials. They go by several names, such as Internet presence providers, database marketers and malls. Advertising agencies and CompuServe `http://www.compuserve.com` also offer Web creation and management services.

The advantages of hiring a consultant to create these materials are plentiful. Since they already know how to use the software, they save you the time, expense and hassle of learning to use a new program. Their familiarity with all the features of the software will allow them to use it to its fullest potential so that your products will be displayed in the most advantageous manner available. They also will be able to create and complete the project for you quickly because they are familiar with the tools necessary to do a good job. Because they have designed projects for other companies, they will be able to draw on that experience to create a better presentation for you. Finally, since their businesses depend on their being well informed, they will know about the latest improvements in the technology and how these can help you.

Select a consultant for designing the Web home page as you would choose any consultant: Ask for referrals from your colleagues, ask the consultants for references, look at their previous work, determine your level of rapport and ask for the price structure. After you've selected the top two or three consultants you feel can do the job, begin negotiating their fees. Bear in mind that you don't want to cut the price to such a low point that they will not want to work with you or will have to cut corners to complete the task

Budget Considerations

Budgeting for the creation of the Web home page must include line items for creating content, converting it to HTML (Hypertext Markup Language) format and connecting it to the computer server. Here are some important factors to consider.

1. Creating Content

Creating content can be done in–house with the marketing team determining which products and messages should be featured. In–house artists and graphic designers can create the visual elements. Companies that don't have artists can hire consultants and Internet presence providers to aid them.

2. Creative and Technical Consulting

Consultants can help companies create Web home pages from start to finish or just complete various parts of the puzzle. For example, large companies with in–house advertising departments may be quite adept at creating text and graphics files but may lack the expertise to convert files to HTML format or to place the files onto a computer server and connect it to the Internet. That might be the time to call in a consultant.

For smaller companies, farming out the entire process can be a boon as the company can focus on what it does best, and the consulting team can do what it does best.

The cost of hiring a consultant to create a Web home page can vary greatly depending on the size of the material you need to create and the negotiating ability of the consulting firm. For example, if you have a simple home page with few items and links, the consultant might be able to complete the job in a few hours. A more intricate job could take days or weeks. As with any immature industry, prices have yet to become standardized. Consultants can and will charge whatever they think the market can bear. Prices vary across the country, ranging from $50 to $125 an hour, plus expenses. The time to create a home page for a small business or home–based business could range from 6 to 100 hours depending on the complexity of the project.

3. Paying for Updates

A key benefit of creating electronic information is that it can be changed easily whenever you want. However, each time you change information, you will have to pay for the technician's time. Most companies have information that is dynamic; it changes with each modification in the product line, prices or availability. Therefore, your budget should account for the technician's time to update material. If you decide to undertake this task in–house, you will have to account for training and actual time spent on this function.

How to Create a Web Home Page

Creating a Web home page is a relatively direct process. Here are the steps to create a home page.

1. Determine the goal of the home page. Will it be used to sell products, create an image or serve as a library for company information?
2. Create content. Take advantage of interactive tools to make files accessible.
3. Save the file as ASCII.
4. Import the file into an HTML (Hypertext Markup Language) program.
5. Assign codes to the content. These codes will assign font attributes, display pictures, link to other pages and allow forms and e–mail to be sent.
6. Load the home page onto a computer server.

"After a little practice, it is quite straightforward," says Bob Lash, executive vice president of The Internet Roundtable Society, an Internet presence provider, based in San Mateo, California, `http://www.irsociety.com`. "Over time editors will get better. It is amazing how good they are now."

Several companies publish software that creates HTML files. HTML Assistant, published by Brooklyn North Software Works, and HoTMetaL, published by SoftQuad, are two widely used programs that offer freeware versions (no payment required, ever) and commercial versions. For the freeware version of HTML Assistant ftp to `ftp.cs.dal.ca`, look in the directory `/htmlasst/ for the file htmlasst.zip`. To receive the freeware version of HoTMetal ftp to `ftp.ncsa.uiuc.edu`, look in the directory `/Web/html/hotmetal/Windows/` for the file `hotmetal.exe`.

Microsoft and Quarterdeck also announced they will introduce software that will create HTML files. SkiSoft Publishing of Lexington, Massachusetts `71466.1655@compuserve.com`, `617-863-1876`, announced it would publish a program to automatically convert files to HTML, complete with heading levels, pictures and hotlinks to other sites.

For an example of a finished home page and the HTML file, look at the codes below and Fig. 7–15. The first shows what the computer sees; the second shows what you see.

Table 7–1. HTML commands for a home page.

```
<HTML>
<HEAD>
<TITLE>InfoPlace - Internet Consulting Services</TITLE>
</HEAD><BODY>
<IMG SRC="ip-symbol-tr.gif"
ALT="InfoPlace symbol">
<IMG SRC="ip-logo-tr.gif" ALT="InfoPlace(tm)">
<HR>


<H2> We are consultants to information providers and consumers
     on the Internet </H2>


<H3> Our specialty is publishing information on the World Wide
     Web. </H3>
<UL>
<LI><B>InfoPlace delivers the
<A HREF="ip-services.html#benefits">benefits</A> of publishing
     on the fast lane of the Information Super-Highway</B>
<LI> <B>InfoPlace provides a one-stop
<A HREF="ip-services.html#services">service</A> for setting up
     World Wide Web servers.</B>
```

```
<LI> <B>Infoplace offers other Internet
<A HREF="ip-services.html#other">services</A></B>
</UL>
<H3> Our clients provide examples of the business use of the
     World Wide Web </H3>
<UL>
<LI> Technology Promotion
<DIR>
<LI> <A HREF="http://www.taligent.com/">Taligent, Inc.</A>
</DIR>
<LI> Public Relations
<DIR>
<LI><AHREF="http://www.infoplace.com/infoplace/winklermcmanus/h
     ome.html">Winkler McManus - the Virtual Agency</A>
</DIR>
<LI> Software Distribution
<DIR>
<LI><A  HREF="http://www.marketmind.com/">  Intelligent  Market
     Analytics, Inc.</A>
</DIR>
</UL>
<STRONG>
Contact<BR>
Ameet Zaveri - <I>zaveri@netcom.com </I><BR>
408-371-1540<BR>
2276 Shelley Ave, San Jose,  CA 95124
</STRONG>
</BODY>
</HTML>
```

Codes are used to set typeface commands that affect the way text will appear on the screen. Sample codes stand for titles, headlines, lists, and links to other pages and functions, such as creating e–mail or filling out an order form. The basic codes are:

<HEADER>	Every home page has two elements: the header and the body. The header is the information containing the page's address so that computers can find the page. This command starts the header command.
</HEADER>	Ends the header command.

<BODY>	The body is the text and the commands the browser needs to use to find material. This is the beginning of the body command.
</BODY>	End the body command.
<TITLE>	Display home page name.
</TITLE>	End display of home page name.
<IMG SCR= "xxx"	Displays an image called "xxx".
<H1>	Displays a type 1 heading.
</H1>	Ends the type 1 heading.
<Hx>	Displays a type x heading.
</Hx>	Ends a type x heading.
<ahref="xxx">	Creates an anchor that connects readers to "xxx".
</a>	Ends anchor.
<I>	Displays text in italics.
</I>	Ends italics.
<ul>	Starts list of bullets.
</ul>	Ends list of bullets.
<li>	Starts list of numbers (called an "ordered" list).
</li>	Ends list of numbers.
<p>	Begins a paragraph.
</p>	Ends a paragraph.
<address>	Starts address in bold.
</address>	Ends address in bold.
<dir>	Directory listing—creates indentation.
</dir>	Ends directory listing.
<strong>	Displays in emphasis depends on client.
</strong>	Ends emphasis.
 	Line break.
<b>	Displays boldfaced text.
</b>	Ends boldfaced text.
<mailto>	Creates an e–mail note.

Note:

- HTML supports six heading level commands.
- To end a line, use the BR hard return.
- Don't assume the line will wrap properly.
- Put anchors near the page top so people can find them easily.

Connecting to the Internet

Now that you have your Web home page created and all the supporting materials created, you need to place the information onto your computer in a way that is connected to the Web so other customers can view the information. This section will explore the various options:

- Do it yourself (become a host).
- Rent space from a host.
- Join a mall.

Do It Yourself

You have several options for determining how to connect with the Internet. You can be a host, which means you have a direct connection, or you can dial into someone else's host. As you might expect, there are advantages and disadvantages to each method. Generally speaking, the faster and more direct the connection, the more you will pay. Be careful about signing a long–term contract because prices are beginning to fall rapidly. *As more companies get involved in the Internet and competition heats up, prices will fall, terms will get better and service options will become an important factor in your decision.*

The least expensive way to get started is with a 14.4 SLIP (Serial Line Interface Protocol) connection to an Internet provider. Access will be slow—especially for graphics—and only a few people will be able to access your site simultaneously. If you are charged by the minute, this arrangement can become quite costly.

The second best step is to maintain a direct connection with a leased line supporting a 56–kilobyte data frame relay. Here is a list of approximate sample costs:

Internet access	$300 per month and up
Phone lease	$125 per month
Telephone company setup charge	$1,000
Internet setup charge	$1,000

Digital modem $1,000

The third option is to purchase a T1 connection from the phone company. This dedicated line can handle much more traffic than either of the two previous systems described. This system operates at the blinding speed of 1.54 Mb per second, compared to 56K on option 2. If you are expecting a great deal of traffic, either in terms of customers or the number of files they can retrieve, then this option might fit your needs.

Installation	$4,000
Monthly fee	$1,000
Phone company installation	$1,854
Monthly fee	$500
CSU/DSU modem	$350/56Kbps
TI line	$1,750
Router	$2,600/56Kbps

If you operate your own server, you will need software. A recommended shareware program is KA9K. You can retrieve it from the Case Western University Web. The address is `biochemistry.bioc.cwru.edu`.

If you use a DOS or Macintosh computer, you will have to dedicate one machine to running the Web home page. If you have a UNIX system, it can perform several functions at the same time (multitasking) and you don't need to dedicate a machine to run the Web. Many servers are available for UNIX systems. For a list, check the user home page at CERN.

As with other Net software and operations, this is tricky and best left to a professional. To do this is very technical and not for the faint of heart. While a fair amount of energy has gone into creating friendlier interfaces to access information on the Internet, very little effort has gone into making servers friendly. Today, there are too many parameters to set. To put this in perspective, if the thought of installing a network for your office computers is too daunting, then connecting your Web home page to the Internet server is beyond your abilities. In fact, it is so complicated that the instructions go well outside the realm of this book. You really do need to hire a consultant to do this task.

If this warning hasn't dissuaded you, you might want to read "Internet Servers: A Step–by–Step Guide on How to Build Them," by Greg Bean, Cyber Group, 6400 Baltimore National Pike, Baltimore, MD 21228.

Rent Space from a Host

For companies that don't want to get involved in the technical aspects of connecting their home page to a server, renting space from another company is an option. This method also might help companies keep costs under control as they would not have to lay out the money for expensive computer components. Don't worry about looking like a renter. If you register for a domain name, the customer has no way of knowing you are on someone else's machine. A domain name is your company's address on the Internet. The Domain Name System is the method used by the Internet to administer names of computer networks. Cool companies have their own domain name, which is usually the same name as the company with ".com" added to the end, e.g., mycompany.com.

Companies might want to rent out their space for several reasons: Renting space is their core business, or they might be merchants who have more space than needed to operate their own business and want the extra income. Some companies have even written this into their business plans. They expect to turn unused server space into a profit center.

The major advantage to renting space is the same as renting space in an office building—it is far less expensive to rent than to own. Also, you won't have to put up the expensive fees involved in creating the server or connecting it to the Web or renting the expensive direct phone connections to the phone company. The advantage to ownership is that you can have complete control over the system and make a profit on unused space that you resell. Finally, you won't have to hire a network administrator to oversee the operation of computers.

Disadvantages of renting include paying fees every time you want to change the home page (for example, to add or delete products or change prices). This might not be a major consideration if your home page is composed of information that does not change often. Another consideration is that if the owner creates a lot of traffic, response time will be slow. Your customers might find it takes too long to get information. This is because performance slows down when more people are using the system.

Join a Mall

Virtual malls on the Internet are gaining in popularity and scope. Many companies are creating their own electronic realty offices and starting malls. These malls are collections of many businesses that are accessed by the consumer through a common address. Here are brief profiles of several malls.

Examples of Malls

The Electronic Newsstand `http://enews.com` was created in July 1993 by netResults, an Internet presence provider, to serve as a "pain–free" way for publishers and major corporations to gain an Internet presence. The Newsstand, launched with a modest eight publications, now has more than 175 titles and is accessed more than 50,000 times per day—over one million times per month, making it one of the most popular sites on the Web. Titles include *Business Week*, 15 titles from Miller Freeman; 10 titles from Phillips Business Information, Inc.; 18 titles from BRP Publications, *Air & Space*, *Smithsonian*, *Canoe & Kayak*, *Yankee* and the complete IEEE book catalog.

NETCENTER `http://netcenter` maintains several malls:

- 1st Online Trade Show.
- The Barter Network.
- The Finance Center.
- The International Trade Center.
- The Health Center.
- The Mall.

Other examples of malls include:

- Shopping 2000 from Contentware includes catalogs from Tower Records, Spiegel and others. `http://www.shopping2000.com`
- Digital's Electronic Shopping Mall includes the Vermont Teddy Bear Company and DEC's Interactive Catalog. `http://service.digital.com/html/emall.html`

- Internet Shopping Network `http://www.Interent.net` offers products for computers.

How to Select a Mall

A good mall provides management, marketing and security for its merchants. If you decide to select a mall, make sure it offer these features:

- Affordable, high–quality connectivity through T1 lines—and lots of them if the mall has many merchants. As more merchants sign on, and more consumers join, the transmission times slow considerably. If the mall doesn't offer fast access, your consumers could get turned off by long transmission delays.
- Attractive and easy user interface.
- Software tools for providers that make it easy to put up and maintain the site, or access to technicians who will update the pages for you at a reasonable cost.
- Security mechanisms, including authentication and encryption, supported within applications, such as Mosaic using RSA public key cryptography.
- Experience in the business. Many start–up companies are billing themselves as malls but don't have the depth of knowledge, expertise or hardware needed to help a merchant.
- Experience in publicizing and promoting the site.
- Reliability of hardware systems and the ability to fix hardware problems quickly. If the page is down, no one can buy from you.
- An easy to type address. For example, an easy address is:

  `http:///www.myhomepage.com`

- A difficult address has a long name filled with odd characters:

  `http://www.samplepage.com/users/mall/0c:/~mypage.htm|`

This address could be particularly confusing:
- Is the first character in *Oc* the number zero or the letter *o* ?

- They hunt for the ～ character (it is called a tilde and resides over the accent key to the right of the number 1 key on PC–style keyboards.
- Is the last character in the line the letter *l* or the double vertical bars (which sits above the backslash key)?

If your address takes this much explanation, you can bet people will get lost trying to find it. Choose a simple address that anyone can type easily.

Other Business Models

There are many ways to make money on the Web. Operating a mall, renting space on your server and providing consulting services to companies entering the market have been explored. Here are additional business models to explore.

Strategy: Sell Promotional Space on an Information Product

Best for: Information providers

A business model that is popular on the Internet is creating information product that is updated frequently, sending it free to subscribers, and charging sponsors a fee for a special listing. For example, "What's On Tonight" is a listing of television programs that is sent every day to subscribers via e–mail for free. Sponsors pay a fee to have their service listed at the top of the message. For information, send e–mail to: `editor@paperboy.com`.

Several services that provide directory listings of Internet sites, and links to those sites also charge a promotional fee to a designated sponsor, although listings are free. Examples of this model can be found at the Global Network Navigator's Personal Finance Center `http://gnn.com/meta/finance/index.html`, GNN Travel Center `http://gnn.com/meta/travel/index.html`, and the "NCSA What's New Page" `http://gnn.com/wn/whats-new.html`.

While all companies can be listed for free, sponsors can pay extra to have their listing highlighted in boldface, italics or a larger font.

Strategy: Create and Distribute a Sample Product; Charge for the Full Version

Best for: Software Publishers

Software publishers can create their own Web home page, Gopher site or FTP Site to offer free downloads of new software programs. These files can contain complete software programs, shareware versions of full programs, or demo programs. To make money, the publisher could attach an unlocking code to the file. This code would allow the consumer to try the product for a period of time and then lock the program so it could not be reused. If the consumer wanted to use the product again, he would have to call the publisher, pay for the product and receive the keys to the lock.

Using the Internet and commercial online services to distribute software has been a boon for many publishers of software distributed as shareware. Examples of products that began as shareware and have become retail products that have sold hundreds of thousands of copies include Procomm, Virus Scan, Doom, PC Write and AutoMenu.

The commercial online services offer many opportunities for shareware vendors to post files, as they can get free content that benefits their subscribers.

Strategy: Attract an Audience; Sell Advertising Space to Merchants

Best for: Any Industry with a Dedicated Following

E–wine doesn't sell wine; they sell advertising. They want to be known as the site where people can get information about wine, visit wineries, travel to Wine Country, find information about bed and breakfasts and anything else a wine connoisseur would like. The company in Napa, California `http://e-wine.com/e-wine.html`, sells advertising space on its home page to wineries in the form of home pages. When you click on those pages, you get to see the winery, its wines, reviews and current information about what is going on at the winery. You can order wines directly from the winery. The page will have links to other wine sites to build traffic.

This site is interesting because the vendor, E–wine, is not creating an editorial product to attract consumers, as a traditional magazine would. Instead, it is creating a wealth of advertiser–supplied information content to draw consumers.

The synergy of each winery actually draws people to the area because they know it is a one–stop resource center.

The company plans to advertise the page in the trade press to attract wineries and will go directly to wineries to sign them up. To reach consumers, they will put ads in *Wine Spectator*. This example illustrates the need for online sites to use ads and publicity strategies in traditional media to boost online performance.

Strategy: Create Editorial Content; Sell Advertising Space and Subscriptions

Best for: Information Publishers

Publishers of books, magazines, 'zines, newsletters, and reports can make money using the Internet by creating Web home pages that offer readers the chance to read current and historical issues. While some publications offer only a few key articles, others print the entire issue online. This strategy introduces new readers to the publications. The publishers hope to make money either by selling subscriptions to the print edition or by selling online advertising in the form of cyberads or paid sponsorships.

Strategy: Create Information Products

Best for: Consultants, Speakers, Trainers

By writing informative articles and reports, consultants, speakers and trainers can build their credibility and gain exposure that can lead to revenue from selling their services. These articles can be posted to mailing lists and newsgroups, or posted on Web home pages—theirs and others—and create links to and from complementary sites.

Strategy: Create Your Own Business Model

Best for: Entrepreneurs

The Web is an emerging medium. Everyone can become a publisher. In this immature market, the field is wide open for new ideas, creativity and services that lead to sales. As the new medium emerges and new paradigms erupt, entrepreneurs who seize the initiative can forge new business models that are unlike any we know of today. One element will remain constant: If you help consumers get what they need, they'll help you get what you need.

Other Internet Tools for Online Sales

Gopher

If you drop the multimedia aspects of the Web, you have the Gopher. The Gopher is a database of information that the user accesses through a menu structure. One advantage of the Gopher is that information can be searched by keywords, so that your customers can find information quickly. Today, there are more Gopher sites than Web home pages. However, thanks to the beauty of multimedia, Web home pages are growing faster.

If you have a home page, you can easily create a Gopher site since much of the text will be the same. In fact, several popular malls connect to Gopher sites, where their information sits in text form.

FTP

The third way of creating a shopping experience on the Internet is through FTP (File Transfer Protocol). This is even more bare–bones than Gopher. Basically, you would create files that contain information about your products and services. Customers and prospects would access the area and read those files. They could then send electronic mail to you for more information or call your order number via telephone.

Summary

The World Wide Web on the Internet offers incredibly exciting and versatile options for companies to sell products and create relationships with new and prospective companies in a cost–effective manner.

CompuServe's The Electronic Mall

CompuServe boasts of having the oldest and most established online shopping center. The Electronic Mall has been in existence since 1985, when the concept of home shopping with a personal computer was virtually unknown. It started as a test in 1984 with a handful of merchants.

Today, about 130 merchants are online, ranging from well–known retailers, like J.C. Penney and Land's End to specialty stores that offer merchandise and services in virtually every category, including apparel, arts, automotive parts, books, computer software, cosmetics and jewelry, gifts and flowers, hobbies, toys, pets, office supplies, sports and fitness and travel and vacations.

Although CompuServe would not disclose gross revenues, a spokesman said The Electronic Mall is consistently one the most popular areas. CompuServe says it never releases any absolutes in terms of dollars spent online and the number of orders transacted across the system.

"I can tell you that, of the 2,000+ areas on CompuServe, The Electronic Mall is always in the top 12 most popular areas online. That gives you some perspective. That puts us in there with things like PC support for IBM/DOS and Macintosh platforms, electronic mail, the newswires, interactive conferencing and the like," says Keith Arnold of CompuServe.

About 3.8% of the people who browse the Mall make a purchase, which compares favorably to catalogs and direct mail which have an average response rate of 1%. The average purchase is $71.04. The Mall has seen an increase in orders of about 50% over last year; an increase of 80% in accesses. CompuServe reports the number of accesses to The Electronic Mall increased 81% over 1992.

"Part of the Mall's success can be attributed to broader consumer acceptance of home shopping, which has resulted in dramatic growth across many categories of direct marketing, including catalog, direct mail and 800–number telephone ordering," says Regina Brady, CompuServe's director of customer promotion. "We're certainly not immune to the economic factors that affect consumer buying habits, but we may be less vulnerable than some other retailers because our members tend to have high disposable incomes. For them, time is the commodity in short supply. They'll take advantage of any method that frees them for other pursuits, such as spending time with the family."

A Mall merchant who opens a virtual storefront can expect to find shoppers at the highest ends of the demographic spectrum. CompuServe lists its average Mall buyer with the following pedigree:

- Average household income: $93,000.
- Average age 40–44.
- Most married with children.
- College–educated. Most have at least a 4–year degree; about 90% of members are male. ("We are actively looking for applications to attract the female user," Arnold says.)
- Most are active users of catalogs and direct mail offers.
- Early adopters of new technology and high–tech.

CompuServe promotes Mall merchants by printing a full–color illustrated guide to the Mall that is sent to all members each month in the *CompuServe Magazine*. The guide announces new merchants, alerts members to contests and special promotions and includes photographs and descriptions of several featured items. In addition, each issue offers a listing of all merchants, including such information as which merchants offer express delivery and which credit cards each accepts.

CompuServe is taking advantage of advances in technology to enhance the shopping experience. It has featured a text–based system since its inception but added graphical user interfaces that make using the system easy. In late 1994 it began using graphics, sound and video in conjunction with the CompuServe CD, which must be purchased separately.

"Technology is a huge enhancer of the shopping experience," says Arnold. "The addition of the CompuServe Information Manager interface has been a tremendous boon to us. Also, over the past two years, we have added high–resolution product images to the Mall's stores. People are definitely willing to wait the 30–45 seconds it takes to view images if the picture adds value to the shopping experience. They do not want to see gratuitous graphics that don't help sell the products."

CompuServe is looking toward integrating advertising with a CD–ROM. CompuServe released its first edition of the CompuServe CD in late 1994. "The introduction of CompuServe CD (CCD) was one of our most significant events this year. It is the first CD–ROM that is fully interactive with an online service. There is a shopping section on the disc as well," Arnold says. "The CCD product is a multimedia magazine–like extension of the CompuServe Information Service with content that goes beyond just shopping. It has feature articles from across the various parts of the service."

The future looks bright for online shopping.

"With the propagation of new and better technology, especially in the realm of multimedia, we will see shopping become better than ever. When the day comes that we can deliver full–motion video it will be truly spectacular," says Arnold.

CompuServe is always looking for an opportunity to expand its offerings.

"Our primary focus is on the large, significant catalog and direct marketing companies—the household names," he says. "We look at each opportunity and make sure it fits well with the mix of companies we have online already. We strive to keep a balance within the various departments and do what we can to ensure everyone's success."

Each merchant's presentation is priced according to his or her particular needs. On average, the annual investment, with advertising in *CompuServe Magazine*, is $20,000 to $80,000. Merchants pay CompuServe a 2% commission on each sale.

Electronic Mall merchants don't have to worry about becoming technology whizzes to go online. As part of the service you buy when getting on The Mall, you get full account management from CompuServe, which builds maintains and updates the databases. "We work in cooperation with the merchants to make this as streamlined as possible," Arnold says.

America Online

In late 1994, America Online announced the formation of AOL Services Company, whose mission is, in part to develop new revenue streams from interactive advertising and transactions. "By continuing to expand the diversity and quality of the content and by making the content more useful and engaging through innovations in navigation, personalization and multimedia presentation, we believe we can move the AOL brand into the lead as the Number One consumer online service in the United States," says AOL president Steven Case. "We will then be well positioned to develop 'electronic markets' that marry information, communications and transactional capabilities. These electronic markets will be valued by our subscribers, as they will help them make better decisions more conveniently, and they will be valued by our partners, as they will be the source of new revenue streams that can increase their profits."

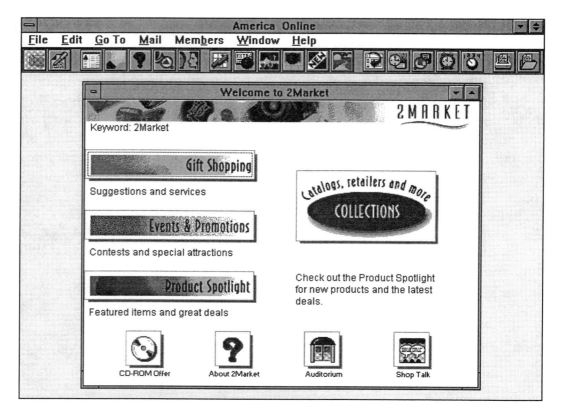

Figure 7–35. 2Market features catalog shopping. *(Courtesy of America Online)*

America Online does not operate a "mall" per se, but rather a shopping department. America Online, Apple Computer, Inc., and Medior, Inc., formed 2Market, Inc., a company that provides interactive shopping services for CD–ROM and online. It debuted on America Online and eWorld (Fig. 7–35). Other commercial online services are in discussion to add this service as well. Some 25 companies are offering products online, including Land's End, 800–Flowers, Crutchfield, Hammacher Schlemmer, the Metropolitan Museum of Art, the Museum of Modern Art, Sony Music, Windham Hill Records, The Sharper Image and Spiegel (Figures 7–36, 7–37).

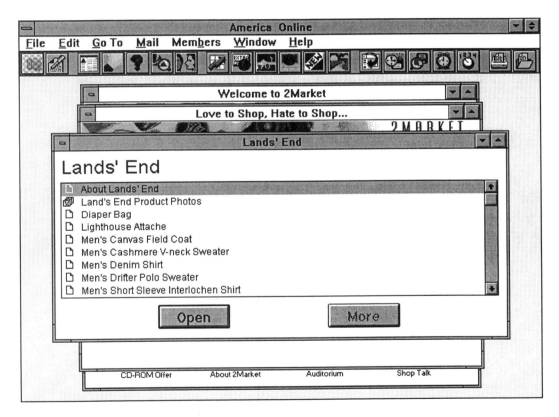

Figure 7–36. Select a product from a menu . . . (Courtesy of America Online)

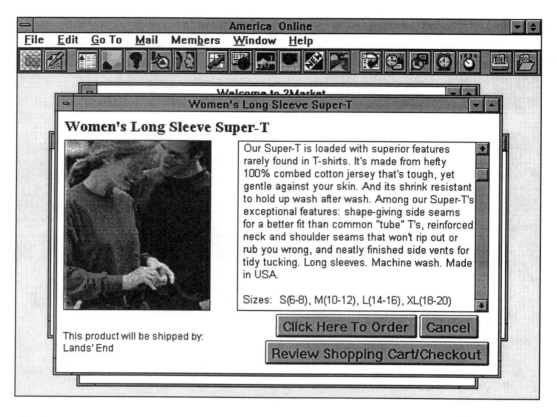

Figure 7–37 . . . to see a color ad and short description. (Courtesy of America Online)

AOL does not discuss growth figures, revenues, dollars spent, and so forth, nor does it speculate on the future of this market, the costs of operating an online "store" or shopper demographics (the last because of privacy concerns).

Prodigy

From the minute members sign on to Prodigy, they see "leader ads" flashing on the bottom third of their computer screen. These ads resemble little billboards that promote a company's products. Although marketers can buy just the leader ad, many companies choose to add additional screens of information that the member can read if he presses an icon.

Prodigy offers a robust environment for creating a virtual shopping experience (Fig. 7–38). Prodigy's mall of merchants includes heavyweight anchors such as J.C. Penney, Land's End, Spiegel and Patagonia, plus dozens of specialty shops like PC Flowers. Adding to the momentum of online retailing, Home Shopping Network also began selling on Prodigy in 1994 by offering 100 products and 80 color photos of products. By the end of the year, the number of products increased to 1,000 and the number of color photos jumped to 800.

Figure 7–38. Prodigy offers extensive sales opportunities. (Courtesy of Prodigy)

PC Flowers has been a "runaway hit," says Carol Wallace, program manager, communications, for Prodigy. It offered the convenience of online ordering coupled with overnight delivery.

"The real goal is to realize and understand the behavior of the customer sitting at the computer. When you can figure that out, you can make money," says Wallace, who added that Prodigy's research can't be shared.

Prodigy allows its vendors to send direct mail via e–mail to selected groups of members. Prodigy will, for example, capture the name and e–mail address of everyone who enters the auto mall and then offer the list to Toyota. To protect members, Prodigy won't give the name or address to the vendor. Prodigy forwards the mail. If customers want to reply with their addresses directly to the vendor, that's fine. The fee varies.

Advertising rates range from $20,000–$40,000 a month. However, every case is different and Prodigy barters with selected companies. For instance, Prodigy might offer free or discounted space to a company that can promote Prodigy with advertising time on its services, says Wallace.

Virtually any company can become an advertiser, from a large national company like Kraft foods to a local gourmet seafood store.

First, you must decide if the market will support your product. Prodigy found that online grocery shopping didn't work, for example. People wanted to pick their own tomatoes.

Prodigy offers sophisticated technology solutions to advertisers. Companies can use video, sound, graphics and multimedia to promote their products. To promote an online interview with Mick Jagger of the Rolling Stones, the rock star recorded a sound clip saying "Hi. This is Mick Jagger. Join me on Prodigy." Sound can be downloaded fairly quickly. Video is a reality, but it can take an hour to download a file that plays for just a few minutes.

"That is going to revolutionize shopping because you will be able to see it online," says Wallace. "A graphic image of a blue blazer does maybe half the selling job that a picture of a model wearing a blue blazer does."

Prodigy's advertisers can use multimedia in their ads but many are going slowly. "It is a function of becoming more comfortable with the medium," says Wallace. "Madison Avenue is still getting comfortable with this medium. All the rules of marketing online are different. We are just scratching the surface of what we can do with multimedia. The technology is here. People are not taking advantage of it as much as they could. There is a learning curve. As online services enter the mainstream of society, I think the advertising element is also maturing."

Regarding the future, Prodigy looks to its customers.

"We are always careful about making predictions," she says. "Our members drive our actions. Consumers will surprise us in a lot of ways."

Other Marketing Opportunities

Free Offer Store

The Free Offer Store on Prodigy `Prodigy: Jump FREE OFFER` works as a lead generator, allowing merchants to find consumers interested in purchasing products and services by giving away something in exchange for the consumer's name and address. Many of the advertisers distribute catalogs, informational videos, sample products and brochures. The store is comparable to a billboard or card pack, but it is interactive and provides an immediate response. Companies purchase space for $2,100 per month, plus a 25 cent fee per lead with a three–month minimum commitment. Marketers receive consumers' names and addresses in either electronic or label format. Potential clientele are lured to the mall through leader ads, which appear on the bottom of all Prodigy users screens, except when they are in the bulletin board areas. A variety of companies are online including:

- The Sporting News
- Tiger Software
- Globe Life Insurance
- Paper Direct
- Lens Express

"This service is wide open to any kind of company appealing to Prodigy's demographics," says John Ballantine, executive vice president of Online Interactive, an online shopping and direct marketing company based in Seattle.

A_2Z Multimedia SuperShop

Computer hardware and software companies can reach audiences on virtually all major online services with the A_2Z Multimedia SuperShop, which is available on Prodigy `Prodigy: Jump A2Z MULTIMEDIA`, and `CompuServe: Go A2Z`. The company plans to expand to America Online, Interchange, eWorld, Microsoft Network and Genie.

"This store will become the largest multimedia CD–ROM store in the country," says Ballantine. "It is a one–stop shopping center for all multimedia products. The store offers competitive pricing and rerun privileges, and plans to add editorial content, ratings and multimedia news to help consumers make informed decisions. Products are included in the appropriate categories of the A$_2$Z Multimedia SuperShop. Typical categories include: Entertainment, Education, Productivity, Graphics and Business. The benefits of this store are:

- *Advertising value:* The company will market, promote and advertise products. The rate works out to be less than five cents per month compared to $20 per month for catalogs, according to Ballantine. Consumers will be attracted to the store through ads and mall promotions.
- *Unlimited space to showcase products:* Stores have a limited amount of shelf space to display products. Therefore, customers can find more products, especially hard–to–find products.
- *Build sales:* Increase retail sales from customers who prefer to buy in stores but first learn of the product through the online store.
- *Convenience for customers:* The online store is always open, 24 hours a day, 365 days a year.

"It also allows companies to get involved in the Information Superhighway without large start–up costs," he says. "Furthermore, there aren't any channel conflicts as the A$_2$Z Multimedia Superstore is another retail outlet."

Summary

The Internet and commercial online services offer tremendous benefits for consumers in terms of shopping convenience. Consumers have responded by purchasing an estimated $50 million in products. Technology offers marketers the chance to build strong relationships with consumers. The promise of technology to come will enhance this relationship. For businesses of all sizes that need to reach audiences of all kinds, the Internet and commercial online services have tools that can be effective in meeting their goals.

CHAPTER 8

Forums: Marketing Opportunities for Information Providers

"Forums can provide companies with a great base to provide customer support, answer questions and post news and new information. All this speaks well for promoting customer relations," says Prodigy's Carol Wallace, program manager, communications.

In this chapter, you will learn:

- How companies and associations can build relationships and a profit center with forums.
- What a forum is.
- How a company can benefit from creating a forum.
- What kinds of companies are best equipped to create a forum.
- How to make the best financial deal.
- How to publicize a forum.
- How to make money on a forum.

Forums are online message and library centers on the commercial online services. USENET newsgroups and mailing lists perform similar services on the Internet. They may be run by businesses and associations for the use of the general public or may be accessible only to customers and employees. While these companies might be called publishers, broadcasters or just plain old companies in the analog world, the commercial online services have a new name for them: "information providers."

Forums can provide companies and associations with a great way to accomplish many marketing goals, such as creating, building and maintaining positive relationships with customers. For example, companies with forums can:

- Publish information, such as press releases, earnings reports, new product information, data sheets, and the like.

- Give away free samples, like information, software and music recordings.
- Offer sneak previews of new products and services.
- Provide customer support for technical questions and make company executives and experts available to customers.
- Sell products.

Software publishers take note: Online services give you a way to deliver a wide variety of information to customers, including:

- Software updates, such as drivers, patches, utilities and templates.
- Marketing and educational materials, such as press releases, product reviews, position papers and online catalogs.
- Technical support materials, such as technical tips, frequently asked questions and lists of authorized training centers.
- Professional development information, including schedules and registration information for upcoming seminars and industry conferences.
- Discussion forums where members can exchange ideas with technical experts, company or association representatives and other members.

Not only can Information providers build rapport with their customers, they can make money at the same time. The business model for an online system is based on usage, just like the telephone. The longer the subscriber stays online, the more money the commercial online service will make. To stimulate the meter, commercial online services need to attract Information providers who can, in turn, attract new members and keep them online as the meter ticks. This is a partnership made in heaven as both sides win: The online service rings up sales and the Information provider helps its customers while taking a percentage of the meter as well.

The Internet's World Wide Web can also be used to create a forum for a company. All the benefits of customer support and goodwill apply. The major difference is the financial terms. Web users pay an access provider to sign on to the Internet. This Internet provider doesn't share the money with any companies that operate a Web home page. Also, the start–up costs on the Web are borne entirely by the Information provider. There isn't any hand–holding for technical support problems, as there is on the commercial online services. On the other hand, there is no restriction on what you can do on the Web in terms of information you present or how it is presented. You can create your own unique design, which vendors on commercial online services cannot do.

Similarly, BBSes, or bulletin boards, can be operated by companies. These BBSes are completely independent of any commercial online service. They are run by the company themselves on their computers, with special BBS software, which costs anywhere from $100 for a one–line service to $1,000 for a system that can accommodate 250 callers. Total costs for hardware and phone lines can be much higher. The advantage is that the company has complete control over content. However, it must bear the costs of maintaining the system.

Examples of Information Providers

Forums can be created to discuss matters of interest on virtually any topic under the sun, including business, lifestyle and hobbies. Here are examples of several forums and what services they provide.

U.S. News & World Report. This highly regarded weekly magazine has a forum on CompuServe CompuServe: Go USNEWS. It is a way for *U.S. News* to extend their printed product and interact with current readers in a way they can't in print. CompuServe operates more than 2,000 forums. This is a way for the reader to interact directly with the editors. Users can debate editorials and submit letters to the editor. It enables the editors to have an even more intimate relationship with their readers. It also provides them with a marketing tool to find out what their readers think about issues.

The Holistic Health Forum CompuServe: Go Holistic is operated by a health care professional, who provides readers with information on nontraditional health methods, such as Chinese herbs and acupuncture. Members can ask questions about medications, treatments and resources. They can also participate in live conferences with professionals to learn from people immediately.

CNN CompuServe: Go CNN blends a forum with its television show "Talkback Live." A TV host acts as a facilitator who fields questions from people in the audience and from members on the forum on CompuServe for 40 minutes. For the next 20 minutes, a guest joins the dialogue.

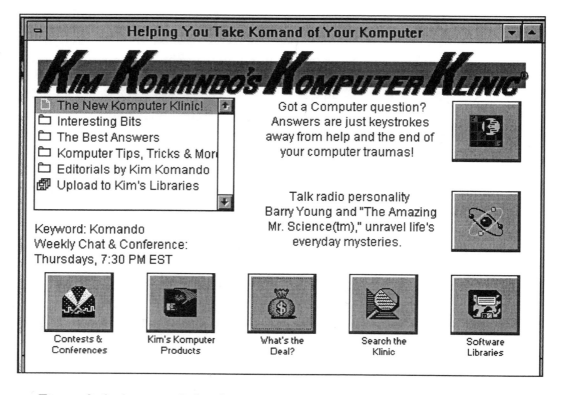

Figure 8–1. America Online's Komando Forum features info and shopping.
(Courtesy of America Online)

Entrepreneur and radio personality Kim Komando launched the Komando Forum `America Online: Keyword KOMANDO` as an answer center for people with questions about their computers. Her service gets 1,500 questions on busy days. That's just fine with her. She funnels the material into a book she is writing about people's most frequently asked questions. Her audience is so large now that she has begun offering computer products for sale to her members, usually at a steep discount (Fig. 8–1). Her business has grown to support a staff of seven.

Toyota maintains a private forum for the exclusive use of its customers `Prodigy: JUMP TOYOTA`. In fact, to gain access, you must type in your car's vehicle identification number. "This is the best application of relationship marketing," says Prodigy's Wallace. Once in the forum, members can see color photos of new cars and read information about cars. Messages are a very active part of the forum. Members can read messages from executives and discuss good and bad things about the cars. "Owners sell each other. It is an awesome endorsement."

Prodigy also has forums for Saturn, AAA of Southern California, Fidelity Investments and others. "It works out well for companies in many different areas, especially in auto and financial where people tend to be intimidated about purchasing. They need to learn about products. These forums add value to the customer."

CompuServe also is the site for private forums for IBM, Novell, Computer Associates, Microsoft, Compaq and several other high–technology companies. These forums should not be confused with the forums that can be accessed by the public. These private forums are for customers who have special arrangements with the information provider. Information providers can either pay the online service, share revenue or a per–charge use.

Who Should be an Information Provider?

CompuServe, Prodigy and America Online look for companies that can attract new members and keep existing members online. In return, companies receive electronic real estate to communicate with members. Online services are looking for companies that have name recognition, clout, brand awareness and are easily identified.

Small wonder that the commercial online services are courting media companies, that have huge name recognition and can provide advertising in its pages. Examples of magazines with forums include *Car and Driver* AOL: Keyword CAR AND DRIVER; *Consumer Reports* (available on CompuServe, AOL and Prodigy with same access keyword: CONSUMER REPORTS); and *American Woodworker* AOL: Keyword Woodworker. Virtually every computer magazine operates a forum.

Associations also are operating forums, including the Association of Shareware Professionals CompuServe: Go SHARE, the Windows User Group Network CompuServe: Go WUGNET, Software Publishers Association CompuServe: Go SPA and Interchange and the Electronic Frontier Foundation CompuServe: Go EFF, an organization dedicated to protecting the privacy of computer users and the right to free speech.

Case Study: The Software Publishers Association

The Software Publishers Association plans to use a forum on Interchange as:

- A newsroom where members can read press releases on late–breaking news.
- A briefing room in which members can talk with association staffers about software industry issues that impact computer users, including game ratings, government regulation and intellectual property rights.
- A research center where members can read current market reports tracking the education, consumer and business software market segments and a data program covering the online services industry.
- An information center about SPA programs, conferences and seminars.

"Online services are fundamental to our charter of educating and informing the public about the latest software industry developments," says Ken Wasch, executive director of the SPA. "Interchange offers us some exciting new ways to deliver information, including linking it to related information from our member companies as well as content from Ziff–Davis and other publications. People will be able to hear our position on an issue, read about what software vendors and *PC Week* have to say, and then discuss the issue with our staff and other Interchange members."

What Topics Are Covered in Forums?

The range of information providers is vast. Topics range from activities like bicycles and model airplanes, to lifestyle activities like gourmet cooking and wine tasting, from professional forums on marketing and law to support groups for sexuality and muscular dystrophy, from matters of belief like philosophy and religion, to financial concerns like financing and investing. More and more entertainment–oriented companies are coming online, as seen by the emergence of

Hollywood Online, Warner Bros. Records and others. The range of possibilities is as broad as human interests.

Some enterprising companies are taking a different tack in creating forums. The previous examples showed how companies are directly promoting their products and services—even calling their forums by company names. A new trend is for companies to create forums that show the benefits of their products. Owens–Corning created HouseNet to let do–it–yourselfers discuss home repair and find out about products. This example follows a pattern launched early in this century by Michelin, which created travel guides to motivate people to travel—and buy tires to replace the worn–out ones!

The question for you is: Does your company offer a topic that can generate significant interest—and cash? If the answer is yes, your company might be a good candidate for becoming an information provider and creating and operating a forum. The rest of the chapter will discuss how to negotiate the best deal and how to maintain an active forum. Forums also can be used as a product support center, which will be discussed in Chapter 13.

Negotiating the Deal to Go Online

When you consider all the benefits that accrue to an information provider, you might be surprised to learn that online services pay information providers to be online! With the technical tools in place to service their customers, you might think that companies would pay the commercial online services for the expertise and computer space to service their customers. As a matter of fact, on the Internet, you would have to pay an Internet presence provider a fee to create and maintain the forum, as well as pay for the storage space your forum's data occupies on a computer server. However, because the commercial online services make money from information providers' customers, your company can operate a forum—and make a profit.

The commercial online services were quite hesitant to reveal financial terms for this book. Each deal is different, they say. Analysts believe the average split on royalties is 80–20 in favor of the commercial online service.

However, the commercial online services are eager to sign new information providers to attract new customers and to give them a competitive advantage over the rival services, so you might have considerable leverage in negotiating with the commercial online services.

If you decide to create a forum online, here are the steps to take and the factors to consider.

Step 1: Decide which online service to use

The most important factor in deciding which online service should house your forum is determining which service currently has members who match your target market. For example, CompuServe has a large business market; Prodigy has a large home, children and women's market; and AOL seems to appeal to people at the cutting edge of technology, literature and the arts. Before signing on with an online system, find out much more about the demographics of their subscribers.

Step 2: Negotiate the best deal

There are two revenue streams to discuss. Online systems make money when members sign on to the system. The longer they are online, the more money the online system makes. Your company could get a slice of both those pies—new member enrollment and online time. How much money you receive is determined by many factors. Every deal, representatives say, is different. Here are some factors that affect the terms of an agreement with an online service:

- *Can your forum recruit new members to the online service?* If it can, the service will pay a "bounty" for each new member. Bounties can vary widely, from a few cents to several dollars. Newer services are more likely to make sweetheart deals than older, established online services.
- *Can your business help promote the online service by bartering services?* For instance, a radio station, television station, newspaper or magazine can offer to trade advertising space for additional financial consideration. A large association could send notices to members or place an ad in its newsletter or magazine.

- ***Is the information provider exclusive to one service?*** If so, the commercial online service will offer more favorable terms. Some companies would rather extend their reach. For example, *Consumer Reports* is on CompuServe, Prodigy and America Online.

- ***Does the forum provide information that can't be obtained from competitors?*** If so, you have enviable bargaining position.

- ***Does the forum attract highly desirable consumers (high–income) or hard–to–attract consumers (women)?*** Women have been slow to sign on to online commercial services and are poorly represented. If your forum can draw women, you have an impressive bargaining chip.

- ***Does your forum appeal to a large number of members?*** Operating the tiddlywinks forum might not give you as much bargaining force as having information that many people want, like baseball statistics for a fantasy league.

- ***Does your forum have a high degree of name awareness and brand awareness?*** If consumers know your company instantly, you bring credibility to the online service. Members will already have a preconceived notion of the quality products your company makes and could spend time in your forum. For example, I was immediately drawn to the Real Time Marketing Forum on eWorld because it was sponsored by high–tech marketing guru Regis McKenna. I've read his books, so the forum had a natural appeal for me. If it had been operated by a collection of people with lower profiles, I wouldn't have been so enthusiastic about checking out the service.

- ***How stable is your company and its commitment to online services?*** Has your company been around for a while, or is it a relatively new start–up? The longer your company has been in business, the better. Start–ups will have a much more difficult time bargaining with the commercial online services.

- ***Another factor to consider in negotiating royalty rates is what will happen if the hourly rate charged to consumers falls***. This is quite likely as the competition heats up among the top players. The economics of your business plan change dramatically if income is based on 20% of a rate $9.95 per hour versus a $4 an hour.

Step 3: Maintain the forum

Maintaining the system involves issues of technology, user interface, personnel and content.

The technology involves creating the look and feel of the forum, connecting information to the server and other nerdy issues. Unlike the Web, these factors are out of your control. The online service creates the software, interface and other tools and training needed to operate the forum. It also maintains billing records.

You will need to consider what the user interface looks like. Will you have any say in the way it looks or will it look the same as every other forum? Using an online service's software is a double–edged sword. It is a blessing because these services know what works and what doesn't, so you get the benefit of their knowledge and experience. You also don't have to create tools from the ground up or spend massive amounts of time learning to program new software. Your readers, who are familiar with other forums on that service will easily be able to use your forum's tools, which are identical to every other forum's way of doing things.

On the other hand, your forum will look pretty much like everyone else's forum—a distinct disadvantage to companies and publishers that have their own corporate look and feel. For that very reason, the *San Jose Mercury News* created an Internet World Wide Web home page in addition to the forum it provides on America Online. The company wanted to create a unique look and feel. The technical and artistic tools on the Web will allow the publisher to reach its goal.

Online systems probably will adapt to a hybrid forum that allows information providers leeway in designing their forums. For example, America Online permits Hollywood Online to maintain a unique interface designed to take advantage of its multimedia offerings.

Human factors also must be considered. Your company hires a system manager to create content and organize the forum's messages, libraries and conferences, as well as check files for viruses, answer readers' questions and perform other housekeeping tasks. The employee is your responsibility in terms of paying a salary and defining the work schedule. Nuts and bolts issues about manpower must be discussed. How many people will be needed to maintain the forum? Who will it be? Is this a primary or secondary part of this person's job? How much time should she or he devote to this forum each day? What happens when your system manager goes on vacation? How will the employee be trained?

Finally—and most important—content must continually be created. People will not go to a forum where nothing is going on. You must do interesting things that draw people to the forum. For example, CompuServe featured a press conference with Vice President Al Gore. Forums on America Online have hosted Jay Leno and Jerry Seinfeld. Mick Jagger appeared on Prodigy.

"It is not about selling," says Leslie Laredo, director, advertising development for AT&T Interchange Online Network. "It is about telling. Subscribers are paying to be online. They better be rewarded."

The creative issues include: What content will be provided? What will be the names of the sections on the message board and library? What information can be installed by the first day of operation? What information can be added and when? Will special events, like conferences, be held?

Step 4: Keep members online longer

The longer people stay in your forum, the more money you will make. How can you keep people longer, especially when they are watching the meter? Here are several ways:

1. Be interesting: If you have new information, lively discussions, contests and promotions, people will come around regularly.

2. Promote discussion: People like to chat online. They like to interact with people from around the country who are interested in the same topics they are. To increase the chat function, the moderators should always ask questions of readers. Even when he answers a reader's question, the final line should invite a response, such as "What do you think of this?" or "What else have you tried?" or "Let me know if you need additional information." These types of messages can generate more conversation and more entry points for other readers to join the conversation while the meter runs.

3. Promote controversy: People love to talk and debate online with other members. To stimulate conversations, you should create controversial messages that people can respond to. Typical uses would call for the moderator to raise a question about an arguable issue from the day's news that would be of interest to the forum members. For instance, a health forum could ask people what they think about some aspect of health care reform. A forum for business professionals could ask people what they think about the effects of the economy on their business. People also like to discuss current trends in their industry, such as new technology, salaries and personalities.

4. *Create interesting files:* Libraries are collections of files of documents, sounds and photographs. These files can be retrieved by members at their discretion. The more interesting files you have, the more retrievals you will have.

5. *Create large files:* The larger the files, the longer they take to download and the more time people will spend online. Photo and sound files can be quite large. A 60–second sample sound clip of a song can take 60 minutes to download! Marvel Comics created a file that contained the 48–page comic book of Generation X, which took 90 minutes to download. Remember, the longer the meter ticks, the more money you will make.

6. *Offer free sample:* Software is a great giveaway online for obvious reasons—everyone has a computer! Borland introduced its Sidekick for Windows personal information manager program by offering 5,000 free downloads of the entire working edition. By the end of the first day, that number had been reached and the company extended the promotion to 10,000 downloads! Borland won on at least three counts:

- It built a large installed base of users, who will pay to upgrade to new versions in the future.
- These people will tell their friends and company peers, who will buy the software.
- The promotion created a large number of articles in daily newspapers, trade publications and online discussion forums.

In addition to software companies embracing the Internet and commercial online services, the music recording industry has achieved phenomenal success online as well. In 1994, Aerosmith made music history with its online debut on CompuServe's Recording Industry Forum of the previously unreleased song "Head First." Recorded during sessions for the album "Get a Grip," the song was available for eight days on CompuServe. More than 10,000 CompuServe members took advantage of the free download.

7. *Conduct conferences with famous people.* @times, the *New York Times* Forum on America Online, hosts live interviews in its @times Auditorium on a regular basis. Guests have included Public Theater producer and *Angels In America* director George C. Wolfe and Geoffrey Ward, who co–authored *Baseball*, the nine–episode PBS series and best–selling book. The forum also provides publicity opportunities for its staffers who appear in interviews. Guests have included Rebecca Sinkler, editor of *The New York Times Book Review* and Will Shortz, the *Times* crossword editor. Prodigy has conducted live interviews with actors William Shatner, Jerry Seinfeld and Jay Leno, author Sidney Sheldon and rock legend Mick Jagger of the Rolling Stones.

8. ***Host conferences and educational seminars with leaders in your industry or with people who can provide value to your members.*** The Public Relations and Marketing Forum CompuServe: Go PRSIG regularly has online seminars. Recent topics covered were "How to Write a Press Release in the Electronic Age," and "Crisis Communications."

9. ***Contests are a great way to build interest in a forum.*** For example, America Online hosts a stock market contest in which subscribers are given $10,000 in play money and told to build the best portfolio. To play, they must sign on and check prices regularly. They also probably will chat with other members and leave messages. They can also invite other friends to play, thus increasing traffic even more.

- To promote the 100th year of Gibson guitars, CompuServe subscribers could enter a contest to win a limited–edition 100th Anniversary Les Paul Special Guitar valued at $10,000. To enter the contest, subscribers must answer a different Gibson trivia question each week. Clues to questions are available in Library 6, "Gibson Guitar Corp." of the Music Industry Forum. This is a great example of marketing because the contest draws people to the forum, which creates cash flow; subscribers must learn about the company to answer questions, thereby building awareness of the company and its products. Finally, the prize is highly valued— a limited edition of a musical instrument that cannot be found in the stores in the contest area after that date. Finally, the contest was promoted to the entire CompuServe audience in the "What's New" message that displays to all users each time they begin a session.

- Universal Pictures and CompuServe cosponsored a contest, with the grand prize two tickets to attend special CompuServe members–only showings of the film *Junior* in five U.S. cities. Members could also win a T–Shirt and hat, and access production notes and GIF images of the stars.

10. ***Surveys are another way to build online time.*** Prodigy conducts surveys on current event topics, such as "Is IQ related to race?" Survey respondents can spend even more time online to view the results, which are contained on several computer screen pages, by age, race, gender and educational level. Prodigy uses

this tactic frequently on a variety of topics, ranging from politics to sports (Fig. 8–2). Not only does it build time as readers respond to the questions, but additional time clicks on the meter as people view the results of previous polls.

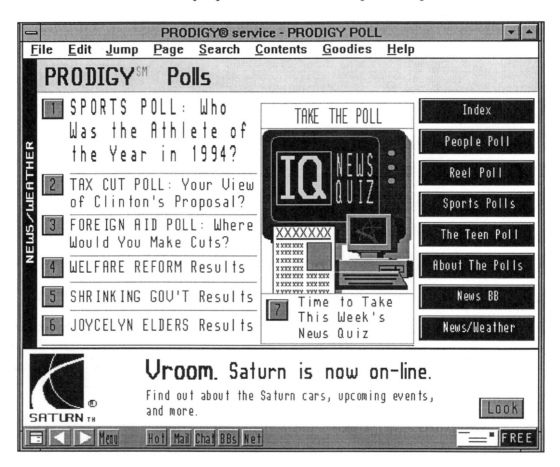

Figure 8–2. Polls and surveys keep people online. (Courtesy of Prodigy)

11. ***"Sublease" space on your forum to complementary companies or associations whose members can visit your area.*** By doing this, you will help a smaller group that might not otherwise be able to afford the time to manage a forum, or you might convince the commercial online service that they can generate enough traffic to earn them a spot online. You will benefit by having more people come to your forum and ring up time online.

Step 5: Publicize the forum

To be successful, information providers must promote the forums. One tactic that works well is to find a niche and market to it, like holistic health. It offers specific content. The information provider goes to conventions and promotes the forum. The more successful sysops create a great deal of content.

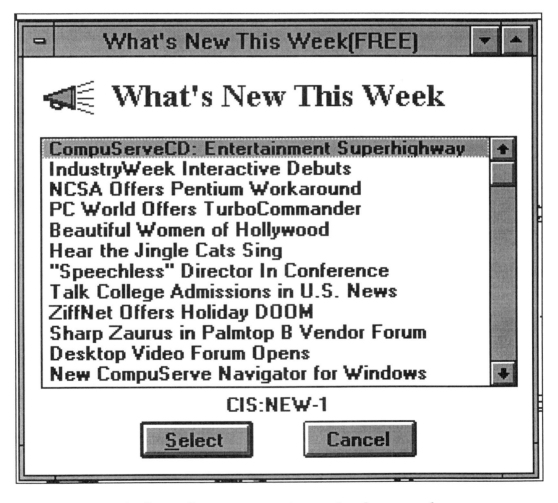

Figure 8–3. CompuServe promotes interesting forums and events.
(Compliments of CompuServe)

CompuServe offers several ways to promote forums. The "What's New" section (Fig. 8–3) lists upcoming events and items of interest. It appears on the screen each time a member signs on. To get your forum listed, you must work with your product manager. *CompuServe Magazine* also writes articles about forums in the monthly publication. To get an article written, work with the product manager or send a note to the editor.

America Online promotes its new Information providers in the "What's New" and "What's Hot" sections. Prodigy sends e–mail notices to members' mailboxes.

To promote the forum, you can and should use public relations strategies both online and off. Online tactics include:

- Dropping notes in related forums telling the readers that your forum exists, that a new file of interest to them has been added that a guest who would fascinate them will appear in a conference.
- Send notes to your subscribers' mailboxes telling them of interesting events and to mark their calendars.
- Post bulletins that automatically appear when readers sign on to the forum. The content can include new material, interesting discussions and upcoming events.

Off–line publicity tactics include:

- Writing and sending press releases to media that reaches your target market. For example, a car magazine can promote itself by sending press releases to automotive editors of daily newspapers. Computer forums can list events in newsletters sent to consumers.
- Sending press releases to opinion leaders and other VIPs who can tell their audiences and people in their sphere of influence about your forum. More detailed instructions for publicity can be found in Chapter 12, Public Relations.

Summary

Forums can become profit centers for companies that can offer information or entertainment. The online centers can also provide a way to build rapport with existing customers and provide information for potential customers.

CHAPTER 9

Building Relationships with E-mail

E-mail is the common denominator for reaching targeted groups of people and creating relationships online. Whether companies are large or small, home-based or consultants, e-mail can help deliver messages in a cost-effective manner. However, please be advised not to confuse e-mail with direct mail. The direct mail marketing techniques that work so well in the analog world are viewed with disdain in the online world. Mass mailings and unsolicited advertisements are the kiss of death on the Internet. However, you can use e-mail and messages in newsgroups, forums and the like to create long-lasting relationships with customers and prospects. This chapter will show you how.

In this chapter, you will learn:

- What mailing lists, newsgroups, forums and bulletin boards are.
- How e-mail can be used effectively.
- The benefits of using these tools in your marketing plan.
- What kinds of activities are forbidden or allowed.
- Examples of successful communications.
- How to find groups.

A major strength of the Internet and commercial online services is the ability for online marketers to target messages to audiences with pinpoint accuracy. Unlike TV, newspaper and magazine advertising which depend on broadcasting your message, the online media allow you to narrowcast. In fact, these electronic bulletin boards possess the tools that permit you to market one-on-one to create rewarding long-term relationships with customers, one at a time. This will help small companies that realize the economic value of a long-term relationship. For the successful online marketer, the motto is "Make a customer today, keep him for life." For a consultant, small business or retail center, the lifetime value of a customer can be thousands of dollars. That is the key to this kind of marketing to an online audience. You must think in the long term. You are not just selling a bouquet of flowers for $45 today; you are selling five bouquets a year for the next 40 years! Think of the sales opportunity as a chance to sell a bouquet to the same person for every birthday, Mother's Day, Valentine's Day, wedding and anniversary for years to come! That's the real value of this kind of marketing.

Companies that sell expensive products with high margins, like luxury cars, airplanes and consulting services can also benefit from this kind of marketing. Consider that, while large and small businesses might broadcast their messages to thousands of people, these deals must be closed one customer at a time. In this manner, one-to-one marketing is a familiar concept indeed.

Electronic Messages in the Marketing Mix

Electronic messages are a terrific way for online marketers to interact with consumers. A variety of tools exist for marketers, including e-mail, forums, bulletin boards, newsgroups and mailing lists. These tools can be used to dispense information to consumers about new products and services, company background, help files and any other material you can create to foster a relationship.

The benefits of using e-mail to converse with consumers include:

- Prospecting for leads by introducing consumers to your product or service.
- Converting prospects to customers by providing them with requested information, such as company overviews, product backgrounders, press releases, reports, surveys and media reviews.
- Building relationships and developing brand loyalty by informing consumers of new products or services, sales, discounts, seminars, events and the like.
- Conducting market research by reading consumers' messages.

Let's look at these methods of creating relationships.

E-mail

E-mail is the most universal application on the Internet and commercial online systems. It is the first online tool people use and, for many, the only tool they will ever use. People are introduced to e-mail through their companies, which communicate with others via e-mail. A leading reason for people to subscribe to online systems is to converse with other people. E-mail is one of the key tools people use to build relationships with one another. For online marketers, e-mail is the common denominator for reaching people. After all, e-mail is the one tool that everyone has and it's easy to use. Using e-mail, you encounter no technical barriers. There aren't any confusing commands to learn or navigation routes to be guided through. E-mail doesn't even care whether you use a PC or a Mac or UNIX computer system. E-mail can also be sent to people on different online systems. E-mail, therefore, is the way many companies will communicate with consumers to create relationships.

Benefits of E-mail

E-mail helps companies by permitting the free flow of information without the barriers of time and space. People can send and receive e-mail at any time of the day or night. The recipients can answer at their leisure. Any kind of file can be sent via e-mail, whether it be text, photo or sound. E-mail is inexpensive on the commercial online services, and free on the Internet.

This section will explore some of the more exotic and interesting ways to use e-mail to create and maintain relationships with prospects and customers.

Automated Mail and Semiautomated Mail

Striking while the iron is hot is a key point in sales. The Internet and commercial online services have great tools to make this happen by giving people information when they need it.

The Internet has automated mail servers called Mailbots (short for mail autoresponder robot) that automatically send mail, just as a fax-back system does. For example, let's say that you print the message `for information, send e-mail to infopack1@mycompany.com` in the body of an e-mail message, your signature file or a Web home page. People send an e-mail note to your mailbot, and the mailbot will send a prewritten message back—even if the note was sent at 2 A.M. on Sunday.

For truly effective use of e-mail, the address should be on every piece of literature produced by your company: business cards, envelopes, letterheads, memo pads, press releases, advertisements and brochures. E-mail can create a new channel of communication with customers if the address is presented to them.

To create a mailbot, contact your Internet service provider.

The commercial online services do not have this feature automated; however, it still makes sense for marketers to create the information files and promote them. If people send mail to your address, you can manually send the files to them. You might lose some time, but you will get your message out in an effective manner.

The tactic of using a separate mailbox for information replies can also be used to track the number of responses from a particular source. For example, if you have two ads written about your company and you list a different mailbox address in each ad, you'll be able to see which ad drew more responses. You can do this with articles, fliers, brochures and any other marketing material.

You can use the power of e-mail and interactive e-mail and direct-response e-mail to build relationships with customers, one at a time.

What Are Mailing Lists, Newsgroups, Forums and Bulletin Boards?

Communities of like-minded people form on the Internet and the commercial online services just as naturally as cliques form in high school. In the online world, these people join certain message areas where they read and write messages to one another.

Each system's services are remarkably similar in nature, although their structures and name conventions are not. In fact, based on the names, you wouldn't even guess that we were talking about the same areas. To help you get up to speed quickly, here is a table showing each service and the names given to each message area:

Service	Name
Internet	USENET Newsgroups (also called newsgroups), and mailing lists
CompuServe	Forums or SIGs (special interest groups)
America Online	Forums and Clubs
Prodigy	Forums and Bulletin Boards

For simplicity's sake, let's call them forums, except when we're pointing to specific matters concerning the individual area. We'll also discuss newsgroups and mailing lists in greater detail. Whatever the terminology, these are places where marketers can find potential prospects for their products.

Topics can range from activities like sports, tennis, water sports, music, baseball, collectibles and cars; to professions, including lawyers, marketers, investors and home-based businesses; and special interests, such as physical disabilities, single mothers, the environment, current events and religion; to computers, software and computer games.

Finding people online with special interests can be relatively easy to do if they participate in forums catering to their needs. For example, you can find people who have specific interests, like bicycling, mountain climbing, sports, cooking, gardening and wine, or people from ethnic groups, such as:

- International House AOL: Keyword International is a discussion area for people who speak German, Portuguese, Spanish and Russian
- African-American Forum CompuServe: Go AFRO.
- Cultures Bulletin Board Prodigy: Jump CULTURES BB. Topics include Native American, African-American, Latin American, Jewish, Eastern European, British and Asian.

People can also be grouped according to their stage in life, such as senior citizens PRODIGY: JUMP AARP. The online world is full of niches of senior citizens, bike riders, marketing professionals, veterans, gardeners, cooks, photographers, small airplane pilots, teenagers, working women, people who work at home, fans of every sport under the sun and computer users. People have congregated into niche markets, which online marketers can harvest if they follow the right steps.

How to Find Target Groups Online

Hundreds of different target audiences are online in USENET newsgroups and mailing lists and in the forums and bulletin boards on the commercial online services. You can find groups easily by reading the names of the forums. Check the directory of any commercial online service to find your audience. The following table explains how to find forum topics:

Service	To find groups, type:
CompuServe	GO DIRECTORY; select menu option for either SEARCH FOR LIST by typing a TOPIC, or list all indexed topics for a complete list with keywords. For newsgroups: GO USENET, select NEWS READER, select SUBSCRIBE, then either search by keyword or browse topics. For mailing lists: Follow instructions for Internet mailing lists below. Add INTERNET: before each e-mail address.
America Online	Select GOTO from menu bar; select Directory of Services, type TOPIC, press enter key. For newsgroups: Keyword NEWSGROUPS, select icon labeled SEARCH NEWSGROUPS, type TOPIC, press enter key; For newsgroups: Keyword NEWSGROUPS, select icon labeled ADD NEWSGROUPS, browse through menu listing main topics. For mailing lists: Keyword MAILING LISTS, select icon labeled SEARCH FOR TOPICS, type TOPIC, press enter key.
Prodigy	Pull down Jump menu select A-Z index, search by topic

(Continued)

Internet newsgroups	Send e-mail to: `internet:mail-server@rtfm.mit.edu` In the subject line, type `send information`. In the body of the message, type: `send USENET/news.answers/active-newsgroups/*` (The asterisk is part of the address.)
Internet mailing lists	1. `http://www.neosoft.com/internet/paml` 2. Send e-mail to: `internet:mail-server@rtfm.mit.edu` In the subject line, type `send information`. In the body of the message, type: `send USENET/news.answers/mail/mailing-lists/*` 3. Send e-mail to: `internet:mail-server@sri.com` In the subject line, type `send information`. In the body of the message, type: `send interest-groups` 4. A printed, indexed version is available from Prentice Hall under the title *Internet: Mailing Lists* (ISBN 0-13-327941-3).

Benefits of Using These Tools in Your Marketing Plan

Online marketers might consider forums virtual gold mines on the digital frontier. They can benefit from reading messages in these highly focused forums by:

- ***Prospecting and retaining customers:*** Marketers can reach hundreds and thousands of current customers and potential consumers with one message.
- ***Market research:*** By reading messages, you can find out what is hot, what people are talking about, and what their feelings are. While most messages will be placed by members who are interested in finding answers to problems, you can also raise your own questions to find out what people are thinking about a topic of interest to you.
- ***Crisis control and prevention:*** By monitoring conversations, you can find out what people are saying about your company and its products. If the word is bad, you can attempt to control the crisis by providing information and trying to solve the problem.
- ***Building relationships:*** By answering customers' questions, you can help solve problems. By providing them with information, you can enrich their experiences or empower them.
- ***Publicity:*** You can lead people to your related forum, Web home page or commercial site provided that you do so in an informative, nonintrusive manner.

Companies, consultants and home-based business executives can also create their own forums to:

- ***Build relationships:*** By answering customer's questions and providing product support and company information, marketers can build long-lasting relationships.
- ***Become a recognized expert or leader in an industry:*** This is a good strategy for consultants and home-based businesses, as they can become known to hundreds or thousands of people, or a select number of people in their specialized area of interest.

Forbidden Activities

Once you locate your audience, take heed. There is a strong negative sentiment against direct advertising among users of newsgroups and mailing lists as well as forums or bulletin boards. This is understandable if you look at it from the consumer's point of view. Since people are paying to be online and it takes time to read mail, they object to receiving mail that they didn't ask for, but that they must pay for in terms of connect time charges. If you use the Internet to send mail to someone on CompuServe, they have to *pay* to receive your message. Imagine how happy they'll be to find out they've just paid $15 to read your unsolicited 40-page message, complete with picture files!

Remember that online systems allow members to post messages to people with similar interests—provided the note contains information, not advertising. All the commercial online services prohibit commercial messages in their forums. That's right. Prohibit. It is against their law, despite what other books falsely proclaim. Each subscriber agrees to a method of behavior when they agree to be a part of the service, whether it be CompuServe, Prodigy, America Online or other services. These subscriber agreements specifically prohibit advertising on the message boards. Here is the message Prodigy offers to its members:

```
    "Please, no advertising or soliciting. Members use the boards
to communicate with other members. You've told us that you don't
want  the  boards  cluttered  with  commercial  messages—it's  like
having  an  unwelcome  salesperson  show  up  at  your  door.  For  this
reason,  please  do  not  post  commercial  or  classified  ads  on  the
public  boards.  This  includes  solicitations  or  offers  to  buy,  sell
or  trade  goods  and  services  of  significant  value.  If  you  have  a
commercial  interest  in  a  product  or  service,  please  don't  post
unsolicited  notes  about  it.  But  if  a  member  has  asked  a  question
about  it,  feel  free  to  answer—just  be  sure  to  disclose  the  nature
of  your  interest."
```

Since few people actually read these agreements, many sysops will drive the point home by telling people of the policy when they join the forum, as you can see from this example from the Public Relations and Marketing Forum CompuServe: Go PRSIG:

```
    SOLICITATION IS PROHIBITED ON OUR FORUM'S MESSAGE BOARD. This
means that our forum members should not actively promote their
respective businesses on the message board. A member may upload a
brief piece publicizing his/her biz in PRODUCTS/SERVICES, LIB 11,
provided it's related to the field of professional communications.
Of course, members are always free to discuss their work,
responding to questions and queries of others.
    If anyone has a question about the policy, ask a Sysop for
clarification.
```

If this isn't enough, sysops have the authority to kill messages that violate this provision. In other words, if you are stupid enough to waste your time writing an ad and posting it on a forum, you will not see it appear, because the sysop will kill it. The offender will get a stern warning from the sysop—in private. Another violation could lead the sysop to ban the offender from the forum forever. Here is an example from a real message that someone tried to post to PRSIG (company information has been obscured for obvious reasons).

```
    02-Aug-94 15:49:03
    Sb: # Generous Finder's Fee!
    Fm: The Unnamed Company 12345,1234
    To: All

    Our client Unnamed Company of America bought over 300 top of
the line heavy duty Fax Machines that arrived too late for tax
season so are reboxed for liquidation. (They're commercial rated
Sharp Mode FO-235, still with original fax paper etc., with most
advanced features.) January retail was legit $695 but these 300
are now at liquidation price of $269 including shipping (two day
delivery and 90 day free replacement warranty)

    The Finder's Fee? You can order for yourself, no problem, but
if any brilliant brain out there knows a way to move the whole
bunch, then $1,000 is yours via FedEx the same day the deal is
done! For one or all, best contact is Gary at Unnamed at (555)
555-1212.
```

```
Sb: #220484-
# Generous Finder's Fee!
Fm: Bill Lutholtz, Asst. Sys 76424,3655
To: The Unnamed Company

We do not allow advertising of this type on our Forum—it's
against the rules that we've clearly stated in our introductory
bulletins. All duplicate copies have been deleted except for one
copy which is being moved to the Sysops Section, out of public
view.

Please don't post this kind of message on our Forum in the
future.
```

The Internet's USENET Newsgroups lack the security of the commercial online services in regard to unwanted advertising. However, the net culture is dead set against advertising in newsgroups. Nearly all newsgroups are noncommercially oriented. Posting commercial ads or solicitations in these newsgroups is inappropriate and will not be welcomed. Furthermore, some newsgroups (examples being misc.consumers and alt.business.multi-level) may appear to be receptive to advertising or solicitation at first glance, but in fact they are not. They are meant for discussion, not commercial activities.

On moderated newsgroups, in which the list owner reads all messages before releasing them to the public, improper messages will never see the light of day. On unmoderated newsgroups, where messages are not censored, advertisements will be seen by all. But that might be your biggest nightmare.

Posting ads on newsgroups or mailing lists is not illegal, but it is definitely counterproductive, as the culture will either flame you or ignore you. Just as it is not illegal to stand on the busiest intersection downtown and beg people for money, neither are you likely to persuade people to part with their cash. So why waste your time and theirs? Follow the rule! Obey netiquette.

Members can also use cancelbots to block messages from people they don't want to hear from. In this manner, even if you post a message to the group, they can avoid you and your messages in the future.

The most flagrant abuse of netiquette occurred when two lawyers sent e-mail to thousands of newsgroups. People were outraged and sent flames to the lawyers. E-mail traffic was so heavy that systems actually slowed down. Readers also sent letters to the Internet provider and the lawyers were thrown off the system. The moral of the story is that people will react negatively to unsolicited direct mail. A footnote to the story is that the lawyers say they received $100,000 in new business, became convinced of the power of Internet marketing and set up a company to advertise on the Internet.

Legal Activities

To make sure you don't violate the netiquette, lurk (read) around the newsgroup for a few days to see if ads would violate the netiquette. This is not a contradiction of the stern warning just issued. Some newsgroups *do* permit advertising, such as the classified advertising areas, which are covered in Chapter 10, Classified Ads.

Furthermore, some commercial and quasi-commercial activities are permitted on newsgroups and forums. For example, some people and companies that need to hire consultants and freelancers post notices to that effect. Other people can post messages in which they ask for information about products or for recommendations on competing products. As a marketer, you can freely join such a conversation and offer to send samples or literature. Sometimes, people talk about products and that leads a third party to order it. For example, I was lurking in the alt.anagram newsgroup and read of a software program that creates anagrams called Anagram Genius info@genius.demon.co.uk. Simply by typing a person's name, the software would compile a massive list of words and phrases found by rearranging the letters in the person's name. In this manner, former Vice President Spiro Agnew, who was thrown out of office and later found to have embezzled money as governor of Maryland, has the following anagrams contained in his name: A power sign, Gains power and Prison wage. I ordered it.

People also post resumes in discussion areas. This strategy can help you market yourself or find a new employee.

Relationship Marketing with Messages

Marketers can reach these highly targeted groups to create meaningful relationships. Your goal as an online direct marketer is to reach a highly focused audience with electronic messages that will convince these people to buy your product or service. These messages are designed to build a relationship with potential customers, one customer at a time. Service providers can build a customer base when prospects are convinced you know your stuff, you are trusted and you participate in the community. You can be a success with direct marketing if you make the commitment in time, resources and information necessary to build relationships with prospects. Remember the cardinal rule about direct marketing: Members of online services want information, not advertisements. Let's look at a few case studies of proven ways to successfully interact with people online that will increase your sales.

Case Study: Bates Information Service

You can build rapport with people by answering questions people raise, just as Mary Ellen Bates of Bates Information Services did. She finds information for people who don't have the time or expertise to find the information themselves. She is an active member of several communities on the Internet and CompuServe.

"I participate when appropriate, usually giving recommendations of places to find information, names of trade associations and the like and add that I'm an independent researcher who also does this for a living," says Bates. There's plenty of value when I say, for example, in response to someone's query about finding market information on the XYZ industry 'Here are several sources: the XYZ Trade Association, the XYZ Office at Dept. of Commerce, try BUSDB database on CompuServe. You might also want to contact an independent researcher to handle this research.' This establishes that I am enough of an expert that he can trust my advice and if he decides he doesn't want to do the work himself, he knows someone who can. I never post my phone number in these messages—just my name and company name. People e-mail me if they want more information."

She has landed clients on CompuServe and the Internet by using this approach.

"There's a big difference between posting an ad, on the one hand, and posting an informative message with a mention at the end that this is what I do for a living. I've gotten some great clients this way and they're already convinced that I know what I'm doing because they've seen me in action," she says. "The bottom line is that people will listen to your messages and will think well of you if you add value to the discussion. There's no value added when someone posts an ad."

Case Study: Canyon InterWorks

Online marketers are master searchers. They search through forums that reach their target audiences, read messages to get a sense of the group and wait for a relevant topic. They join the discussion with information about what they do. For instance, let's say your audience is small businesses and you see this note:

```
Subj: business cards
Date 94-07-29
From: Daniel241


Gee, I wish I had a business card. Does anyone know where I can
get them good but cheap?
```

You could respond as Chris Erichson did

```
Subj:      daily Internet commerce
Date:      94-07-30 20:35:30 EDT
From:      CANYONIWORKS@delphi.com
To: Daniel241


My company sells 'Internet Laser Cards' - perforated cardstock
sheets of 10 business cards - 50 sheets per box. Each card
displays a colorful "INTERNET CITIZEN" design-just feed the sheet
through your Laser or Inkjet printer, print your Internet address,
name/company, telephone etc. And pop them out. Crisp, clean edges,
very professional and EXTREMELY useful.
     If you want to get a better idea of what I am talking about,
just leave mail, include your street address and I will make sure
we send you a sample.
```

"The key points are to answer their questions and help them," says Erichson `CANYONIWORKS@delphi.com`. "I offer my service/product in a way that relates to their needs. People pitch to me when I ask questions. I know they pitched me but they provided a highly probable solution to my problem in a helpful, non-aggressive way. It's all *tact*."

"I learned the Golden Rule: Net etiquette = Net success. Treat people with respect and read the FAQs," says Erichson, whose cards contain a beautiful design and the words "Internet Citizen," along with space to laser-print your name and address. "I advertise on carefully researched USENETs and offer my product tactfully in related discussion threads. From this alone, I receive e-mail requests for info/samples with street addresses from around the world. I promptly mail them info and receive orders through the mail quickly and with a very high request-to-order ratio."

Case Study: Christina O'Connell

Newsgroups, forums, mailing lists, and the like can give PR pros considerable access directly to their customer base. "Bringing your message, in your own words, to these audiences can be extremely successful," says Christina O'Connell, an online public relations consultant. "If you know what you're doing! Hype, sales pitches, rehashes of stilted press releases don't cut it online but ongoing availability to your customers, providing a genuine resource to appropriate audiences, etc., does.

"As Corporate Communications Manager for a computer hardware company, I initiated a broad online campaign which included daily monitoring of appropriate CompuServe forums, participation in discussions which involved our product line, e-mailed product information when requested, etc.

"One area where we were really successful was the promotion of new memory products. At the time, Apple was introducing several new PowerBooks, each with different memory configurations. Our company manufactured PowerBook memory boards. In a section of AOL which focused on PowerBook topics, I posted messages explaining the new configurations, giving advice on how to identify 'in spec' memory boards and what to do if you were sold 'out–of–spec' boards. These messages were not pitches for our product but rather consumer oriented posts on the lines of 'No matter who you buy memory from, here's what to ask when ordering.'

"The results included increased sales. Folks trusted us since we knew what we were talking about and they knew where to find us; great corporate image boost as consumer oriented and as engineering pros; a better informed consumer base which was valuable to us as quality manufacturers; and a nomination as 'Service Heroes' for being so helpful."

Netiquette for Discussion Groups

As we've discussed in Chapter 4, netiquette is extremely important to marketers, who always risk being intrusive or unwelcome in discussion areas. Here are additional pointers that can increase your effectiveness in communicating with people through newsgroups, according to Christina O'Connell, a steering committee member of the HTMARCOM list (this stands for High Tech Marketing Communications).

- When responding to a post, think carefully whether your reply is best directed to the entire list or to the original poster.

    Example: If the original post says:

    ```
    I've got this brilliant brochure I'd be happy to send
    to HTMARCOM folks.
    ```

    send your reply to the brilliant brochure maker, *not* the entire list! (If courtesy does not stop you, think twice about posting your snail mail details to the whole list.)

- When pitching your services to an HTMARCOM request for help with a marketing problem, e-mail to the poster again, *not* the list!

    Example: Original post reads:

    ```
    We've got this enormous budget and no idea how to
    spend it. Any hints?
    ```

    Your reply suggesting new programs to consider, say a TV ad blitz, should go only to the whole list but your response, My agency is superb at spending bucks, should only go via private e-mail to the original poster. (And if courtesy does not stop you, consider whether you want all your competitors on the list reading your pitch for new business.)

- When commenting on a post, please quote only as much as absolutely necessary to make your points. Usually a line or two will do the trick.

Example: Instead of a full repeat of original post, try

```
So&So asked about methods for planning trade show
booths.
```

"When reading your reply, we all want to see your new contribution to the discussion, not the message we have already read," she says. "Remember that many HTMARCOM members pay per message or per character for each and every post, so when you waste bandwidth by ignoring the above, you also cost members money. This is not the way to make a good impression on your professional colleagues on HTMARCOM."

Strategies: How to Create Messages That Work!

Despite the rules and restrictions on advertising on forums, there are many ways to go with the flow of the online community and promote your business. Here are strategies to increase effectiveness for one-on-one marketing:

Strategy: Create Signature Files to Add Positioning Statements to Your Messages

Benefit: A signature file tells people who you are and what you do.

Discussion: While every online system lets you put your name and e-mail address in the mail header, that information is next to useless to the reader. That's because there is no context for, say, joe@yourcompany.com. Is he the chief cook or bottle washer? And just what does his company do, anyway?

Fortunately, netiquette does allow mail senders to include a signature, but don't confuse this with your John Hancock. An online signature or tagline is a four-line message printed at the bottom of your message area in which you can present information of any kind. It is commonly used by people in business to tell others who they are and what they do. A suitable use for online marketers is to print your positioning statement and contact information. The benefit of this signature is that you can subtly let people know who you are and what you do without being a pest about it. There are little if any downside risks since netiquette deems this an acceptable practice. Examples:

```
Rhode Island Soft Systems * P.O.Box 748 * Woonsocket,RI 02895
Ph:401-767-3106 Fax: 401-767-3108 CompuServe:Go RISS,Section/Lib 5
```

```
>>>>>>>>>>>>>>>>>>>>>>>>>>>>>>>>>>>>>>>>>>>>>>>>>>>>>>>>>>>>>>>>>
Daniel Janal    *    Janal Communications    *    510-831-0900
           Public Relations agency for high-tech companies
                      Author, Speaker, Trainer
"Online Marketing Handbook" * "Online Marketing Update Newsletter"
           "How to Publicize High Tech Products"
http://www.janal-communications.com/janal.html update@janalpr.com
>>>>>>>>>>>>>>>>>>>>>>>>>>>>>>>>>>>>>>>>>>>>>>>>>>>>>>>>>>>>>>>>>
```

Action: Create a signature file. Each software system allows for a different method. It would be impossible to list them all here. Here are several simple methods:

Method 1: Create the signature file in your off-line mail reader, if it permits. For example, Pipeline, an Internet service provider, has an option for creating the signature file under the e-mail menu. You simply select the signature file option and type your message. It will be automatically appended to your messages.

Method 2: With Windows, create the signature in a word processing file. When you want to use it, open the file and capture the signature to the clipboard. Paste it into your message.

Method 3: On CompuServe, you can create a signature file by typing Go USENET, select USENET reader, select Set USENET Options, fill in the form. The signature will be attached to each article your write.

Method 4: On a UNIX-based system, you can create a signature file for the Internet by following these steps:

1. Type `pico`.
2. Write the signature file.
3. When finished, hit ^x
4. When asked to save buffer, type `y`
5. When asked for name of file type `x.signature` where x is the first name of the file.
6. To test the signature file, go into Pine and compose a letter. You should see your signature after the message section.

Typing this signature or tag line a dozen times a day would take a lot of time. You can save the time by creating a macro with your word processor that inserts the text when you run the macro. Another time-saver would be to create a word processing file with the signature in it. When you want to use it, use the command to insert a file. To save even more time, give the file a small name, like S.DOC so you only have to type the fewest number of characters. Check the manuals of your online systems to see if they can provide shortcuts or automatic solutions.

Note: Do *not* include your fax number or 800 number. At this point in online marketing, there is a potential for attacks by people who think online systems should not have any commercial material. These people are small in number, but vindictive in nature. Some have been known to jam fax machines, ring up large phone bills or stuff e-mail boxes. Don't give them the chance. This warning might be overly cautious. Please use your own discretion.

Strategy: Answer Messages on Forums, Even If You Can't Promote Your Product

Benefit: Introduces you to the community as a model citizen. You raise your credibility when you answer questions that don't benefit you.

Action: Read message boards and answer questions that other members raise.

Discussion: Be a helpful neighbor. The best way to build credibility is to offer information. You might not actually be promoting your business or service, but you will be promoting yourself and building credibility. That will come in handy when people ask you what you do. They will be more apt to believe you because you are a member of the community. Example:

> "I need to find a sales trainer who can teach my sales staff how to prospect without wasting time. Does anyone know someone who can do this?"

You answer:

> Gordy Allen of Leads Plus conducts great sales seminars and has written great workbooks for the sales staff and for the sales manager. You can reach him at 800-548-4571.

You also get exposure by displaying your signature file.

Strategy: Monitor Message Boards

Benefit: You won't get flamed.

Discussion: By reading messages for a few days or weeks, you'll find out what the community is all about, the netiquette of the board and what topics are discussed.

Action: Go to your A List of message boards; read messages, library files, FAQs (Frequently Asked Questions) and other background files.

Strategy: Write Descriptive Headlines with Keywords

Benefit: Your message will stand out from the rest in format. If people aren't interested, they'll pass on by. You won't have to worry about getting flamed.

Discussion: Online systems let you put a subject line in e-mail messages. This is the only information a person will see before making a decision to read or kill the message. When consumers and reporters view their mail, they see the headlines and the online name of the sender but not the full text. If they want to read the full text, they must be prompted to do so by a compelling headline. Using keywords as the first word gives readers an even better idea of the subject matter. Examples:

```
News: My Company introduces new tape recorder
AD: Surplus Ski Equipment for Sale
FYI: Online Marketing Seminar Set for San Jose
```

Action: Write an appropriate headline for each message you send.

Strategy: Answer Questions from Members That Lead Them to Your Product or Service

Benefit: Prospecting and increased exposure.

Action: Look for messages that you can answer with authority and that allow you to promote your product or service. For example:

```
I have to write a business plan and I've never done one. Can
someone suggest a software program that will do this?

Answer: Yes, try Biz Plan Builder from JIAN Software for Tools.

Answer: I write business plans for a living. My clients have
included many startups and medium sized companies. Please send a
note if you would like more information.
```


Creating Your Own Mailing List on the Internet

Businesses can start their own mailing lists on the Internet. It is probably the fastest and least expensive method available. The commercial online services, for example, probably won't even want to talk to a small company because the forum wouldn't generate significant traffic. Newsgroups, by contrast, must be approved by a central committee of newsgroup operators. Companies can create alt.newsgroups much more easily. However, many systems don't run a full list of those newsgroups. Also, companies might prefer the mailing list route because it can be closed off from the general public and can therefore be targeted.

By starting a list, a small company or consultant can:

- Keep in touch with clients and customers.
- Send press releases and product information.

- Answer questions.
- Let customers talk among themselves to help solve problems.
- Let them know what's new on your Web home page.

As a mailing list owner, you are a publisher who can freely distribute marketing materials without fear of reprisals or flames. After all, people want to be on your list because they want to receive information in the first place.

To create a mailing list, you must work with an Internet service provider who has the proper software, which keeps track of subscriptions as well as managing the mailing functions. The three major programs are Listserv, Listproc and Majordomo.

You will also need to create an information/welcoming message to new members. This message tells new and prospective subscribers what the list covers and who should join. This will help you and them make the best use of their time and resources so they don't join a list that doesn't meet their needs, or yours. The message also should contain information on how to unsubscribe. Also, the list should contain FAQs about the mailing list itself. This message should also be set up as an information piece that is sent automatically to anyone who sends mail to information@your address.

The next step is to get members. You'll have to publicize the mailing list to attract subscribers. Consider these strategies:

- Posting notices in relevant newsgroups and mailing lists.
- Including information in your signature file.
- Letting your customers know about the mailing list through press releases, letters, newsletters, ads and other communications.

These strategies will help to create word of mouth, which is one of the best marketing methods, as satisfied subscribers will tell their colleagues.

Case Study: HTMARCOM

Creating a mailing list can help a small company make contacts, develop an international reputation and build credibility. Mailing lists can also help companies and consultants who want to position themselves as experts on a topic or discuss specialized issues. Here's the story of how Kim Bayne created the

HTMARCOM Mailing List for high-tech marketers and what the list has meant to her.

"It started out as a good idea. I'm president of the Colorado Marcom Network, a statewide professional association of high-tech marketing communicators. I thought, I should be doing a version of the Marcom Network on the Internet and expand my contacts to a worldwide base," she says. "My Masters Degree is in Computer Resources and Information Management so learning new technologies is a natural. And I wanted to create a central location for high-tech marketers to network. I felt that if we (high-tech marketers) were spending the time to promote the technology, we should be using it as well. Starting and operating a list seemed like a good way to do that."

HTMARCOM features online discussions about high-tech marketing and has online archives for marketing articles and resource lists. An online monthly newsletter, HTM, is posted to HTMARCOM and is available to others via e-mail. (To receive a copy, send e-mail to `kimmik@bayne.com` with `SEND HTMARCOM-NEWS` in the subject line.)

The list has been a success from the start, attracting a number of subscribers.

"When I started, I had no idea how successful it would be. We grew to 80 subscribers the first week, and we're growing at about 150 a month now."

The mailing list is getting national exposure as well. HTMARCOM, started in February 1994, had been featured in *Advertising Age*, *Marketing Computers*, *Marketing Technology*, *American Demographics' Marketing Tools*, *PR News* and *Jack O'Dwyer's Newsletter*. Its messages provide the basis for a monthly column in *Marketing Computers* magazine. Editors of that publication ask a question online and print the most interesting answers in their magazine.

Starting a mailing list and running it doesn't happen by itself. List owners have to be dedicated. Bayne lists the requirements as:

"Time, commitment, a willingness to moderate, a good high-speed modem for downloading lots of e-mail messages, and a good off-line mail reader," she says. "My Internet service provider doesn't charge me anything other than my connect time at this point. Internet Express views it as a good business development tool for them, as well."

Operating a mailing list requires a person who understands the technical aspects of the Internet.

"I started out being totally dependent on Internet Express for the technical aspects until I came up to speed. I read tons of online manuals, surfed the Net, joined lists for list owners, and immersed myself totally in the online world. Now I'm glad I did," says Bayne.

To create a mailing list, check with your Internet service provider who must have the proper software to operate a Mailing List. "Internet Express did the initial setup for HTMARCOM. I handle subscription approval, archiving, discussion facilitation, and subscriber configuration requests. Internet Express handles error messages, software maintenance and system operation."

Bayne is a firm believer in the power of Mailing Lists for marketing.

"Now that I've seen how much visibility I have achieved, I think it's become a good business development tool for wolfBayne."

To subscribe to HTMARCOM, send the message `subscribe HTMARCOM YOUR NAME` to the address: `listserv@rmii.com`.

Bayne has created a World Wide Web home page for HTMARCOM, which is located at `http://www.bayne.com/wolfBayne/htmarcom`.

Strategy: Create Private Mailing Lists

Benefit: Maintain close relationships with customers, retailers, editors and other VIPs.

Discussion: If your customers are on a variety of online systems, you can create a mailing list with the e-mail functions of any or all of the commercial online services. In this strategy, you would create a list of customers, prospects, editors and other key contacts who have asked to be on your list. Next, you would create and send messages to them. They could respond to you for additional information or to create a dialogue. Companies must be committed to maintaining this dialogue for the relationship-building process to work.

Key to the success of this plan is that people have asked to be on the list. If you put people on the list without permission, you might suffer the slings and arrows of flames, and destroy the very relationships you hoped to cultivate.

Here is a table showing the mailing address formats to and from the Internet.

Provider	To Internet from provider	From Internet to provider
America Online	`username@host`	`username@aol.com`
AppleLink	`username@host@address`	`username@applelink.apple.com`
CompuServe	`internet:username@host`	`nnnnnnn.nnnn@compuserve.com`

MCI	`TO: username (EMS)`
	`EMS: Internet`
	`MBX: user-id`
		`username@mcimail.com`

Prodigy	`username@host`	`username@prodigy.com`

Strategy: Create Your Own Newsgroup

Benefit: Builds relationships with prospects and customers.

Discussion: You can create newsgroups with your company's name or with the area in which the company participates. The benefits to the first tactic are obvious. The benefits to the second tactic are that your company will be seen as a promoter of an important issue of concern to your audience. For example, a home building supply company could create a newsgroup for do-it-yourselfers.

Action: Discuss with your Internet service provider. Read the FAQ "How to Create a New USENET Newsgroup" available via anonymous FTP from `rtfm.mit.edu`. Follow the path `/pub/usenet/news.answers/creating-newsgroups/*`

Finger

The Internet's Finger tool provides marketers with a quick way for prospects to read about your company. When prospects invoke the finger command, they can read the .plan (pronounced "dot plan") file. This file can contain about a screen's worth of text. You can tell people about your company and its products or provide e-mail, phone and Web home page addresses for more information.

To create a Finger, talk to your Internet provider. Fingers can be created only on UNIX-based machines.

To invoke Finger, the consumer would type `Finger info@yourcompany.com`. She would see a message that could look like this:

```
    Thank you for your interest in Publicity Builder Software. It's
the only software program that will turn your PC into a public
relations agency. You get a complete publicity manual plus a
software disk that contains more than two dozen sample press
release templates that let you simply write press releases.
    Publicity Builder is available for PCs and Macintoshes for only
$49.95 directly from Janal Communications. For more information,
please    visit    our    Web    home    page,    http://www.janal-
communications.com/janal.html; send e-mail to update@janalpr.com,
CompuServe 76004,1046, AOL djanal, or call 510-831-0900.
```

More imaginative uses of Finger would be to use it to provide contest information, jokes or other information and light material that people would want to read. Finger has been used by many people to provide such esoteric information. If your company is really dedicated to maintaining a daily update of useful or fun information, then Finger might be a good marketing tool to attract people and begin to build brand awareness and loyalty.

Online Conferences

The Internet and commercial online services can hold conferences with their customers using a variety of tools. Companies that have their own forums can use those resources, as well as the chat areas of the commercial online services. The Internet has Internet Relay Chat as well as Virtual Places, a software program from Ubique, San Francisco, that enables conferencing on the World Wide Web. One of the more interesting tools is WebChat which enables conference participants to add pictures and sound to their text-based discussions. Using this tool, a company's support personnel could, for example, send FAQs that explain how to correct a problem and show a screen shot showing what the finished product would look like. Salespeople could conduct real-time chats with prospects by showing them pictures of products and send audio clips of testimonials from consumers. `Internet: http://www.irsociety.com/webchat.html.`

To hold a successful conference, companies should take a great deal of care to let consumers know what will be discussed, when it will take place and how to use the tools. This information can be placed in a FAQ file that consumers can read at their convenience.

Summary

Message areas, such as mailing lists, forums, bulletin boards and clubs, are the biggest two-edged sword in online marketing. To take advantage of this vast resource, you must become a member of the community who contributes to the general flow of information. If you provide people with answers to their questions, they will be quite receptive to learn more about your company and its services. Online marketers will succeed if they become active members of the community who obey the rules of netiquette and provide information—not persuasion to make sales. To do otherwise is to proceed at your own risk

You can also create your own mailing list on the Internet and publish information that your customers and prospects find useful, as well as letting them discuss matters with company executives and other customers.

CHAPTER 10

Selling Products and Services with Online Classified Ads

Created in the 1700s, classified advertising is the oldest form of advertising and was responsible for the development of the first newspapers—which consisted entirely of these ads! Today, classified advertisements are the agora for the modern age—a place where buyers and sellers meet to sell useful products and services. These ads, a few scant lines long, have been responsible for companies finding a never-ending supply of prospects. Now they are available online and can reach a worldwide audience.

In this chapter, you will learn:

- How classified advertising can help a business.
- Tips for writing effective online classifieds.
- How to avoid writing bad ads and offending people.
- How each major online system offers classifieds.

Classified advertising has always been an effective, low-cost method of promoting products to large numbers of people. Classified advertisements in newspapers have been used to announce sales, products, events and services. Your company can use online classifieds to sell products and services or call attention to new products, announce end-of-season price cuts and close-outs. Because of the demographics of online systems, your company can target highly specialized marketplaces faster and less expensively than any print media. Because online classifieds can be read by anyone in the country—or the world—they offer a broader reach than a classified ad in their local newspapers. Also, with many large city newspapers going online, you can reach readers in those cities for a low price.

There are many similarities between online classified advertising and its print cousin. Both charge by the number of words and number of insertions. Both rely on the consumer contacting the advertiser. Both are placed in subject categories for easy browsing. Both invite the reader to respond either to order or to gather more information. Because of the low cost of classified advertising compared to display advertising, businesses find it useful to create interest with a classified and then close the deal after sending a follow-up package of promotional materials, either by electronic mail sent directly to the customer's e-mail box or via traditional mail carriers to the customer's home or office.

Online advertising can target just as print advertising can. You can specify the category in which your message appears, such as automobile, computers or exercise equipment. CompuServe also lets you designate the state or country of origin so that it attracts the right audience. America Online permits text searches for easy access to all ads.

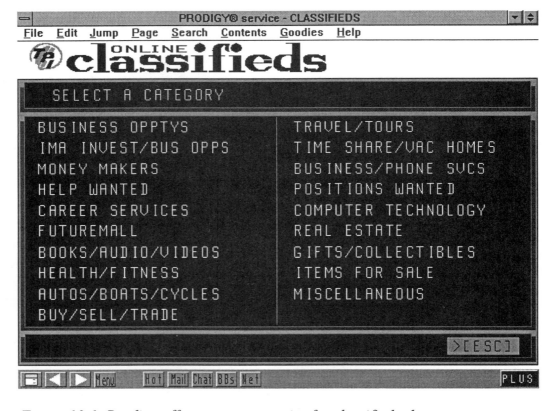

Figure 10-1. Prodigy offers many categories for classified ads. (Courtesy of Prodigy)

Products that seem to sell well include computer equipment (new and used), computer software, information products (such as books and reports) and music. Ads can be placed in all the traditional categories found in newspapers including computer equipment, arts and crafts, books, clothing, cosmetics, jewelry, collectibles, gifts, art supplies, hobby electronics, health items, appliances, housewares, furniture, music, video games, pets, recipes, religious items, sports equipment, tickets for events and travel, children's toys and consumer electronics. Other categories to advertise include real estate and mortgages, transportation, electronics and collectibles, computing services, communications, consulting, financial, tax issues, investments, legal, investigative, office equipment, advertising and promotions (Fig. 10-1).

Rules and Regulations Governing Classified Advertising

Merchants should be aware that the same laws that govern retail sales and mail order apply to online sales. Ad directors at the online services, who approve ads, take a dim view of ads that feature headlines promising to "make money with your modem."

Additionally, each commercial online service has its own rules regarding ads that are acceptable. Ads are subject to the approval of the classified advertising manager. Objectionable ads include:

- Ads that suggest any illegal activity.
- Ads that have sexual connotation, implied or stated.
- Ads that are generally considered to be inappropriate, abusive or sexually offensive.
- Ads to buy/sell/trade firearms, or alcoholic products.

Case Study: Barry House Hotel, London

Classifieds don't have to be wordy to work. The Barry House Hotel in London placed the following ad on CompuServe, which has received inquiries and sales from around the world.

```
   *** London Budget Hotel ***

   Comfortable  B&B  in  Central  London.  Please  send  your  mailing
address for brochure
```

"I placed a one line ad because it is cheaper," says B.S. Bhasin. "I then sent out one of our brochures and booking form in response."

The company also uses online services to promote its business by placing information files in online libraries, including the Inn & Lodging Forum: Small Elegant Hotels Section and UK Forum: Travel Info Section.

How to Write a Great Classified Ad

Let's examine the steps you need to take to create a great classified ad. An online classified advertisement has three main parts:

- Headline.
- Body.
- Call to action.

Headline

Whereas print classifieds allow the reader to read an entire ad at a single glance, online classifieds are presented as a series of headlines in a menu. Readers scan headlines and select the ads they want to read. For this reason, it is vitally important to create a clever, appealing headline. Headlines are the first, and perhaps only, chance of reaching your audience.

The best headlines are those that are straightforward and honest. These actual headlines come from the computing for sale section of CompuServe. They certainly do get their point across, even if they are not terribly exciting.

```
1  14.4 C.P.M. 1+LD & 800# Peak/OffPeak
2  *FREE FAX-ON-DEMAND SERVICE IN EUROPE*
3   LifeTime Income - Telecommunications
4  800#,18 CPM,FREE Setup,6 Sec.Billing
5  Calling Card, 17.5 CPM, No Surcharges
```

"The headline should be succinct. It should get to the point," says Randy Padawer, host of the Classifieds on America Online, which draws 90,000 ads each month. "I find that listing a price is a good thing. That is debated. For example, if you have an old fossil computer you want to sell, make your headline say "Mac Plus, first $200," rather than something cute like "Your kid's first computer.""

Body

The body of the classified ad contains a description of the product or service and the offer. While browsing hundreds of online ads, several trends emerge:

1. Teaser. The message is short, about one line, and asks the reader to call, fax or e-mail for more information. For example:

```
For free information on how to improve your telephone sales,
call 1-800-555-1212.
```

2. Full disclosure. The message is several pages long. This appeals to the type of consumer who buys on information, not emotion. This approach also works for technical products that need to convey a great deal of information.

The jury is out on whether long messages work better than short. No comprehensive data has been studied to this point.

"In the body copy, the specifications should be made clear and should be complete, whether you are selling a car or a home appliance or a computer," says Padawer. "If you are willing to deal in terms of price, you might include the words 'or best offer.' "

Here are a few examples of ads from the Internet that could be placed by a small business, a real estate agent and a car dealer.

```
Subject: ELVIS WALL CLOCK FOR SALE
Date: Wed, 10 Aug 1994 19:05:13 GMT
Sender:

I have an ELVIS wall clock that I would like to sell. It is brand
new and in its original box. Great gift idea for ELVIS fans. I am
looking to get $25 shipped for it. If interested please e-mail me.
```

From:
Subject: Townhouse for Rent/Sale - Old Bridge, NJ
Date: Fri, 12 Aug 1994 02:00:57 GMT

 TOWNHOUSE FOR RENT/SALE
 Matawan/Old Bridge, NJ Area
 + Three Bedrooms (large master bedroom)
 + Two and a Half Bathrooms (two upstairs, one downstairs)
 + Eat-In Kitchen
 + Fireplace in Living Room
 + Rent: $1075/mo. + Utils.
 + Sale: $97,900 (assumable 6.5% 23 yr. ARM)
 + Call Tom at 908-555-1212(W)or 908-555-1212(H)

From:
Subject: 1988 Dodge Shadow for sale (NJ)
Date: Wed, 10 Aug 1994 16:32:43 GMT

****************FOR SALE*************************

1988 Dodge Shadow 68,000 miles
Automatic transmission Air Conditioning Cruise Control 4 Door
AM/FM Stereo Radio 2 Brand New Tires $2300. negotiable
Call 201 827-1485 After 4 p.m.

From:
Subject: IBM VGA 14" Color Monitor $125
Date: Sat, 06 Aug 94 18:29:24 EDT

FOR SALE: IBM VGA 14" Color Monitor, $125

This is the genuine article, IBM Model 8512, in good condition.
It is regular VGA, up to 640x480x256 at .39 dot pitch, and cannot
do Super VGA.

Price: $125 + shipping
Reply here or call Lonny at 305-555-1212

Call to Action

All classified ads should have a call to action and a feedback mechanism. This means that your ad should ask people to do something, such as send e-mail for more information or call an 800 number to order the product. CompuServe and Prodigy ads tend to be short because people are charged by the word. Therefore, many of these ads ask readers to send or call for information. Those information packages can be several pages long. Since ads are free on America Online, ads tend to be long enough to tell a complete story about the product.

Increasing the Response Rate

Improving your response rate by 1% can be a big number indeed to an online audience that reaches millions of people. Here are several hints on how to write an effective online classified advertisement:

- Emphasize how the product will benefit the customer. Don't stress features at the expense of benefits, a common mistake, because people buy products on the basis of how they will feel after they experience the benefits of the product.
- Give complete, accurate, specific details. Vagueness won't work. Omitting important information, like miles on a car, will make readers wonder what's wrong, missing, or misleading.
- Give readers an accurate picture of what your offer includes. What will they get and how much will it cost? When and how will it be delivered?
- Advertise in more than one category and online service. Increased exposure means increased response. Give the ad a chance to work by letting it sit online for a test period. You might wait longer than you would in a newspaper because some online consumers browse the classifieds only once a month. The longer you place the ad, the more chance it will be seen.
- Ask readers to reply via e-mail to encourage immediate response. Create an auto response system, such as a fax-back system or

mailbot (automatic mail response system available to Internet users). Avoid requiring readers to invest additional time and money for snail mail or long distance phone calls.

- Offer free samples. They are one of the best ways to get people to respond. If you are in the service industry, consider creating an information report that readers can get free. This report should have information of value and contain sales material to convince prospects to hire you.

Converting Inquiries to Sales

Getting people to respond to your ad is just the first step. To make money, you must convince them to buy your product. This can be done by writing clever sales copy that convinces them to part with their cash. Direct mail copywriters can write a letter for you for a few hundred dollars.

Testing ad copy must be done to ensure high sales. You might have a great product, but if you can't tell people about it in a convincing manner, you are wasting your time. By testing every factor involved with the sale—from product name, pricing, headline, body copy, response mechanism, offer—you can affect the response rate.

The price of the product also needs to be tested. Product pricing is a sensitive issue. Some people might like to buy the product but aren't convinced it should cost beyond a certain price. By testing the price, you won't alienate your prospects. Some people might be wondering if it is better to sell fewer copies at a higher price than more copies at a lower price. The answer depends on your costs and goals. If your cost of goods drops dramatically after a certain point, you would want to sell as many as possible. Likewise, if your goal is to expose as many people as possible to your service, you might consider selling your book or report at a lower price. Then again, people relate value to price; so if you charge too little, people might not think your product has value. As we've said, pricing is a touchy area, so your best bet is to test, test and test. The beauty of online classified ads is that they cost so little, you can afford to test until you find the right message, price and audience.

People also need to have confidence in the seller.

"An ad should represent directly and honestly what is being sold or offered," says Padawer. "That integrity should be reflected in the headline and body copy. Taking this approach inspires confidence in buyers who will see that you are somebody they trust dealing with. That's what makes a great classified ad, more than good writing or a snappy paragraph. I think people can tell when someone is honestly trying to transact with integrity."

"If you are selling something, you should be willing to provide the buyer with personal information that is verifiable, like your name, home phone number and work number. This makes your buyer feel comfortable with you," he says. "I find that people who tend to steal from others online are not willing to come forth with information.

"If they don't, then let it go," says Paul Hopkins, the other host on Classifieds Online. "There will always be another bargain around the corner."

Case Study: Sheila Danzig

Sheila Danzig, a direct mail specialist, is a member of the Entrepreneurs Forum on CompuServe Go: USEN. For a copy of her free report on "How to Turn Your PC into a Money Machine," send e-mail to CompuServe: 74637,374.

Here is her advice for making sales:

"I found that not converting from inquiries to orders was the biggest problem among advertisers. That was because of two things: selling something that had no market—just because you want to sell it, does not mean anyone wants to buy it—and selling it with poor, boring, or unbelievable copy. This is not too hard to repair, but does take some work. It is too easy to get "tire kickers" in the classifieds, *but* people really only answer ads that they at least have some interest in. And after the first round of 200 replies to ad requests, people slow down a bit and start discriminating. (Didn't we all?)

"If you can get the inquiries, you can convert them with the right copy. But you really have to be selling something of value, with the right copy. The cost per inquiry is *soooo* low that it allows you to test all different approaches, and prices, until you find one that hits.

"I have sold some things that others told me can't sell online. Like my express envelopes. How do I sell envelopes online. My ad tells them how I increased response to my mailings by XX% and to leave their name and address for a free sample.

"Free samples work, free reports work; give something of value free, and then sell something of value with that. It has worked for many. Yes more people have failed than succeeded. But that is true of direct mail too. That does not mean direct mail does not work. It means that people are not working it properly."

How to Avoid Writing Bad Ads and Offending People

Writing a bad classified ad is easy. Just think of all the things that turn you off about advertising and you'll be right on target.

"Bad ads are mysterious and hedge with regard to the product or the person offering the product," says Padawer. "A bad ad invites the buyer to make the first step to bid on the product or goes on and on and on like some sales con."

Here are examples of bad classified headlines and what not do. Online denizens have a very low tolerance for get-rich-quick schemes and each of these headlines seems to promise more than they ever could deliver. Also, note the dollar sign, exclamation point and asterisk. The writers think these will draw attention but, to a wary reader, these symbols create an atmosphere of hucksters. To their credit, online services do not limit the rights to free speech and they protect the quality of the online environment by placing these ads in a separate section, where only the truly interested would ever venture.

None of the entries in the menu shown here has been edited. Would you read any of them?

```
 1 The best-kept secret in Direct Marketing
 2 'em BIG Profits on the Info SuperHwy ***
 3 NEED PEOPLE FOR NEW GIFTING PROGRAM NOW!
 4 I MADE $16 MILLION
 5 Japan To Be Conquered.
 6 HI-QUALITY TV COMMERCIAL ONLY 30.000 $
 7 Oz & Kiwi to be Conquered.
 8 Mexico to Be Conquered.
 9 **** Personalized Children's Books ****
10 YOUR OWN 900#--FREE $10K/month possible
```

Measurement

There are no known statistics for measuring the effectiveness of online classifieds. However, the costs are so low that a test can be conducted without wagering a great deal of money.

Classified Advertising Opportunities

Here is an overview of classified advertising areas on the Internet and commercial online services. There are many similarities and differences.

Internet

Classified advertising on the Internet is free on selected newsgroups. However, as we've said many times before, you cannot post intrusive ads anywhere else on the system! These newsgroups exist solely for the purpose of placing classifieds:

```
misc.forsale
misc.forsale.computers
misc.forsale.computers.d
misc.forsale.computers.mac
misc.forsale.computers.other
misc.forsale.computers.pc-clone
misc.forsale.computers.workstation
misc.kids.computer
misc.legal.computing
us.forsale.computers
biz.comp.software
```

You can subscribe or place notices in these newsgroups by following the directions of your news reader or Internet software.

Some regional newsgroups allow classified advertising as well. As you explore newsgroups, you might find others that are amenable to classified advertising. For example, a San Francisco regional newsgroup `rec.arts.sf.marketplace` permits notices from people wanting to sell books, works of art and cars. No one was flamed. Another group, `rec.music.marketplace` seems to exist solely for people to sell their products. Check them out!

The *New York Times* announced that it will test help-wanted ads on the Internet. The ads will be accessible through the Pipeline, an online services company that provides access to the Internet. If this test is successful, can other classified ads be far behind?

CompuServe

CompuServe maintains a classifieds area, `GO:CLASSIFIEDS`. The cost of listing an ad in the Classifieds area depends on the length of the message and the time length the message will be displayed.

The cost per line for a 7-day (1-week) listing is $1.00.
The cost per line for a 14-day (2-week) listing is $1.50.
The cost per line for a 56-day (8-week) listing is $5.20.
The cost per line for a 182-day (26-week) listing is $14.30.

Note: One line equals up to 68 characters.
Example: Three lines of text submitted for 1 week = $3.00.
Three lines of text submitted for 8 weeks = $15.60.

America Online

America Online offers several areas in which to place classified ads, including:

Classified AOL: Keyword CLASSIFIEDS
Chicago Online Marketplace AOL: Keyword CHICAGO
San Jose Mercury News AOL: Keyword MERCURY CENTER
Photoforum AOL: Keyword PHOTO

Unlike most other online services that host classified ads, AOL does not charge for posting classified ads. The section gets about 90,000 new ads each month.

"We hope to see a multiscreen Classifieds Online with more areas to post and chat," says Padawer. "We hope to have a Trader's Lounge chat room before long, with regularly scheduled formal and informal events; more gateways to newspapers joining AOL over the next year; and, as the membership continues to grow, far more bargains to peruse every day. When systemwide software allows keyword search capability for AOL messaging, we'll add that here too, of course."

Prodigy

Prodigy maintains a vast database of classified ads `Jump: Classifieds`. Advertisers can place ads in the online versions of these newspapers:

Atlanta Constitution `Prodigy: Jump: ACCESS ATLANTA`
Milwaukee Journal `Prodigy: Jump MILWAUKEE`
New York Newsday `Prodigy: Jump NEWSDAY DIRECT`
Los Angeles Times `PRODIGY: Jump TIMESLINK.`

Advertisers on Prodigy's service can place up to six "pages" of information about their product or service. A page consists of about 40 words, as displayed with 7 lines per page. Ads are charged at these rates:

Total number of days	Max number of pages	1st page rate	Additional page rate
30	6	$ 50	$5
60	6	$ 80	$5
90	6	$100	$5

Summary

Online classified advertisements can help you announce new products, services and sales to local, national or international audiences. Online classifieds are easy to write and are inexpensive or free, so that marketers can test headlines, body copy, call to action and price. The Internet and commercial online services offer classified advertising sections that are either free (AOL and the Internet) or modestly priced (CompuServe and Prodigy). Classified ads can provide online marketers with a good bang for their buck.

SECTION 3

Marketing Tools for Building Relationships

The old rules for advertising and public relations don't always work online. The new medium is allowing marketers to use new strategies and tactics to reach and influence consumers. This section will show you how to think about your favorite marketing tools in such a way as to take advantage of the power of the new medium.

CHAPTER 11

The New Advertising: Creating Effective Advertising Messages

"Cyberadvertising introduces a new set of paradigms to advertising. It is different in every way from print and broadcast advertising—creatively, functionally and economically," says Leslie Laredo, Director, Advertising Development for AT&T Interchange Online Network and a recognized expert on online advertising. "The interactive capabilities of 'cyberads' offer key advantages for vendors to establish and maintain dialogues with customers."

In this chapter, you will learn:

- What "interactive" really means.
- Why traditional advertising won't work online.
- What kinds of appeals please online members.
- The difference between "intrusive" advertising and sought-after information.
- The problems facing advertising agencies trying to understand the new medium.
- What works and what doesn't according to several case studies.

Interview: CKS Interactive

When one thinks of interactive advertising, the first advertising agency that comes to many minds is CKS Interactive in Cupertino, California., which has virtually created the term "interactive advertising." To give you the best view of what interactive advertising is, I interviewed Pete Snell, general manager of CKS Interactive, one of the companies of the CKS Group 4 which has conducted advertising campaigns for Apple Computer, Ziff-Davis and many others.

Janal: What is interactive advertising?

Snell: There are so many definitions. I would use this one: Interactive advertising is the ability to interact with the source of the message you are receiving to either stop the playing of the message, to divert it to another area within the message for additional info, and to have the source of the message respond to your desires.

For example, let's take an interactive advertisement aimed at direct response. The prospect looks at it and says, "I've seen enough. I want to buy." They can get information on where to purchase the product. The delivery of the message must be able to react to the message recipient's desires.

We much prefer interactive information delivery. Our belief is that, whether we are using online or interactive television, the emphasis must be on information delivery and not on classical persuasion. The term "advertising" has come to mean things that people see on TV: a commodity product that delivers little information but attempts through images and persuasion techniques to get people to buy the product. For example, beer ads feature bikini-clad women playing volleyball on the beach. Infiniti ads don't even show the car; they create a feeling about the car.

That is inappropriate for online services and interactive TV.

Marketers who want to get a message across should not think absolute persuasion, but rather serving the online service's customer through the efficient and intuitive delivery of information about the product.

The first thing a marketer must understand is the expectation and mindset of the users of this communications medium. The Internet is the classic example at the farthest end of the spectrum. It has grown due to the sharing of information. The people who use it are engineers, scientists, UNIX programmers, the university community, and now business-oriented professionals are coming online. The Internet is a fantastic place to go for people who want information. They see strings of messages on a BBS, engage in a chat or download files. They go to the Internet to get unbiased information—pure honest information on a product, hobby or a lifestyle. What facilitates that is that people can hide behind a screen and not reveal their true identity. These people are information seekers and absolutely will not tolerate the Net as a delivery mechanism for commercialism.

Janal: Nevertheless, commerce is coming to the Internet and is being embraced by many consumers, as seen in the case studies and testimonials in this book, as well as in articles in many daily newspapers and magazines. How is this possible if the Internet community is antibusiness?

Snell: Let's look at CommerceNet. It is a closed off environment for commercial transactions. It is kept out of the mainstream of Net activity.

Janal: What guidelines should marketers use to create effective messages?

Snell: The marketer needs to blend his objectives and messages to meet the users' needs. For example, an engineer needs information on chips to design a board. Rather than rely on the manufacturer's printed information, he can download detailed information, including a technical manual, schematics and performance models. By putting current technical literature and product information online, the chip company does a service to the customer.

Janal: Does this model work for the commercial online services as well?

Snell: The commercial online services are more family-oriented. Something happens in the minds of users when they move away from the TV to the computer. They are in control and don't want to be interrupted by commercials. A fast way to create ill will is to interrupt their work with a commercial. People don't want more intrusions. In their minds, the computer is one of the last areas where they are in control and can make decisions about what they want to see.

On the other hand, online services can create sales but not in the way that TV has done. Marketers must think about how to interact very, very differently.

Janal: How?

Snell: 1. Throw away the commercialism. The marketer must think about how he can deliver information in a reactive, not proactive, mode. Establish a forum or area where people can go, using ads to attract people to your forum, where you can create one-to-one or one-to-many dialogues.

2. The power of word of mouth. This is the best way to sell a product. Online services give marketers that ability. The recommendation of satisfied users is essential. Amplify that a thousandfold to a millionfold. Unbiased, unsolicited people going on a forum and saying, "I love this thing and love the customer service and if you have this problem, I'd recommend this product." You have 5,000 people on a forum who'll see that message! What an incredibly powerful way to sell a product! It gets back to the idea of serving the customer—an idea that has been lost in this country.

3. Serve, don't manipulate, the consumer. Be accessible.

4. Creating a forum for people who have a passion (for such topics as *Melrose Place, The Simpsons* and *Seinfeld*). Enthusiasm is infectious. If you are the facilitator to creating excitement, people will want to check it out. Manufacturers

can create an environment where happy customers can tell everyone else about their great transaction with the company.

Janal: Is this really advertising?

Snell: It is not advertising at all. It is the delivery of information and customer service. It is a spin-off of event marketing—creating a forum for excitement. Prodigy announced it would eliminate leader ads from its bulletin boards. That's because consumers didn't want it. They didn't expect it. However, if a consumer proactively goes to an advertisement, that's okay. He grants permission to receive these messages. That's a big deal. If people haven't given their permission, that's offensive.

Janal: What concerns should marketers have over the design and interface?

Snell: First, no shovelware. Don't take the stuff you've done in print and put it up on the Internet without any thought to the medium and how people will access the information. A print brochure has a layout that shows what information we want to deliver to the customer. The same questions must be asked when you place electronic information—for example, product information, a message from the president on the vision of the company, investor relations information, press releases, FAQs from customers, seminar schedules, training schedules and customer testimonials.

In regard to interfaces, there are no manuals for your forum. Consumers can't read how to use it. So it must have these elements:

1. It must be intuitive.
2. It must look good.
3. Icons must do the communicating.
4. It must integrate into the rest of the marketing pieces which must all have the same messages.

The New Advertising Plan

Ad agencies must adopt a new mindset to deal with online advertising. For example, online advertising is not good for image advertising. The very way of doing business is undergoing a massive change, says Leslie Laredo.

Online services can create ads that evolve into two-way communications because e-mail is easy and immediate. People will respond to contests and surveys. "How many times do you think about calling Honda and telling them about what you think about the car, car servicing, etc? People don't think of calling unless there is a problem," she says. "On online services, people will respond. There is constant dialogue."

New paradigms must be established. "Agencies can't use traditional thinking, such as buying advertising space," says Laredo. "They must think of an online service as a brand asset. It is a place to dialogue with customers, announce products, conduct sweepstakes, promote discussions and build a community. It is a way to create relationship marketing."

In Laredo's view, advertising agencies should view the ad as a product. "The ad can be really cool, dynamic and responsive. The online advertisement can become a living part of the product."

One need only look at the several examples to see that the creation of online ads led to massive amounts of publicity for companies like McDonald's and Pizza Hut when they announced ads on the Internet and America Online. Virtually every major newspaper, television channel and radio station reported the ad.

There will be a need for new and different approaches to the creative process. "People want information before pictures," she says. The interactive nature of the World Wide Web means information can be accessed in any number of ways, not the traditional page-turning approach of multipage magazine ads or brochures.

"You need to interview the best salespeople and create an expert system for sales," she says. "You have to anticipate what you would do logically and where you want them to go next. People get confused easily."

The traditional method of buying advertising on the cost per thousand readers, CPM, does not apply to cyberspace.

"There is no easy answer," she says. The price of an ad changes based on each medium's main attribute. For example, computer ads are more valuable in a computer section, where they are more likely to be read by interested buyers. Questions linger as to how to charge for ads. Is it by the time consumer spend on the system? Number of screens? Number of times a person accesses the information? What about off-line usage, in which customers copy and send information ads to colleagues?

Other differences between traditional advertising and cyberadvertising include:

- The dimensions of time and space take on completely new and different perspectives online. Space is virtually unlimited, and time is what the customer takes from you, not what you buy for delivery. Ads can consume the amount of space that is appropriate to the message, not to the confines of a page or 30-second commercial, Laredo says.
- Online ads are easily measured by hits—the number of times a reader accesses the ad.
- Frequency and learning are different online because people seek out ads. No longer is it necessary to have high frequency levels to ensure a hit-or-miss learning experience.
- Targeting to highly defined markets is a key benefit. Communities of people gather around common interests and topics, naturally creating qualified audiences.
- Advertising online creates a new time frame. Messages can be created, posted and revised in minutes, not months.

The Case for Static Ads

John Ballantine has three words for people who think static ads are dead.

"It's not true," says Ballantine, executive vice president of Online Interactive Inc., an online shopping center and direct marketing company based in Seattle. Online Interactive provides convenient, quality shopping options for consumers via online services. He has developed and managed numerous online shopping applications with various commercial services such as Prodigy, America Online, CompuServe and Genie. He believes intrusive advertising works.

"Millions of dollars of merchandise are being purchased online on a daily basis," he says. "More than 100,000 customers per month visit the A₂Z Multimedia SuperShop and the Free Offer Store located on Prodigy Prodigy: Jump FREE OFFER, ATOZ. The Free Offer Store has one of the highest conversion rates on Prodigy. This is due in part to advertising online, driving people from leader ads, Prodigy direct mail, and highlight screens. While some people consider ads intrusive, many people enjoy viewing the ads and learning how to locate the best bargains online."

He thinks the Prodigy model is the one for all online services to follow. "Prodigy is the clear leader in the family advertising, shopper category," he says. "This is because of the way advertising and shopping are integrated into the service through leader ads, highlights and other promotional vehicles."

The New Advertising Agency

The need for interactive advertising on the Internet and the commercial online services is sending a new message to Madison Avenue, but they don't quite know what to make of that message.

"They are in fear and scramble mode," says Laredo. "It is downright scary to the agencies. Agencies are always slow to adopt new technology. Clients are dragging them into this."

Meanwhile, large agencies are taking steps to keep pace with the new interactive advertising by buying small agencies or forming internal divisions.

"They are all doing that," she says. "They are staffed by the multimedia world, the CD-ROM world, not the online world."

The agencies are living in fear, she asserts. "Who do we hire? Do we have the talent? How will we make money?" are questions the agencies are asking. No one has the answers yet.

"Agencies are looking at their ROI (return on investment). It will be decades before online services will be worth billions of dollars. It will be years before interactive TV and the Information Superhighway are the medium of choice and a mass medium," Laredo says of the traditional advertising industry, which is a $148 billion industry. "I don't think traditional advertising will go away."

"Agencies spend $100,000 to get an account; they need annuities," she says. "Online services can create potential for long-term clients. It is difficult to get rid of an agency that is handling day-to-day activities."

She sees a new advertising agency emerging—one that values integrated marketing. "We'll see a return to full-service advertising agencies. The ad agency will do all the research, media buying and creative. Statistics will come back from online usage. This material must be analyzed. These are high–margin items."

Another advantage of online services is that ads can be measured in terms of how many times the information was accessed. You can see if an ad is working or not. This activity will lead to new demands on ad agencies, she asserts.

"You must have dialogues with customers and respond to them. You must be on call," she says. This will lead to new job titles, and people required to service the online customer. "Companies can tie the messages to a customer support center and take advantage of idle time. They can also create links to e-mail agents that can automatically send requested information to a person's e-mail box."

Most importantly, agencies should realize that the future is made up of interactive communications—daily interactions that lead to lifelong relationships.

Examples

The online world has a myriad of ads that make good case studies of what works, what doesn't and why. There seem to be two types of ads—ads that look like ads as we know them from print advertising, and ads that are really online stores. Let's look at a few examples.

Case History: Hollywood Online

One of the most successful and universally acclaimed interactive ads is the *Forrest Gump* Interactive Multimedia Press Kit. The award-winning ad is effective because consumers interact with the ad and enjoy it.

"It is a wonderful advertising and promotional tool," says Jonathan M. Pajion, executive vice president, marketing, for 2-Lane Media, of Los Angeles, which created the *Forrest Gump* promotion for Hollywood Online. "It is designed for the viewing public to download it, be enticed by it and go see the movie. It is designed to help sustain word of mouth. People can make copies of the program and give it to friends."

2-Lane Media began the project with clear goals from its clients, Hollywood Online, which was created in 1993 to set up special online areas to promote Hollywood film releases AOL: Keyword HOLLYWOOD. This plan offers the studios a novel and effective way to market their films. In the course of a few months, Hollywood Online had signed up most of the major film studios and had an online area secured on America Online.

"The marketing goal of the *Forrest Gump* Press Kit (and the others, as well) was to generate and sustain interest in the film in a new method—online—and to provide online users with an alternative method of obtaining information about film releases, and an environment in which to discuss the films," says Pajion. The kit also informs the media and creates word-of-mouth advertising for the public. "It does make for a wonderful distribution method for the press. They are more likely to view this than to look at pieces of paper."

2-Lane Media saw its challenge as adding value to the material.

"For our part, the steps we took to reach that goal were to make all the multimedia kits as complete, interesting and fun as possible, given the memory space limits. Since *Gump* was predicted to be a big film, we decided to give it a prestige feel, and since the film spans so many years, we decided upon a unique and interesting timeline/collage interface to convey the highlights of the film. Beyond that, Hollywood Online was responsible for the distribution of our finished project on their numerous online locations for downloading and viewing by the public," he says.

The elements that go into each kit consist of the elements in the standardized film electronic press kit: the script, cast, production stills, production notes, video trailers and occasionally other ancillary materials like lobby cards and posters. We then took these elements and used various programs to create the finished product. The online promotion for the films generally consists of several components, based on the standard EPK (electronic press kit): a text-only magazine based on the EPK's text, a text and photo magazine, several short (15-20) second Quick Time and .AVI format trailers and a cross-platform interactive media press kit.

The kit was designed to be as small as possible for quick and easy downloading by the public. The file can fit on a single floppy disk and the company encourages fans to copy it for friends. The program is available in Macintosh and Windows formats and does not require any additional software.

Hollywood Online placed the kit on its online forums on CompuServe and America Online. Consumers can download the file and they have done so in droves—more than 10,000 people have retrieved the files in about four months, even though instructions clearly indicate that the file size and the amount of time it will take to download on a 9600-baud modem will be about 28 minutes.

"The kits are not sold per se, but are accessed or downloaded via modem from the online services. The kits we have done for Hollywood Online have been among the most successful in terms of downloads. Obviously, if the film is successful and highly anticipated, the kit and the ancillary materials will be downloaded more than those for a burst at the box office," says Pajion.

Let's look at the various components of the ad.

- Theme song. As the program loads, you hear the *Forrest Gump* theme song. This is the first indication that this is no ordinary advertisement online. It involves hearing. The more senses you appeal to, the more interesting it is to consumers and the better environment you have created in which to sell.
- Interface. A picture of Forrest Gump sitting on a park bench appears in the middle of the screen. He says the opening line of the movie, which sets the stage: "Hello, my name is Forrest. Forrest Gump. It's funny what a young man recollects." On the top of the screen is a display of still images from the movie which, we learn, is a timeline. By moving a slide bar, consumers can see videos and still pictures as well as sound from the key points in the movie. This helps tell the story to consumers and gets them interested in the film. The interface is easy to use and intuitive, even though it doesn't come with an instruction manual, nor does it need to, thanks to good design.
- Along the right side is a series of icons that, when pressed, reveal information about the cast, extensive production notes and credits. This information is vital to reporters and film buffs alike.
- A quiz about the movie is located in the icon labeled "History." Pick the correct answer and you hear Forrest Gump offer you a chocolate. Answer incorrectly and he says "I'm not a smart man," or "Mama says, 'Stupid is as stupid does.' "

The *Gump* files are a good example of using the online services as part of the entire marketing program.

"It won't open a movie. It is another marketing tool," says Pajion.

The work has received accolades from the advertising industry.

"If you want to know what an interactive ad is, then the answer is here: Whatever it takes to get people wanting to explore the product. Here is the neat, just-as-much-as-you-need-to-know-interface, the humor and the use of a timeline highlighting the special advantages of interactive media," said the judges in the Marcom Awards for excellence in high-technology advertising, PR and marketing communications. "Not only did some judges want to hire this company, they expect its sense of economy, humor and purposefulness to be widely imitated."

The business model to create the piece was that of a traditional ad agency.

"We did all the creative work for them," says Pajion. "They used the finished product. For each film project. Hollywood Online would give us the EPK from the appropriate studio, and we would then brainstorm and storyboard our concept for each kit, taking into account the type of film and target audience. Our storyboards were then given to the proper executive at the studios for review and approval. After approval, we would then design, assemble and program each kit from scratch, and assemble and digitize the necessary components for each project (e.g., as trailers or magazines). The final pieces were sold to Hollywood Online.

"In every case we attempted to give each multimedia kit its own look and feel relative to the film and incorporate some type of gamelike aspect so that users would be encouraged to explore each kit thoroughly and look at the kit more than once, perhaps even showing it or recommending it to others for download."

The "ad" has led to a spin-off business in selling clothing bearing the film's logos. As part of the Hollywood Online forum, consumers can go to the adjoining Bubba Gump Shrimp Company Store and order baseball caps, sweatshirts and T-shirts. The ordering system is constructed with a menu system that lists all products and then leads to a description of the item, with links to the ordering system. Pictures of the products can be downloaded and viewed offline. A better system would be to display the photo with the description. This was probably done as a tradeoff between time and convenience.

Although the *Forrest Gump* piece is called "an interactive multimedia press kit" by its producers, the industry calls it an ad. This shows the blurring of definitions of marketing in the online world. On the one hand, it contains a mountain of information that reporters can use to write stories about the film; on the other, it is a tool that can persuade consumers to see the film. Based on the successful sales of Bubba Gump baseball caps, and the number of downloads, the *Gump* piece successfully meets the needs of the press and consumers.

Case Study: Aerosmith

Rock group Aerosmith launched its world tour with a first stop in cyberspace as guests on CompuServe's Convention Center. In addition to talking directly with band members during the one-hour conference, participants could win Aerosmith prizes, including the latest Columbia release "Box of Fire" and Geffen Records' compilation album and home video "Big Ones." Other prizes included an interactive CD-ROM game and a CD-ROM music video puzzle game. Proceeds from connect-time charges and the sale of limited-edition "Aerosmith Cyberspace Tour" T-shirts benefited Electronic Frontier Foundation (EFF), an organization dedicated to protecting the privacy of computer users and the right to free speech.

This strategy highlights several important marketing tactics:

- Interactivity. People could talk to the group.
- Contests and prizes. These tools create excitement, draw an audience and create goodwill.
- Donations to a worthy cause. Creates goodwill.

Case Study: NBC and McDonald's

NBC and McDonald's launched a joint promotion that blends television with online services on America Online. The "Go Interactive!" campaign was the first-ever online marketing effort integrating advertising, promotion, communications and interactivity. Highlights of the campaign included:

- Special online McDonald's commercials, among the first commercials to go online. This tactic garnered millions of inches of copy in newspapers. However, the file was very long and took a great deal of time to retrieve. Few consumers downloaded the file. Marketers might wonder why people spend 45 minutes to retrieve a 30-second ad.
- A sweepstakes for $10,000 worth of computer hardware and software as first prize. This tactic appeals to the primary audience, which is united in its use of computers and software. The prize money is substantial enough to warrant attention.
- "Talk to McDonald's" private e-mail box, where consumers can communicate with McDonald's. "NBC & McAuditorium" live interactive chat events promises interactivity between consumers and the company, a good step.
- "NBC & McDonald's Multimedia Gallery" includes an interactive media kit with information on each of NBC's new shows and a trivia game with questions about McDonald's, NBC and new

technologies and other interactive activities. Contests are a good vehicle to attract consumers to forums. Using the company's material as answers to contests might wear thin after a while, as the answers can be self-serving. However, done correctly, this tactic can increase a consumer's awareness of a product's benefits or a company's reputation.

- Children and families can read a guide to the Information Superhighway that teaches them about the interactive world of online computer services. This is another good tactic that brings families together in an educational environment. The result of their learning will be a more informed user of online services.
- RMCC Pen Pal, which enables kids to print, color and mail greetings from a special online coloring book to children at Ronald McDonald Houses. Special activities for kids will draw people to the forum. Creating a paper printout was a successful program for the company, as there were many downloads. Other companies can create similar materials and tie them into an integrated marketing program that draws consumers to the stores as well, perhaps by giving a free prize to children who complete the drawing. While in the store, they become potential consumers and build relationships with the company.

McDonald's placed a full-page ad in *USA Today* to promote its online forum on America Online. This is a good example of integrated marketing in which one medium promotes the message in another.

Sharper Image

The Sharper Image ad for a shower massager (Fig. 11-1) on America Online shows that static ads aren't dead yet. The advertising copy reads as any catalog copy would. The picture with the ad has nice color and shows up well on a computer screen. However, the information is static. There is no depth of information. In many ways, this ad is a repurposed magazine ad. Ordering is conducted through push buttons, and consumers can review their purchases, see a running total and cancel any orders.

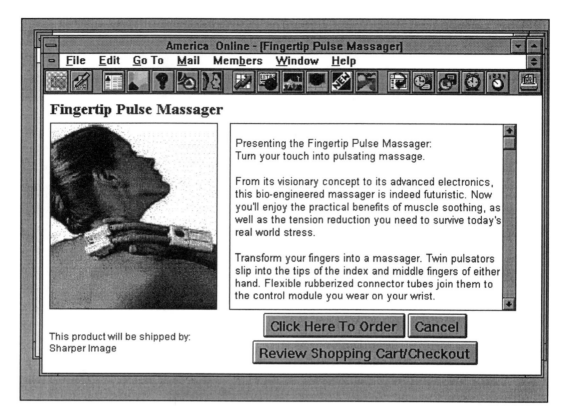

Figure 11-1. Static ads aren't dead yet. (Courtesy of America Online)

Promotions

Promotional tactics from large companies show that consumers are genuinely interested in online promotions. The following examples can help your company brainstorm tactics that can help you reach your target audiences with clever promotions that take advantage of the dynamic, interactive nature of the online medium. Generally speaking, online promotions cover these strategies:

- Free product samples.
- Contests.
- Information.

Strategy: Free Samples

Everyone loves free samples. People online probably like them more than most. The culture of the Internet and the commercial online services has evolved around the idea that members can get something free, whether it be advice, information, news, or software. This time-honored tradition has been embraced by companies from various industries hoping to appeal to their audiences. For example, most major record studios have offered free cuts of new releases, often before the singles are released to the general public. Fans of the groups can download the files, which can take a considerable amount of time. However, given the enormous popularity of this tactic, and its widespread adoption by rival record producers, music fans seem not to mind the wait. For example:

Warner Bros. Music `CompuServe: Go WBPREVIEW` has prereleased several music clips on CompuServe before stores or radio stations get their copies. A 30-second sound clip of Eric Clapton's "I'm Tore Down," from the unreleased album "From the Cradle," was available first to online users. Other online previews greeted fans of the artist formerly known as Prince, Dinosaur Jr., Grant Lee Buffalo, Karyn White, Neil Young, American Music Club and Laurie Anderson.

Warner Bros. also promotes its music groups by creating "multimedia showcase screen savers" that members can download (receive) to their computers for free. Featured groups include Rolling Meat and Beastie Boys, who drew almost 1,000 orders in one day.

On CompuServe, RCA Records previewed country superstar Clint Black's "One Emotion" with a 58-second sound sample of the single "Untanglin' My Mind," which was cowritten by Black and country music legend Merle Haggard. The sound sample was available until the CD appeared in stores.

In one of the most widespread promotions, Madonna fans could download a sound clip of "Secret" from the "Bedtime Stories" album on the Warner Bros. Records forums on America Online, CompuServe and Internet's World Wide Web. To appeal to the online members' desire to be treated as a special group, Madonna recorded a special message.

Aerosmith prereleased "Head First" on CompuServe. The song was available for eight days, and more than 10,000 members downloaded the file, which was free, except for connect time charges.

Many software companies offer free programs or demonstration versions to people through the Internet and commercial online services. For example, Epic

MegaGames `CompuServe:` `Go` `EPIC` lets users download Jazz Jackrabbit free of connect time charges. Jazz Jackrabbit is a high-action run-and-jump game that captures the fun and action of games played on most popular video game consoles today. Borland released more than 10,000 copies of its Sidekick program through CompuServe on a first-come, first-served basis. These promotions can help create awareness and positive images for the sponsoring companies.

By offering a free product on an exclusive basis, these companies are helping to promote brand loyalty.

Case Study: Marvel Comics

Marvel Comics lets subscribers to CompuServe, Internet and America Online download the premiere of the new comic book series *Generation X*, a spin-off of *X-Men*, a successful series about a band of men and women with powers that set them apart from the rest of humanity. To make the offer enticing, the offer is good for a limited time and online readers get to see the strip before newsstand readers. Marvel takes advantage of online publishing by offering the 40-page *Generation X* book number in three formats online: one executable file containing the entire book; multiple-page GIF-image files, each containing several pages; and single-page files. Subscribers to CompuServe could attend an online press conference with Marvel writer Scott Lobdell and illustrator Chris Bachalo and ask questions by typing on their computers. Readers could also share opinions with others and with company executives in CompuServe's Comics Publishers Forum's Section 4, "Marvel Comics," `CompuServe:` `Go` `COMICPUB`. Because it will take nearly 90 minutes for a computer with a fast modem to download the 48-page comic book, the company has no plans to regularly distribute its products that way. This promotion illustrates several key points:

- *Exclusivity:* Online readers see material before anyone else.
- *Compatibility:* The variety of file formats makes the offer appeal to a wider group of people and shows sensitivity to their needs.
- *Interactivity:* Online readers can chat with writers in a special event, as well as with company officials and other fans.
- *Opens new channel:* Because of the long time required to download files, this test won't affect sales in other channels.

Case Study: Car and Driver

Car and Driver AOL: Keyword CAR hosts a conference every Wednesday, in which questions posed by consumers are answered by reporters.

"It's been pretty well received. We get a lot of letters to the editor," says Frank Marcus, columnist. "People seem real interested and pleased. We're selling subscriptions on there as well as merchandise."

This is a good example of a product that is mainstream—cars. For people who wonder if the Internet and commercial online services can deliver messages to mass markets, they need look no further than cars, comics and music.

Information

Information is a key factor in persuading people to buy products online. The major TV networks have created a string of promotions to entice computer users to switch off their monitors and turn on their TVs.

CBS Prodigy: Jump CBS, Internet: http://www.cbs.com promotes its television shows, especially David Letterman, the network's hottest star. Readers can take a *Late Show* trivia quiz, review the Top 10 Lists or send Dave a message. More than 100,000 members viewed the Prodigy area in its first two months.

CBS also maintains an online mall where members can order T-shirts, mugs and hats portraying logos and characters from their favorite shows, such as *Murphy Brown*, *Northern Exposure* and *Picket Fences*. As an indication of how popular promotions can become, members placed more than 2,000 orders in one week, a large sum, Prodigy says, especially since promotions had not yet begun.

Not to be outdone, NBC AOL: Keyword NBC provides information on its shows as well. Viewers can find out how to obtain tickets for all its shows and download pictures of its stars. (*Wings'* Crystal Bernard is the hands-down leader) and read press releases for its shows.

Paramount Pictures created a Web home page promoting the release of *Star Trek: Generations* http://generations.viacom.com/. More than 17,000 people visited the site in the first 10 days, and 3,600 placed orders for products, a company spokeswoman says.

Promotions as a Publicity Tool

Promotions can lead to free publicity in the mainstream media. McDonald's, Pizza Hut and Marvel launched online promotions that were so novel at the time that many newspapers wrote articles about these services. Glowing articles appeared in *USA Today* and other national and local newspapers, thus generating additional exposures. Local companies might be able to get publicity in their local papers, TV and radio as well if their programs are newsworthy.

Summary

When it comes to online marketing, advertising is at the crossroads. Major agencies don't know how to deal with the coming changes. Definitions of the terms are debated. An established way of doing business is changing with the paradigms of online marketing. These are interesting times to watch for changes on Madison Avenue.

CHAPTER 12

Public Relations: Influencing Editors and Your Target Market

Online Public Relations allows you to reach the public directly, without the help of reporters, who are the gatekeepers of information in the traditional media. While your media plan certainly can and should include dealing with the media, the Internet and commercial online services provide the online market with tools to create relationships directly with any number of consumers who are interested in your company and its products or services.

In this chapter, you will learn:

- What publicity is and how it can help you.
- How publicity can be used online to sell products.
- How online publicity differs from traditional publicity.
- How publicity can be used offline to sell online products.
- How to position your company, product or service.
- How to write a press release.
- Where to post your press releases.
- How to build rapport with reporters.
- Public relations strategies for influencing consumers.

What Can Public Relations Do for You?

The most cost-efficient weapon in the marketer's arsenal is public relations, or PR. For a fraction of the cost of advertising, public relations can help accomplish the following objectives:

- Build an image for the company or product.
- Expose the company or product to new audiences.
- Reinforce images and messages within an audience to create demand for products.

- Build relationships with new customers.
- Cement relationships with old customers.

Public relations can build credibility for products and services in a way that advertising cannot. When reporters write a favorable article, they are implicitly or explicitly endorsing your product, company or cause. Advertising doesn't carry that implicit endorsement.

What Public Relations Can't Do

Public relations can't make up for a bad product. It has been said that publicity for a bad product will just let the world know that much faster to avoid that product.

Advantages of Online Over Traditional Public Relations

Online publicity offers many distinct advantages over traditional public relations conducted in the print media of newspapers and magazines and on television and radio. In the traditional media, there is a gatekeeper called an editor, reporter, producer or host, who decides whether your message will see the light of day—and in what context the message will be viewed. The gatekeeper can kill the story because he doesn't think the message would interest her readers, because there isn't enough room in the day's program even though readers would be interested or he's just having a bad day and wants to take it out on a PR person (stranger things have been known to happen).

Online systems offer tremendous opportunities for companies to boost image and sales through publicity. The online world lets you broadcast your message directly to the audience, without the intervention of the media. This is an important distinction. Online systems allow you to tell your story directly to the audience without the biases of the media. You don't have to worry about your message being distorted, misinterpreted or twisted into a negative. You can also work with reporters to promote your message. With online publicity, you get the best of both worlds!

Online publicity puts the public into public relations. Online publicity, in many cases, bypasses the gatekeeper. Companies can disseminate their message by reaching the audience directly through forums, bulletin boards, newsgroups, electronic mail and other methods that will be discussed in this chapter. Public relations beats advertising hands down in forums because advertising is *prohibited* in forums on commercial services. Messages can be killed by system administrators so that your intended readers will never see slick ads. On the Internet, there are no specific rules against advertising, but there is a strong cultural bias against blatant advertising. If you posted an advertisement on an Internet USENET newsgroup, recipients would see the message and probably send "flames," vicious hate mail, to you. Public relations works online in a way that advertising cannot.

Online publicity also has the advantage of creating a one-to-one relationship between the company and the customer or prospect. Thanks to electronic mail, results can be nearly instantaneous. It is a phenomenal tool to develop targeted marketing campaigns.

As with traditional publicity, companies must continue to follow up with prospects to make the sale. However, the next step for the online marketer might involve a combination of cyberspace methods and traditional methods. For example, you might receive a message for more information. You can follow up either by sending e-mail alone or by sending e-mail along with printed materials sent by the post office or overnight courier.

Online public relations also offers advantages in terms of posting content and in gathering information and public opinion.

"The Internet is about content. As with public relations, the message is the message. Public relations doesn't put a message adjacent to the content. Public relations doesn't sponsor content. Public relations is content itself. Content drives the Internet," says Brian Johnson of Alexander Communications, an Atlanta-based public relations agency. "The Internet is about interactivity, a dialogue, and public relations is about interactivity, the give and take of ideas, ideals and information. On the Internet, listening is as important as talking. As public relations professionals know, at least half of our value to clients is helping them understand their current position so that their ideal position can be achieved."

Creating an Online Public Relations Campaign

To create a public relations campaign that works, you need to follow these steps:

- *Goals:* Determine your objective.
- *Research:* Understand the market and competition.
- *Message creation:* What makes your product different?
- *Materials creation:* Writing press releases and other materials.
- *Audience selection:* Who are your target customers and where do they live online?
- *Message dissemination:* How do you send appropriate messages to the right public or audience?
- *Evaluation:* Determine success. Compare achievements to goals.

Let's look at each of these elements.

1. Goals

A goal is the statement of your objective for the marketing campaign. Without goals, you don't know what to shoot for and won't know when or if you have achieved success. Too many marketing plans are sabotaged from the outset because the goals have not been clearly defined. Every marketing plan has at least one goal.

By setting goals, you can focus your marketing campaign, justify approval from management and measure success Your goals can be sales-oriented, financially oriented, or even ego-oriented. For example, publicity can:

- Increase sales.
- Increase the price of company stock.
- Make you famous.
- Provide sales material in the form of reprinted reviews, articles and testimonials from satisfied customers.
- Introduce or increase awareness of your product.

- Lead to joint marketing and distribution arrangements.
- Create opportunities for strategy alliances.
- Attract suitors to buy out your company.
- Create visibility internationally.
- Make your product an overnight sensation.
- Make an established product look new.
- Make a new product look established (not old!).
- Alert people to your special event, news item or promotion.
- Create one-to-one relationships with customers.
- Create long-term customers.
- Build loyalty.
- Establish word-of-mouth (word-of-e-mail) campaigns.
- Make you look so good that your boss promotes you.
- Make you so rich you can retire.

For a goal to be worthwhile, it should be explicit, measurable, achievable, important to you and deadline-oriented. Consider the following:

Explicit: Is your goal clearly defined? Does everyone in the organization know the goal well enough to tell others about it?

Measurable: How will you know when you've reached your goal? You need to set a clear mark—for instance, creating 11 new leads a day.

Achievable: Set goals you can reach. Nothing is more counterproductive than creating goals that can't be attained. Start by setting small, achievable goals. You'll build confidence that your program works, and you can then set larger goals. Be realistic when setting goals by obtaining feedback from associates. This is especially important in regard to time frames and budgets.

Important to you: Is the goal really important to you? If it isn't relevant, you won't work hard to achieve it, or devote the resources necessary to attain the goal. Are you willing to spend the time and effort necessary to make this a reality? If you set a goal that means something to you personally, you are more likely to work for it. For example, the goal of increasing sales by 10% is nice, but doesn't mean anything on a personal level. If you say, "I'll feel good about myself if I make this goal," or "I can buy a new car if I make this goal," then you are more likely to take ownership of that goal and work hard to make it real.

Deadline-oriented: Set a realistic time frame in which to achieve your goal—for example, one month to research the topic, two weeks to create the essential messages and test them inside the company. By assigning due dates, you are more likely to reach the goal. If you don't reach your goal by the target date, you might realize that you need more resources, that the plan isn't working or that you simply needed another two days to accomplish the task.

Goals are not set in stone. They can and should be adjusted frequently to take advantage of new information, changing market conditions and other factors.

All public relations goals should be made in cooperation with the entire marketing department's objectives.

2. Research

Any marketing program that doesn't include solid research is bound to fail. Information about competitors, customers and the market is essential to creating an effective marketing program. Online services offer many avenues to find current and historical information on these topics, as well as census information that might otherwise be hard to find, or very expensive to buy. For a detailed discussion about research and online sources, please refer to Chapter 5.

3. Message Creation

Defining a message can be one of the hardest parts of the marketing process—and one of the most rewarding. How rewarding to hear total strangers at a trade show describing your product exactly as you positioned it! And how disturbing to hear the description mangled by people on your own staff! That's the difference between creating a message that everyone understands and that sounds great compared to a message that is muddy and doesn't roll off the tongue easily.

The best messages are the ones that are remembered easily. After all, if people can't find your message or can't remember it, then all is lost. Unfortunately, many would-be marketers don't adhere to this simple truism. They just don't get the point across. For online marketers, this point cannot be overstated because brevity is the key. People who go online are browsers. They are paying for the time they are online and don't want to spend a second more time than they have to read messages. Time is precious even if they retrieve messages and read them offline when the meter isn't ticking. People get so many messages that they must skim to avoid information overload. If you want to get your message across, it must be memorable. Not surprisingly, the best newspaper headlines are short. Consider:

War!
Peace Declared!
Kennedy Elected!

Pithy messages are essential because people have short attention spans, varying abilities to discern differences between products and a great need to put ideas, people and products into neat pigeonholes. People love to be mind readers. That is, when you tell a group of people you are, say, a writer, one person might think you write novels, another that you write computer manuals and a third that you work for a newspaper. Therefore, you must be specific and not leave anything to chance. If you give people the opportunity to read your mind, chances are they will get the wrong answer every time!

This section will contain exercises for creating meaningful messages. They are:

- Fundamentals of Publicity Writing.
- Features and Benefits Workshop.
- Foolproof Product Positioning Statement Workshop.
- Company Positioning Statement Workshop.

When you complete these exercises, you will have defined clear messages about your product and company that can be used to tell the world what you do!

Fundamentals of Publicity Writing

The first steps in publicity writing are to avoid the two steps that always lead to disaster: lying and overstating the truth. Here are simple rules to avoid disaster.

- ***Tell the truth:*** The first rule for effective public relations is to tell the truth. Reporters and consumers will find out if a product doesn't live up to its claims. Don't oversell and overpromise. Simply say what the product can do and how people will benefit.

If you go beyond this boundary and stretch the truth, people will find out and your credibility will be shot forever.

- *Avoid hype and buzzwords:* People have negative views about advertising and salespeople. They don't believe many claims. By hyping products and adding useless words, fluff and hyperbole, you actually harm your efforts. Here are words and phrases to avoid when writing publicity material:

Next-generation
Revolutionary
Trend-setting
State-of-the-art
One-of-a-kind
Leading edge
Incredible
Ahead of its time

If you use these words and phrases, you are daring reporters and skeptical readers to find products that are better. If you, in fact, do have a product that is revolutionary, reporters and readers will know it is because they have never heard of anything quite so wonderful. Trust them. They'll get the idea. If you tell them you can change water to gasoline, they don't need to be told it is revolutionary! They need to be told where they can buy it!

Features and Benefits Workshop

People don't buy television sets, orange juice or tax preparation services. They buy the benefits of those services. That is, they buy entertainment, refreshment and convenience (or expertise). Unfortunately, many naive marketers stress the features of products and not the benefits. What's the difference between a feature and a benefit? Let's look at a TV remote control. A feature might be that the dimensions are 1 inch wide by 4 inches long. The benefit is that it fits in your hand comfortably. People buy comfort and convenience. They don't buy plastic clickers. If you create this worksheet, you will have a great wealth of material with which to create additional sales tools like data sheets and press releases. You'll also learn far more about the product than you now do!

Foolproof Product Positioning Statement Workshop

Since the beginning of time, marketers have wanted to create the unique selling proposition, also known as the positioning statement or the reason to buy. Whatever the name, the purpose is to create a short message that people will remember whenever they think about your product. Here's an exercise to help marketers get to the point quickly and accurately. I call this exercise the foolproof positioning statement workshop because everyone who has participated in this exercise has created a statement they are pleased with—regardless of their profession or initial skepticism

The foolproof product positioning statement is a two-sentence message: The first sentence tells people what your product is and how they will benefit. The second sentence tells people why your product is different than others.

Here's are a few examples:

    David Letterman is a talk show host who entertains baby
boomers so they can feel good before they go to bed. Unlike other
talk show hosts, he performs a Top Ten List.

    Dento is a toothpaste that helps children fight cavities.
Unlike other toothpaste, Dento has X-45g, the most effective
ingredient in keeping teeth healthy

    Jerry Jackson is a real estate agent who helps medium-sized
businesses and commercial space at premium prices. Unlike other
real estate agents, Jackson specializes in that business segment.

You'll notice a formula. It goes like this: (Company or product or service) is a (category) that/who helps (primary audience) achieve/reach (primary benefit). Unlike other (categories), (company or product or service) has/offers/features (primary difference).

This formula will work. In some cases, you might need to make a few adjustments for the sentence to read properly. Feel free to take some liberties with the wording so that you sound natural when you say it aloud. If it sounds okay when you say it, chances are it will read well in print, too. It should sound as natural as something you would say to a friend on the telephone. It should not sound stiff and formal. It should sound inviting and friendly.

Writing the message is the first step. The second step is to test your message. To do this, you need to read the message to a person who does *not* know your business. Ask that person to put your message in his own words. If you hear an accurate message, you have written a good statement. If you don't, work on it.

Don't test the message with someone who knows your product because that person will be able to assume the answers to holes in your message and will fill the holes automatically. This won't help you when you deal with people who don't have a clue as to your message.

Also, don't ask people, "Did you understand the message?" People will nod yes because they don't want to offend you or appear ignorant. If you follow these rules, you will get your point across. Instead, ask if they can explain in their own words what the product does and who should use it.

Another consideration you might have is what to do if you have several products for several audiences, or one product that fills the needs of many different markets. You can create additional positioning statements. For example:

```
Janal Communications is a public relations agency that helps
software publishers and hardware manufacturers make more sales by
getting their products reviewed in the media. Unlike other public
relations agencies, Janal Communications can work on a project
basis, which saves the client money.
```

```
Janal Communications is an online presence provider that helps
any company create a presence on the Information Superhighway.
Unlike other online presence providers, Janal Communications
offers complete public relations services to effectively market
the company's site online.
```

Company Positioning Statement Workshop

A company positioning statement is a four- or five-word description that accurately describes your company's main purpose.

You should create a positioning statement for your company and for yourself. This is especially important if you are a consultant, home-based business or small business because readers will not know who you are or what to make of you. If you have a personal or company positioning statement, you'll be able to begin carving out a niche for yourself. This is especially important if you follow our rule: be a good neighbor and participate actively in forums.

Here are a few examples:

- Harry Holmes, communications consultant for small businesses.
- Arlene Jackson, art consultant for large corporate offices.
- Gordy Allen, sales prospecting trainer.
- Grant James, advertising copywriter for tangible products.

To create your own statement, write your name, what you do and who you do it for. Simple. Don't make things complicated. You will get your message across!

Companies should create these messages as well. Here are examples for company backgrounders. Notice how they contain information about when the company was founded, what it does, what its mission is, awards it has won, prominent executives and/or where the company is located:

> Founded in 1986, Janal Communications is a public relations agency specializing in computer software publishers and computer hardware manufacturers. Clients have included AT&T, Grolier, and Prentice Hall. Its president, Daniel Janal, has spoken at many industry conferences and has written two books about marketing "How to Publicize High Tech Products and Services," and "Online Marketing Handbook." The company is based in Danville, CA.

> Technopolis® Communications, Inc., provides public relations, marketing communications and marketing services to computer hardware, software and services companies.

> Founded in 1992, Oscar Toys is a leading manufacturer of pet toys. Based on the belief that pets can make people happier and healthier, Oscar Toys markets a full line of high-quality, low-cost toys for cats and their providers. The company's leading products are the Boomerang Mouse, Catapult and Dog Alert.

Summary

Clearly defining your product and company is a task that every marketer must do to convey the proper message to his or her target audience. When you have completed the exercises in this section, you will have the foundation for writing a press release, pitch letter and signature, which will be discussed next.

4. Materials Creation

Online publicity materials can include press releases, company backgrounders and fact sheets, testimonials, data sheets, case histories and financial reports. This section will show you how to create these tools.

Writing Effective Press Releases

A press release is to a product as a business card is to a person or a resume to a job applicant. A press release is a document that tells your story to a specific audience or group of audiences. It tells them what is new, interesting and exciting about your product or service. It includes the features and benefits of the product, information on how the product will be marketed and distributed, and any special requirements the user needs (especially for computers and software, and technical products). A well-written press release is an effective tool in communicating with your prospects and customers. Press releases aren't just for reporters. They really are public information sheets that tell your story to any audience you care to designate—including an online audience.

You need to create press releases for several reasons. First, some forums will let you post your press release in full online. If the message serves the forum's members, the readers will welcome it. Talk about free publicity! It doesn't get any better than this! Second, as you develop relationships with people, they will invariably ask you for more information. A press release is a great way to deliver the message; because it is succinct, it tells your story well. It also has a special aura to it because the reader knows this is privileged information intended for the media. How lucky they think themselves to be getting the same material that Dan Rather would receive! In that way, you are also helping to improve customer relations and the status of your company.

There are two essential steps in creating a press release: writing and formatting. The next sections explain how you can create an effective press release.

Writing the Press Release

There are three steps to writing the press release:

- Determine the message.
- Gather information.
- Write and edit.

This section will explain how to put it all together.

Step 1: Determine the message

The message of the press release ties in with the goals you established in the previous section. What is the purpose of the release? What is new that you want people to know about? That's the primary message of the press release. For many readers, the answer is, "Our company just announced it is shipping a new product." Fine. That's a great start. Now, refer to the Features and Benefits Worksheet to find the most compelling benefits to readers in each market.

Step 2: Gather information

Research is an important factor in writing a good press release. You should research these areas:

1. The product or service. Facts are the mainstay of a press release. What is it? What does it do? Who will benefit from using it? How? Who are the competitors? What advantages does it offer? Where does it fall short? How much will it cost? When will it be available?

2. The market. Statistics give credibility to a press release. How big is the market you are trying to capture? How much will it grow in the next few years?

3. Opinion leaders. Comments by opinion leaders round out the story and provide testimonials and credibility for the product. If reporters reprint the quotes in their stories, they will have created a powerful statement delivered to your readers. Also, by pointing reporters to opinion leaders, you will have tilted the playing field in your direction as these sources will say favorable things about your company. If you don't list sources, reporters might call people who aren't as kind. By listing them, you make the reporters' lives easier, and yours, too!

4. You'll want to ask opinion leaders, analysts and customers what they think about the product and which features they think benefit them most. Don't be surprised if you get different answers from those given by company technicians!

5. Other marketers in your company. Where does the product fit in with the entire product mix at the company? Is the company betting the future on it? Is it a minor product? How will its revenue affect the entire company? Where does publicity fit in the marketing mix? Where does online promotion fit in with the marketing mix?

Press Release Checklist

Reporters need to find information in a hurry because they are always under the pressure of a deadline. If they can't find facts quickly in a press release, they very well might toss out that release and write about another product. If you follow these techniques, you will have a press release that contains the basic information that helps reporters do their jobs.

1.   What is the product name and version number?
2.   Who is the typical user?
3.   How will the consumer benefit?
4.   How does it differ from competitors' products?
5.   How much does it cost?
6.   When will it be available?
7.   Where can people purchase it?
8.   What does it replace?
9.   (For marketing magazines) How will the product be marketed?
10.   (For computer magazines) What computer system does it operate under and what requirements are needed (e.g., operating system, memory, graphics)?

11. Quote a current user on how he or she likes the product.
12. Quote a company official on the usefulness of the product.
13. Quote an industry analyst on the need for this product.
14. Cite independent statistics showing the market potential for this product.
15.. What is the company's background? This final paragraph provides the company's background, positioning statement, product line and other interesting facts. Please refer to the company positioning statement in the previous section.

Step 3: Write and edit

Once you have all this information you are ready to write. Press releases are a lot like the articles you read in the newspaper. In fact, the best press releases read and sound like news articles or short stories. The highest compliment a writer of press releases can receive is seeing the release reprinted virtually word for word in a publication. Therefore, study articles in the newspaper and mimic the ones that you think meet your needs. Ask yourself: Would you want the paper to write that about your company? If so, then that's the right article.

Newspaper articles and press releases are both written in the inverted pyramid style, which means that the most important news is listed first. This is different from a murder mystery where the killer is named in the last chapter. You don't want your readers or reporters to wonder whodunnit. They don't have the time to read that far. You must put the most important news on top. It is followed by quotes, comments and background information.

An important guideline to follow is: Is this interesting to my audience? If it is not, then you have no business sending the press release to reporters or your customers. The press release is not the place for self-congratulatory remarks or for massaging the director's ego. It is a vehicle to make sales or enhance the company image. Any other use and your effort will be wasted—and even detrimental.

To make a press release come alive, use quotes from customers, analysts and company officials. However, be careful when quoting company officials. Too many press releases contain utterly useless and self-serving sentences like "We are pleased to announce." That's not news. If you weren't pleased to announce something, that would be news! Also, this information doesn't advance your cause, which is to make a sale based on the transfer of information.

As I've stressed repeatedly, space is at a premium, so don't junk up the release with useless words. Cut deadwood!

Format

Even before reporters read the press release, they glance at the page and subliminally check it for professionalism. The press release has a distinct look and style see the sample on the next page. If your press release doesn't have a similar look and feel, reporters will dismiss the message as amateurish. Fortunately, the formatting rules are simple.

A printed press release is typed on company letterhead. Online services don't print letterheads with the rich choice of styles available to stationers—at least not yet. Therefore, you should type at the top of the page your company name and address and phone, fax and e-mail numbers. Because ASCII-based systems don't retain formatting characters, don't worry about centering the data.

Skip a line and type `For immediate release`.

Skip another line and type `Contact`. Immediately underneath, type the name, title, phone and e-mail contact information. The contact is the company spokesperson, who could be the public relations professional or the vice-president of sales and marketing, or even the company president. The choice depends on the size of the company and the job duties of each person—as well as the importance of the release. Please don't forget to include the e-mail address. Very few press releases gathered for this book contained e-mail addresses, even though the companies were promoting products online.

Skip another line and type the headline. Capitalize the first letter of each word (except for articles and prepositions). Don't print the entire headline in uppercase. IT APPEARS TO BE SHOUTING! Skip a line and type the name of the city in which your company is located, followed by a pair of hyphens and the date of the release, another pair of hyphens and the first paragraph of the press release

As you type the release, skip a line between paragraphs.

In print press releases, you would type `-more-` at the end of each page. Online, however, there are no page breaks.

At the end of the release, type ### to signify that nothing follows.

Try to keep the press release to two printed pages.

If you follow these steps, your message will look professional and you will get the respect you deserve.

```
Janal Communications
657 Doral Drive
Danville, CA 94526-6206
510-831-0900

For immediate release

Contact

Daniel Janal
Janal Communications
510-831-0900
CIS: 76004,1046; MCI 341-8158; AOL: djanal
Internet: update@janalpr.com

Type the Headline Here in Upper and Lower Case

CITY—DATE—Start typing the first paragraph here. Follow the
guidelines in this chapter for writing style. At the end of the
release, type "###" or "30" without the quotation marks.

   ###
```

Summary

Effective press releases can publicize products to reporters and to consumer. By following these steps, you'll have the basis for great press releases!

5. Audience Selection

Now that you have created your messages, you need to find out where your customers and the reporters live online. This section will give you tips on how to find audiences and strategies to reach them and influence them effectively. The next section will deal with how to build rapport with reporters and convince them to write about your products.

Each commercial online service maintains a nice, neat index of forums and bulletin boards featuring topics of common interest, such as bicycles, Christianity, self-help, investing, marketing, computers and software. Since new forums are added almost daily, you might want to check each service to find out what's been added since your last visit. To find forum topics, please use the table on page 230.

Once you've found the groups that contain your target audience, monitor the discussion in the group for a few days to find out if they really do talk about what the group name implies and if it applies to your product or service. For strategies about how to market to these people, see the Publicity Strategies for the Public section for one-to-one marketing later in this chapter.

6. Finding Reporters Online

Now that you have written your press release, you need to send it to reporters. You can find out which reporters are online by several methods:

- Check the mastheads of the magazines. More and more publications are listing their reporters' e-mail addresses in the print publications.
- Ask reporters for their e-mail addresses when you meet them at trade shows, conventions and press conferences or when you speak to them on the phone.
- Look at their business cards or at the end of their articles.
- Check the directories of the online services. CompuServe maintains a directory for finding people. Type Go DIRECTORY and follow the prompts asking for the person's name and city. MCI Mail generally uses the initial of the first name and complete last name, e.g., jsmith. Naming conventions on Prodigy and America Online don't follow any prescribed format, and are not searchable by subscribers. So you are out of luck if you are trying to find someone on those services. The Internet also doesn't follow a standard naming convention, but many companies are adopting the MCI routine and adding it to their domain name, e.g., yourname@mcimail.com. If you aren't sure of a person's address, you might try this trick. It might work.

The Media List is a collection of newspapers, magazines, TV stations and other media that accept electronic submissions. You can get a copy by sending e-mail to `majordomo@world.std.com`. Leave the subject line blank. In the message area, write: `subscribe medialist`

The Media List is also available at the World Wide Web at `http://cwis.usc.edu/dept/etc/media/`

Most reporters online are those from the technology press, with a smattering of reporters at daily newspapers who cover technology. They are generally found on MCI Mail and CompuServe. Consumer publication editors have not yet jumped onto the Information Superhighway. However, this is changing almost daily. Many publications have realized they can make money by having an online presence on the Internet or a commercial online service. Once they launch the service, their reporters get online and can be contacted. America Online seems to be attracting a good number of consumer reporters.

Case Study: Cyberia Communications

Cyberia Communications, Inc., a consulting service for companies planning to go online, has had success with publicity.

"I have been using online networking since we started our business. I have made contact with many journalists and writers who are interested in what we are doing, and have consequently written articles about us. This gives us more marketing than we could have afforded otherwise," says Adam Viener, head of Cyberia Communications, Inc., based in York, Pennsylvania. "I also posted a few messages a while back, asking people if they would like to receive press releases about the online world. I got a large response, so now, when we have a press release going out, I have about 500 names of editors and journalists who are interested in the online world. Some prefer press releases by e-mail, others snail mail, and some fax. I know how they prefer their releases, and send them out when Cyberia does something new and interesting."

6. Distributing Press Releases

To the Media Only

Fortunately, reporters can be reached through their e-mail boxes, and many welcome press releases and queries are delivered in this manner because:

- *Speed:* They get the release faster than they would by mail.
- *Responsive:* Reporters can send questions by e-mail.
- *Editable:* The information can be imported into the reporter's word processor and edited, reformatted or filed for later use.

You will need to know reporters' e-mail addresses. Reporters use many different e-mail systems, ranging from MCI Mail, CompuServe, American Online, Prodigy and the Internet. Fortunately, you don't need accounts on all these systems. All these systems can send and receive mail from each other.

Newstips, a weekly tipsheet of hot news from the computer industry companies, is distributed to 2,000 reporters. The cost to place a meaty paragraph in the publication starts at $350. For information, send e-mail to `CIS: 75250,3467, Internet:winston@newstips.com, MCI Mail:479-9232,` or call `(216) 338-8400.` Here is a sample reprint from an issue:

```
  QUARTERDECK TO ENABLE WEB AUTHORS; 1ST LOOKS THIS MONTH HTML
(Hypertext Markup Language) is the standard for Web pages, but not
the easiest thing in the world to author. That changes soon,
though, when Quarterdeck unleashes the authoring package in its
Normandy suite of net-smart software. It can run standalone, or
work integrally with the web server if you want to manage & not
just author Web pages. Look for retail release 1Q95 (first looks
after Christmas) at a price tag well under $200.
  Contact: Brad Peppard, QUARTERDECK OFFICE SYSTEMS, INC. (Santa
Monica, CA)310-314-3292; F:314-3219; I:brad@qdeck.com.
```

To Your Audience Only

The next step is to deliver the press release to the right people. You can reach your target audience by posting press releases to:

1. Forums that cover your topic.
2. Company-operated forums, Web home pages and mailing lists.
3. Paid press release distribution services.

This section will explain how to accomplish these tasks.

1. Forums That Cover Your Topic

To reach your customers directly, you will want to post the press release in message boards or USENET newsgroups and mailing lists that appeal to your customers. To do this, you must first find message boards that attract your target audience and make sure the sysop allows press releases. To gain permission, send a private note to the sysop.

Computer software publishers can post press releases on Windows User Group Network Forum CompuServe: Go WUGNET, Compute Online Forum AOL: Keyword COMPUTE and ZiffNet's Computer Gaming World CompuServe: Go ZNT:GAMEWORLD. Tell them you read about them in this book!

WinWay Corp., of Sacramento, California, posted a press release announcing its WinWay Resume for Windows in the WUGNET Forum. "The press releases are still bringing in business," says Erez Carmel, president of WinWay Corp. Consumers can find press releases by looking in the press release section of the library and browsing through a list of titles or conducting a search by keywords. When they see a title that appeals to them, they can see a brief description written by the company (Fig. 12-1). If they want to read the press release (Fig. 12-2), they can do so either by viewing it online or downloading it to their computer.

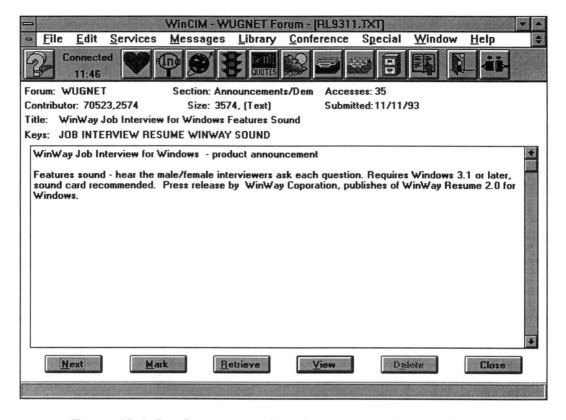

Figure 12-1. Readers can see short descriptions of press releases...
(Compliments of CompuServe)

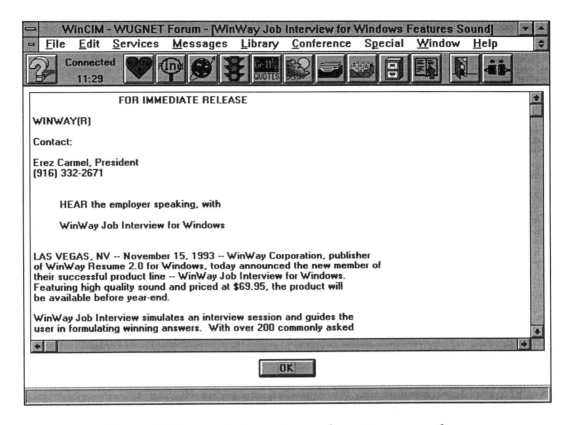

Figure 12-2. . . .and choose to see the entire press release.
(Compliments of CompuServe)

2. Company-Operated Forums, Web Home Pages and Mailing Lists

If your company operates a forum on a commercial service or a Web home page on the Internet, you can post your press releases there. Many computer software companies use their forums to post press releases about new products, updates and company news, such as sales promotions and other newsworthy or interesting topics. Taligent provides a press release section on its home page `http://www.taligent.com/press-releases-archive.html` (Figs. 12-3, 12-4). This is a welcomed service as customers like to know what is going on with their primary vendors. (You can learn how to create a forum on a commercial online service in Chapter 8. You can create a virtual storefront for your company on the Internet's World Wide Web in Chapter 7).

Press Releases

November 1994

Taligent announces Certification and Branding program for Application System
Taligent participates in National Information Infrastructure (NII) research and development projects
Taligent and Developers preview prototype applications for Commonpoint Application System
Abacus Concepts Unveils New CommonPoint Application at Comdex
Taligent and Adamation demonstrate collaboration framework for Commonpoint Application System
Taligent and Brio announce joint development of data access framework for Commonpoint System
Iconix to demonstrate Objectmodeler in Taligent booth at Comdex
Nisus presents Info Bank software for Taligent's Commonpoint Application System at Comdex

---

Figure 12-3. Taligent posts press releases on its home page. Select a headline . . .
(Courtesy of Taligent)

Editorial contacts:

Renée Risch   Ellie Victor
Taligent, Inc.   Cunningham Communication,
(408) 777-5093   (408) 764-0735

Taligent announces Certification and Branding program for Application System

New Product Identity to Provide Developers, OEMs and End-Users With a Common Foundation for Taligent Products

LAS VEGAS, Nevada -- November 14, 1994 -- Moving forward in its mission to deliver an object-oriented programming standard, Taligent, Inc. today announced a certification and branding program for its application system, here at COMDEX/Fall'94.

As part of the announcement, the company unveiled a new product name and logo for the system. Formerly known as the Taligent(R) Application Environment (or TalÆ[TM]), the product was officially named the *CommonPoint*[TM] application system.

Figure 12-4. . . .to see the entire press release. (Courtesy of Taligent)

Another method of reaching your customers directly is to create a mailing list of customers' e-mail addresses. As more of your business comes from online residents, you will develop a database of people who are interested in your products. You can send them press releases, special offers and news they can use to enhance their experience with your product or service. They will appreciate getting this information—especially if they can benefit from the new product or take advantage of a price reduction. Many companies are doing this, both informally and formally. Informally means that the company asks customers for their e-mail addresses and sends material to them. Formally means establishing a presence on the Internet as a newsgroup or a mailing list or as a forum on a commercial online service. For example, Digital Equipment Corporation has created a newsgroup that automatically sends press releases to its subscribers. Ford Explorer Owners' Mailing List promotes discussions of their products.

Having these options available to companies means they have a great way to get the message across directly to your customers without intervention by a third party (editors), who might trim the story or add information about rivals.

To Reporters and the Public

BusinessWire and PR Newswire are two companies that distribute company press releases for a fee. These press releases are posted to several online services and the Internet, where reporters and the public can read them. Both services are so well established that the Securities and Exchange Commission considers transmission of business information on these services to be a primary requirement for complying with its rules to make information available to the public in a timely and equal manner.

There are many advantages to using such a service. You will reach reporters quickly and relatively inexpensively. Many reporters read these wires to get leads for writing news stories and features. You will save a great deal of time, money and labor by not having to print and mail press releases.

PR Newswire is carried on the Internet through a private service called Quote.Com `http://quote.com` and CompuServe's Executive News Service `CompuServe: Go ENS`.

Business Wire is available on `CompuServe: Go TBW`, `AOL: Keyword BUSINESS NEWS`, and `Internet: http://quote.com`.

Many online discussions in marketing forums have been held centering on which service is more effective, and the results have always been split. So you can feel free to select either one and know that the service will be comparable. There is no need to put a release on both services, as there is a great degree of duplication of media outlets.

Both services charge by the word. There is a minimum fee for the first 400 words and an additional fee for each additional 100 words. Different prices exist for selecting specialized news lists, such as those for sports, entertainment, automotive, health, legal markets or for certain parts of the country. Because prices can change, please call the services for more information: Business Wire's number is 800-237-8212. PR Newswire's number is 800-832-5522.

To use either service, follow these basic steps:

1. Create an account with either service.
2. Write your press release.
3. Transmit the press release to the company via either fax or modem.
4. Discuss with your account executive which lists of reporters should receive the press release and when.
5. Your account executive will call you after the release has been sent.
6. Check the online service to make sure the press release has indeed been distributed and there aren't any errors.

Publicity Strategies for Reporters

Strategy: Send E-mail Instead of Calling

Benefit: Build rapport with reporters.

Discussion: Electronic mail is a great way to build rapport with reporters. Here's why.

Reporters spend a good deal of time away from their desks covering stories, attending meetings and—especially if they are in the trade press—at trade shows and conventions that may keep them away for as long as a week.

They could be out of the office for a week at a time. You are more likely to speak to their voice mail than to them. When reporters get back to the office, they are faced with dozens of messages. Naturally, reporters will organize those notes into callbacks and discards. To jump ahead of the pack, you must use e-mail.

Many reporters check their e-mail several times a day, even when they are on the road. E-mail has a sense of urgency to it, so reporters read it first. Since e-mail can be answered quickly, reporters can cut through piles of e-mail quickly.

Reporters who cover high-tech welcome information via e-mail. As time goes on, reporters who cover other topics will be online as well. We are seeing a big leap in use from reporters whose publications are online, such as *The New York Times*, *U.S. News & World Report*, *Chicago Tribune*, *Car and Driver* and others.

There are more advantages to using e-mail to build rapport with reporters. Reaching reporters via e-mail is efficient. That's because you do not have to play phone tag. Time zones are no longer a problem with e-mail, as people can read the mail at their leisure and respond. Answering e-mail is faster and less expensive than calling on the phone.

In fact, I have even conducted pitches for which all the communication took place online. I wrote the pitch letter on MCI Mail to Kerri Karvetski at *Computer Retail Week*. She sent a positive response back via e-mail. I confirmed the time with her. She interviewed Bob Kersey, president of Optical Data Corporation, on the phone a few days later and told me when the article would appear. When the date passed and the article was not in that issue, I sent her e-mail asking her what was up (something I would be too shy to do on the phone). She wrote back that the issues for the next few weeks would be small, but that the article would appear after that time. True to her word, the article did run. This shows that all the phases of product pitching and follow-up can take place online.

E-mail can be used to pitch products, set up appointments, follow on product reviews, answer questions, tell about seminars and dealer programs and provide news, including earnings reports, high-level executive appointments, contracts signed, strategic partnerships and the like.

Strategy: Talk to Reporters Via E-mail on Forums

Benefit: Build rapport.

Discussion: You can create conversations with editors in two ways: (1) privately through their e-mail accounts, or (2) publicly through their publications' online media presence. For example, *Car and Driver* magazine has a forum on America Online. Every Wednesday, an editor goes online for several hours to interact with readers. "It's been pretty well received. We get a lot of letters to the editor," says columnist Frank Marcus. So far, he says, public relations people haven't contacted him online. Many computer magazines have online forums that encourage readers to send notes to editors—including the high-profile writers and top editors. While it might not be appropriate to pitch stories on these open forums, you can begin to develop rapport with reporters by showing them you read their articles, are familiar with their work and are an expert in your field.

Action: To implement this strategy, create a list of the most important editors in your universe. Find out if they have e-mail accounts or if their publications have online forums. Send them notes that would engage them in a dialogue. Examples include product and story ideas, comments on recent articles and columns they have written and suggestions for stories about trends you see emerging. They will value this information as good for background, or as a lead for a story idea. You don't have to plug your own company to build rapport!

Warning: Gratuitous, self-serving messages will not be appreciated. How do you know when you've crossed the line? Ask yourself: "If I were a reporter, would I value this letter, or would I toss it?" The answer is obvious. The second litmus test is the "Oh, what the heck test," as in "I don't know if he'll want to read this, but what the heck, it doesn't cost anything." Wrong. It can cost you your credibility, a commodity that cannot be recovered after it has been spent.

Strategy: Write Effective E-mail Pitch Letters to Reporters

Benefit: Gain the favorable media attention and improve the chances of coverage.

Discussion: The worst way to approach reporters is the traditional method of sending voluminous press kits complete with backgrounders, white papers and copies of previous press releases detailing the company's history. Instead, the proper approach is to send a short note explaining what is new and what you want the reporter to do. The entire note should be less than the depth of a computer screen (about 24 lines). Refer to the positioning workshop in this chapter to help create your message.

An effective e-mail pitch letter should go like this:

```
    Optical Data Corporation is introducing two computer games that
teach science, social studies and math to children ages 3-8 next
week at the Consumer Electronics Show. If you would like to
schedule an appointment, review the games or see the complete
press kit online, please send an e-mail note to me or
info@mycompany for an automatic response, call 555-1212, or visit
our Web site http://www.example.com.
```

This example gets to the heart of the matter quickly (new product introduction), describes the benefits of the product and the target market, and then asks for action. Best yet, it accomplishes this task in less than 60 words! Reporters are intrigued by brevity. When they commit to writing a story, that's when they want tons of data. When the reporter responds, you can then send the appropriate information.

If you are going to send information online, be sure to save the file as ASCII, so that any reporter will be able to read the file into their word processor, whether it be for a PC or a Macintosh. If you are going to send very long files, you can save time for yourself and the reporter by sending compressed files. A compressed file is one that has been truncated for transmission purposes with a program like PKZIP (for PCs), Stuffit (for Macintosh) or UUENCODE (for the Internet). The recipient decompresses the files to see the original. Just be sure to ask the reporter first if he can read those files, and which computer system he uses.

Strategy: Send Personal Pitch Letters to Multiple Recipients

Benefit: Reach many reporters quickly.

Discussion: Another advantage of e-mail is that you can send one pitch letter to hundreds of reporters in the time it takes to send one note. First you target the reporters, find out their e-mail addresses and follow your favorite online service's steps for sending a mailing list.

If you follow this plan, whether sending mail to one reporter or dozens, you'll be able to break through the clutter of phone mail and snail mail to begin to persuade the reporter to accomplish your goals.

Action: Create list, write pitch letter and send letter.

Warning: Make sure that the reporter sees only the copy addressed to her. The last thing you want to do is let the reporter see he is part of a 100-person routing list. Depending on the service, he might see the names of each person on a separate line before he sees your message. That means the reporter sees the first 100 lines, the equivalent of two sheets of paper, or four computAer screens. That is a sure turnoff. For example, MCI's DOC command will hide the routing list, except to people who use CC:Mail. The best action plan here is to send individual messages to those reporters who have that system. As procedures change frequently, check with your e-mail provider to learn the intricacies of this procedure.

Case Study: Technopolis Communications

E-mail is a powerful marketing tool that must be used properly by marketers when communicating with editors.

Steven J. Leon is president of Technopolis Communications Inc., an award-winning public relations agency in Los Angeles that provides public relations, marketing communications and marketing services to computer hardware, software and services companies `MCI:450-43326, CompuServe: 72050,700; Internet: teknopolis@aol.com 310-670-5606`. Since 1987, he has collected, compiled and updated a database of e-mail addresses for editors and reporters.

This includes approximately 300 MCI Mail, 300 CompuServe, 50 America Online and 75 Internet addresses for editors at computer publications, primarily. However, Leon says that the most frequent additions to the database today include Internet addresses from consumer publications, such as *USA Today, U.S. News & World Report*, the *Los Angeles Times*, and others.

Mailroom for MCI Mail from Sierra Solutions and WinCim 1.3 from CompuServe make it extremely easy to send a mass mailing to 2 or 200 editors, in seconds.

Yet Leon has learned the hard way that this should be done carefully, with full knowledge that someone will take offense at seeing his name on a list with 20, 30 or 150 other editors from other publications, all looking for an exclusive scoop.

This is especially important with MCI Mail. In theory, the "DOC" command is supposed to hide the mailing list from recipients. In practice, however, some communications software appears to strip this command from the message, exposing the long list of recipients to everyone on the mailing list. It happens most often with cc:Mail and other gateways used by Ziff-Davis and IDG publications. Leon has raised the problem with MCI Mail, without remedy.

WinCim features a "Show recipients" check box that turns on and off similar mailing list capabilities.

Failure to compensate for these system capabilities transforms what should be private communication into offensive spam.

Instead, Leon tailors each message for each editor, often adding a personal comment relevant to the specific publication and its readers, or a note, when appropriate, that refers to an earlier conversation or e-mail exchange with that editor.

"It takes an hour longer to prepare the e-mail," he says, "but this personal, hands-on approach generates far more news coverage and product reviews."

Strategy: Tailor Your Message to Fit Individual Reporters' Needs

Benefit: Builds rapport with reporters; improves chances of gaining coverage.

Discussion: It is critical for you to realize that each reporter needs to develop her own story for her audience. One size of story does not fit all reporters. Reporters can influence several audiences:

- The online community.
- Vertical markets.
- General consumers.
- Retailers and distributors.

For example, the retail press is looking for a story about how manufacturers are offering incentives to retailers to sell their products; general consumer reporters are interested in new products that their readers will find interesting; the business reporter wants to know how the company's stock will be affected by the introduction of the new product. The list can go on and on for every reporter you target. If you consider the reporter's target audience and realize what that person wants to read, you will be much more successful in dealing with reporters.

Strategy: Be a Reporter's Resource

Benefit: Build rapport, improve chances of gaining coverage.

Discussion: A great way to build rapport with reporters is to become their trusted resource. This means you:

- Return phone calls as soon as possible.
- Provide them with the information or products they need.
- Grant access to people at the company who have information.
- Know everything there is to know about your company and its products and, if you don't, you get the answer by deadline.
- Know about the competitor's products and talk knowledgeably about them.
- Know about the industry and provide gossip and tips.
- Admit when you do not know the answer and promise to find it.
- Never cover up.
- Always tell the truth!

Strategy: Look for Reporters' Queries

Benefit: Get press coverage.

Discussion: Savvy online reporters post query notices in forums to find subjects to interview for articles.

Action: Scan your favorite message areas and answer appropriate queries.

Example: Here's an actual post on a mailing list, reprinted with permission of Scott Hample.

```
Subject: Marketers marketing themselves
Date: 94-10-23 09:21:11 EST
From: scott.hample@ATLWIN.COM (SCOTT HAMPLE)
To: MARKET-L@NERVM.NERDC.UFL.EDU (Multiple recipients of list
MARKET-L)

Marketing Consultants: How do you market yourself or your
company? Relationship marketing? Word of Mouth? Direct Mail?
Database marketing? Ads in the trade journals and other business
press? Does your organization practice TQM?

What are some of the typical methods you use to get your name
known? There's gotta be something more than publishing articles
and/or attending seminars?
    Do you speak at seminars? Publish books and cassettes a la
Nightingale Conant?

What are some of the most unusual ways you market yourselves?

Please respond via e-mail at scott.hample@atlwin.com

Thanks!

Scott
Whaley Research
404-814-3031
```

Strategy: Create a Library of Press Releases

Benefit: Reporters can get information when they need it.

Discussion: Creating a library of press information that includes press releases, annual reports, executive bios and photos will allow reporters to be able to browse and retrieve needed information when they need it, 24 hours a day, from anywhere in the world.

Action: Create a library with the aid of an Internet presence provider.

Case Study: Alexander Communications

Alexander Communications, a high-technology public relations agency, maintains a Gopher server for its clients' press materials so that the press and the public will be exposed to the agency's clients, their messages and materials 24 hours a day, 365 days a year from anywhere in the world. The information will already be in an electronic format, ready for publication.

"These services are specifically designed to help our clients put the Internet to work as a powerful communications medium that informs and persuades. E-mail, online research and news services are fundamental communications tools—Internet services are a natural migration for us," says Pam Alexander, president.

"Whether or not our clients have their own Internet programs, Alexander Communications is aggregating their press information on our agency's Gopher server and adding the value of our relationships with the media. It is the right service at the right time and at the right price," says Brian Johnson, vice president.

The Gopher is a way to present information—text, graphics, sounds, demonstrations, presentations—anything that can be stored on a computer disk—in a simple, menu-driven format. Gopher servers are accessible worldwide through any type of Internet connection and are also accessible to subscribers of CompuServe, America Online and Prodigy. To reach Alexander's Gopher server, point your gopher to `alexander-pr.com 6695`. Alexander Communications charges a start-up fee to format and store materials on the gopher server and ongoing costs for updating information and maintaining the system online.

Publicity Strategies for the Public

Here are strategies that you can use to create one-to-one relationships with online subscribers. These strategies will help you:

- Prospect for new customers.
- Build product awareness.
- Create rapport with the public and current customers.
- Distribute sales and product information to an interested audience.
- Build sales.

Strategy: Create a Member Profile

Benefit: People will get to know you better and faster.

Discussion: Most people online are merely names and numbers. They can be more than that. Forums allow you to create a member profile, which includes your interests, from professional to personal. Member profiles can be searched so that you can find people who have similar interests. If you fill one out on yourself, other people can find you. The policy on this varies from forum to forum and system to system. Professional forums frequently allow you to post a description of yourself, which can include descriptions of your product or service. Check with the forums that feature topic headings like "Resumes," "Introductions" or "I'm new and here's what I do." If you use these options, you'll find prospects and they'll find you.

Action: Find forums that would attract your target audience. Follow the rules for creating a profile for yourself. Follow instructions for finding other members. Send them polite e-mail that strikes up a conversation. For example, let's say that you sell sailboats and supplies. You might send this message: "I see that you like to sail. I do too. I have a model x-200 and sail in San Francisco. Where do you sail?" If you get a response, you can begin to develop a relationship. As this relationship matures, you can then mention what you do and propose ways to help your new friend.

Strategy: Find New Sources of Prospects

Benefit: Prospecting.

Discussion: By posting questions on discussion forums that ask for additional sources of other forums, you might find more opportunities to interact with even more prospects. The answers might lead you to other areas on that system, to other online services or bulletin boards operated by enthusiasts or vendors.

Example: Let's say you sell mountain climbing equipment. You could search for sports, hiking, outdoors, exercise, vacations, and travel. Send a message:

```
Does anyone know of a local BBS that covers mountain climbing?
```

Action: Post questions on those message boards asking if members know of other message boards for that audience.

Strategy: *Look for New Newsletters and 'Zines*

Benefit: Increased opportunities for editorial coverage.

Discussion: Because creating and distributing information is easy and inexpensive, on the Internet, many new publications, such as newsletters and 'zines, are being created every week.

Action: Keep an eye out for these new titles. Smart publishers probably will promote in message areas that you visit. Read the publication to get a feel for its audience and style. Then send the editor a note that proposes they write an article about your area of interest or suggest a topic about which you can write a column for them. New publications frequently need articles and columns. They welcome queries regarding submissions. Don't write the column until you have a confirmed request to write it. That way, you will not waste time if the idea is rejected.

Strategy: *Create Information Files*

Benefit: Increases exposure and credibility. Possible source of leads.

Discussion: Good members of the online community give back to the community. Marketers can do well by doing good. Companies can create information-packed articles and reports that help consumers solve problems. These articles don't sell the company or product directly. Instead, they sell the concept that empowers the company. For example, the Insurance Information Institute places popular consumer brochures, such as "How to Save Money on Your Auto Insurance" on the Internet: gopher.infor.com.

Action: Write a file that helps people solve a problem, or provides them with useful, original information. These files can be stored.

Example: Let's say you are a tour guide who gives walking tours of San Francisco. You could write 500-word articles that describe sample tours with each stop explained. Another idea would be to list areas to avoid because of crime, congestion or image. Since most forums are happy to accept relevant material, send a polite query letter stating your topic and asking if the forum wants to review it for the library. If yes, send it along with a 50-word description of the article. Consultants will want to include their positioning statement as well. This descriptive information will be posted to the library file so that readers can see a description of the material before deciding to read it. For example:

```
Jane Green conducts walking tours of San Francisco for her
company, Green Ways, 800-555-1212.
```

Strategy: Create a "Ten Commandments" Article for Libraries

Benefit: Prospecting. Increases exposure and positions you as an expert.

Discussion: This kind of article is a fact-based information piece that explains a topic of interest, such as: "10 Ways to Cut Your Taxes" for a tax accountant; "Ten Commandments for Reducing Stress" for a psychologist, masseuse, physical therapist or sports trainer; or "10 Keys to Financial Freedom" for a certified financial planner or investment adviser. People love these articles because they contain good information and are easy to read quickly. You'll love them, too, because they are easy to write. The format for the article calls for you to write an opening paragraph that presents a problem. Next, write 10 ways to solve the problem. Other good headline words are: Secrets, Tips, Hints, Rules and Laws.

Action: Propose article, write the article, description and keywords.

Example: Here is an example of a "10-step" article written by a stress management consultant for an audience of accountants and tax professionals:

```
    As April 15 rolls around, accountants are under a great deal of
stress. With the impending deadline of tax filing season, they
work 20 hour days, 7 days a week and must deal with clients who
are disorganized and frenzied. Tax accountants must cope with this
tension. Here are 10 ways to cut agita:
    1. Exercise.
    2. Eat healthy foods.
    3. Avoid caffeine, sugar and other stimulants and depressants.
    4. Breath deeply.
    5. Take short breaks.
    6. Think pleasant thoughts.
    7. Focus on how well you will feel on April 16.
    8. Think of how you are helping people solve their problems.
    9. Think of how you will enjoy the money you are earning.
    10. Think of how you'll appreciate free time when you are done!
```

> This article was written by John Peterson, of Peterson and Associates, an accounting firm based in San Francisco.

Notice that the tips can be as short as one or two words. If you like, this information can be expanded to paragraphs containing several sentences. There is no negative effect in writing a longer article. However, 250–500 words will ensure that your readers won't lose interest.

Here's a sample e-mail pitch letter for the sysop:

> As April 15 rolls around, accountants will be under a great deal of stress. I can help your readers with a 250-word article called "The 10 Rules of Reducing Stress." Can I send a copy to you to post in the library? I am qualified to write this article because I have experience as (FILL IN).
>
> Thanks.
> Your Name
> Signature file

Here's a sample description that would be attached to the file:

> Are you stressed out as April 15 rolls around? This article will show you 10 ways to cut stress. The article is written by John Peterson, of Peterson and Associates, an accounting firm based in San Francisco.

Keywords are words that describe your article. Readers can search libraries by selecting keywords. If the system prompts you for keywords, select as search terms your name, the general field you are writing about and who should read the article. For example:

```
  Keywords:   stress,   accountants,   tax   preparers,   exercise,
bookkeepers, John Peterson.
```

Strategy: Encourage Republication of Your Files

Benefit: Increases exposure and can be a source of leads.

Discussion: If one article in one library is good, then one article in many libraries must be better! Encourage readers to post your articles in other areas of interest, such as local bulletin boards or special interest bulletin boards, newsletters published by nonprofit groups, associations and businesses, and relevant publications. You won't get paid for this editorial service, but you aren't in the business of making money from your writing. You are in business to sell your products or services. That's where the long-term benefit will come. To let people know they can reprint the work, include a line at the end of the article:

```
This article can be reprinted provided it is not edited in any
manner and if proper credit is given. This includes listing my
name as the author and my contact information.
```

If you like, you could instead ask people who want to reprint the article to call you and request permission individually. This way, you will know when and where the article will appear.

To protect your work, place a copyright notice at the beginning of the piece so that people can see it clearly and unmistakably. A sample copyright notice would look like this:

```
Copyright © 1995 Your Company
All Rights Reserved.
Published in the United States of America
```

Action: Attach the preceding copyright information paragraph to your article.

Strategy: Write Articles for Online Magazines and Forums

Benefit: Increased exposure.

Discussion: Online publications welcome editorial content that is objective and useful to their readers. By publishing articles in other venues, you can increase your exposure to audiences of prospects and raise your credibility. For example, a financial planner could write an article about how to save money on taxes and submit the article to the Personal Finance Center on the Global Network Navigator (GNN). To do so, send a letter to abcham@ora.com.

Action: Find appropriate publishing venues, select a topic and query the editor. Based on your conversation with the editor, write the article.

Strategy: Create Online Conferences and Educational Seminars

Benefit: Prospecting and increased exposure.

Discussion: Many forums hold online conferences to help members learn about topics of special interest. They have a lot of time and space to fill. If you submit an appropriate idea, you may be rewarded by getting increased exposure to your audience. Forum operators benefit as well since your session will generate traffic.

Action: Send a query note to the sysop with a conference topic, sample questions and a list of what users will learn. Propose several dates. Example:

```
As companies lay off workers in today's difficult economy,
those workers need to know how to get new jobs. My company helps
people find new jobs by teaching them to write resumes that get
responses. I would like to host an online conference for your
members that will teach them what works and doesn't work in
resumes, which buzzwords are old and tired and which ones are new
and exciting, and how to stand out from the crowd. I've noticed
you hold forums on Thursday evenings. Would Oct. 18 or 25 work?
```

You will want to schedule the conference well enough in advance for the sysop to publicize the meeting to members. This could take about a month. To promote the conference, you might send a file to the library that describes your company and its services or provides tips on your area of expertise.

Strategy: Offer Free Samples

Benefit: Prospecting and increased exposure.

Discussion: As I walked by a bakery in the mall recently, the scent of freshly baked cinnamon rolls pulled me in. I'd never had one of these buns before and, at $2 apiece, I wasn't ready to experiment since I don't like things that are too sweet. However, a sign read "Show us your smile and you get a free sample." As much as I hate to smile, I did want the free sample. After I ate it, I bought a box to take home for $8. Moral: Samples work.

This strategy works well with information products, such as newsletters and magazines, because transmission costs through e-mail are either free or inexpensive, depending on which system you use. There are no materials costs. If you have a product business, you might send a sample product through snail mail.

Some sysops will feel that this violates the no advertising policy, while others will let it pass because it provides a service to their members. Play it safe by reading the FAQs or sending a note to the sysop.

Action: Find message boards composed of your prospects. Post a note to all that they can get a free copy of your product by sending an e-mail note. Follow up with sales and marketing material either by e-mail or snail mail. Example:

```
For a free copy of Dan Janal's Online Marketing Update, send e-
mail to update@janalpr.com or CompuServe: 76004,1046.
```

Strategy: Volunteer to Become a Sysop

Benefit: Increased exposure, credibility and sales.

Discussion: You can increase your credibility and stature in your industry if you are part of the administration of the forum. This is a particularly good strategy for consultants, speakers, trainers and other service providers. To become a sysop, first think of a topic that has long-lasting appeal on a message board that your prospects are likely to visit. This must be a topic that you are an expert on.

Let's pretend you translate business documents into Spanish. Find an international business message board, and propose to the sysop that you host a new section on the forum devoted to translation issues. You would be responsible for answering questions people raise, starting discussions and creating content for the library. In return, you will become an authority in the area to people who use the online service. Members will become prospects and prospects will become customers—if they have a need for your service and if you *don't sell*. By building the relationship, you will get customers.

Action: Scan forums, find an appropriate topic and send message to sysop.

Strategy: Create Your Own Domain Name on the Internet

Benefit: Increased exposure and credibility.

Discussion: Your e-mail address will read like `yourname@yourcompany.com` instead of `yourname@ix.netcom.com`. Some people consider those who have a domain name to have a greater level of credibility.

Action: Contact your Internet provider and ask for details.

Strategy: Track Responses with E-mail

Benefit: Accurate tracking of leads from various sources.

Discussion: The harshest criticism of public relations is that it is difficult to measure. You can begin to measure public relations by creating several e-mail accounts and using them in tandem with each message you use.

Example: Let's say you wanted to test the price of a product and placed ads in printed publications or in legitimately posted messages on online systems. You have three ads and they are the same except for the three different prices and the three different e-mail addresses. People who are interested would see only one ad and would send an e-mail note to the corresponding account. By tallying the number of messages in each mailbox, you could determine which test worked best. This method also works for testing leads or inquiries from articles published about your company or product, or articles you have written and placed in online libraries. You can use this strategy to account for any number of variables. Also, you can then track the respondent's actions after they receive your marketing materials to determine which source of leads works best.

Action: Contact your service provider to create additional accounts.

Strategy: Create Information Packages Available via E-mail and Downloading

Benefit: Prospects get needed information when they want it without delay.

Discussion: The very nature of the interactivity of creating dialogues with consumers means that people will ask you for information about your company and its products or services. You can respond via regular mail or e-mail. Your company might already have such a kit ready to be sent by mail or courier service to hot prospects. The company also will need to have a package for the online consumer. You can let the customer access this information either by creating files and storing them in forums or on your Web home page, Gopher site or FTP site on the Internet. An alternative is to let customers send you e-mail with a note in the subject line saying "send info pack one." You can create an automatic response system through the Internet in which your mailbot (an automated e-mail system similar in concept to a fax-back system) will send the appropriate file to the customer as soon as it receives the query. If you prefer to use a commercial online service, there isn't any automatic mail system. However, you can have an operator check messages and respond as soon as feasible. In either case, prospects will get the information they need in a timely manner—when they are hot to buy.

You must consider what kind of information should be included in this message. Each business will have a different set of considerations. Here are ideas:

- Press releases
- Data sheets
- Sales sheets
- Dealer sheets
- Company annual report and financial information
- Reviews from newspapers and magazines
- Tables of contents (for books)
- Catalogs
- Brochures
- Photos
- Testimonial letters
- Independent reports
- Newsletters
- Annual report
- Message from the president

The final consideration you should make in this matter is: Should the material be the same as the ones you send via mail, or should it be rewritten for an online audience? Could the information be made interactive? Could you add multimedia, sound or video to spice up the presentation? The answer, of course, is "yes"

Action: Create info packages that reinforce the integrated marketing message.

Strategy: Scan Message Areas for Mentions of Your Company

Benefit: Prevent crises.

Discussion: Crises can start online—and companies should take great care in monitoring relevant discussion areas on the Internet and all the commercial online services to find out what people are saying about their company. If negative messages are found, the company can respond to them quickly and put the fire out before getting burned.

For example, a mathematics professor found an error caused by the Pentium chip manufactured by Intel. He posted an article in a newsgroup asking if people could duplicate the error. Word spread and reporters heard about the error. They printed articles in most major newspapers. The company tried to downplay the error as being insignificant. This tactic only added fuel to the fire. The company president, Andrew Grove, wrote a letter and posted it on the Internet. This didn't have the desired effect because the letter carried another executive's header, which led people to wonder if Grove actually wrote it. To make matters worse, people posted notes containing jokes about the Pentium chip. Newspapers printed the jokes as well. Intel finally agreed to replace the chips, but only after admitting that the crisis had taken on a life of its own.

Without debating the merits of its publicity strategy, Intel clearly failed to monitor its key audience and their level of disgust. If they had paid more attention to these messages, the company might have averted a public relations nightmare.

Messages travel quickly online. People write, respond and develop opinions quickly. One of the major problems of this fast communication is that errors and misstatements get repeated frequently. In a short time, these errors look like facts because the information—or misinformation—is repeated. Companies that don't respond quickly can face serious risks.

Action: Create a list of forums on the Internet and each commercial online service that reaches your audience. Assign the task of monitoring these areas to an employee who is trained to deal with sensitive issues and irate customers

Publicity Opportunities

TV talk shows have shown that they can propel anyone into their 15 minutes of fame. The same is true of talk shows online. The Internet and each commercial online service has an area in which personalities and executives can be interviewed live. Just like talk shows, these online shows feature a guest and moderator format. Audience members can type in their questions and comments. The host picks the ones she wants the guest to answer. These moderated forums can offer your company the opportunity to deliver its message, portray the company in a good light and show that it is responsive to the community.

In these early days of online services, just being a guest on a show like this offers the company a chance to get articles written about it for the novelty. The transcripts are saved to the library, where additional members can read the information—tomorrow or next year. In this way, you can find new audiences for your products. If you have an evergreen product, then this is very good news.

These conferences can help both large and small companies. Unlike television, which seeks a broad audience and hence broadcasts its message, online services can both broadcast and narrowcast to highly targeted market. Online services love to feature big-name speakers and celebrities that can attract large markets—and network charges. For example, Vice President Al Gore "spoke" on a moderated conference on CompuServe, which drew 900 people. Jerry Seinfeld and Jay Leno participated in talks on Prodigy's entertainment area. Technology guru Esther Dyson participated in a conference on America Online. Garth Brooks' online conference drew 500 people on the NBC/McDonald's area on America Online. The conference tied in with McDonald's promotion to sell Brooks' CDs at their restaurants.

Best yet, whereas TV broadcasts messages to wide groups of people, online services can be used to broadcast and narrowcast messages. If your company appeals to a broad audience, like an entertainment organization, travel-related company, or the like, a conference can help. Small companies and consultants, speakers and trainers, can talk directly to highly targeted groups of prospects.

Internet Talk Radio was the first moderated talk show on the Internet. Host Carl Malamud interviews the "Geek of the Week" with microphones, converts the show to digital format and sends the file to the Internet, where listeners can retrieve the file and hear it on their computers and its speakers. For information, send a note to `info@radio.com`.

The Internet Round Table `Internet: http://www.IRsociety.com` or `gopher.irsociety.com` bills itself as the *Larry King Live* of the Internet. The program features well-known individuals from the worlds of government, politics, arts and media, including Sen. Arlan Specter, National Public Radio commentator Susan Stamberg and author Anne Lamott. Each guest is interviewed by a host who is an expert in the area. Questions from the audience are taken. A transcriber types all questions and answers for the public to read as the comments are being spoken. After the guest has departed, readers are invited to stay online and continue the discussion. The entire transcript is recorded and can be purchased. To be a guest on the show, send e-mail `to wendie@fununiv.com` and explain why you and your topics would make for a good show.

Conferences also are held in forums and bulletin boards on the commercial services. To be considered to be a guest in a forum, contact the sysop. For example, the Public Relations and Marketing Forum on CompuServe features guests who can share information about public relations and marketing. The online guest fields questions in a moderated format. The transcript is saved to the forum library, where others can read it at their leisure. To be considered for a guest shot, send a message to the sysops at `PRSIG`.

Ziff Executives Online features an opportunity for leaders of computer software and hardware companies to respond to members' questions over a one-week period. Executives can answer questions online during a moderated session and/or answer questions that members send after the session. To be considered for this guest shot, send a note to Ryk Lent of Ziff-Davis Interactive `MCI:ryklent`.

America Online offers several areas (Center Stage, Odeon and Wired) where members can participate in live, interactive events with special guests for lively exchanges of ideas. Guests may be writers, musicians, artists, actors, filmmakers, politicians, athletes, journalists and others. Guests have included Billy Graham, INXS, Olympic Medalist Dan Jansen, David Bowie, Conan O'Brien, Rosie O'Donnell and The Eagles. Major film studios have used these areas to promote their shows. Nickelodeon featured actor Ed Asner on a chat to promote the *Mary Tyler Moore Show*. Filmmaker Oliver Stone (*JFK, The Doors, Talk Radio*) in the Auditorium talked about his stab at culture hacking, *Natural Born Killers.*

Prodigy also interviews many famous people online in various bulletin boards. Guests have included author Sidney Sheldon, comedians Jerry Seinfeld and Jay Leno, as well as *Star Trek's* Capt. James T. Kirk, William Shatner.

Summary

Public relations strategies can be used online to build relationships with reporters, customers and prospects. In some cases, you would use traditional public relations methods. In others, these steps need to be modified to fit the nature of online communications. The online community has devised new methods as well as opportunities for companies and consumers to interact with win–in dialogues.1

CHAPTER 13

Building Relationships with Customer Service

"Answering support questions on the forum is far easier, quicker, and less expensive than answering letters or phone calls," says Eric Robichaud, president of Rhode Island Soft Systems, a software publisher of screen savers, fonts and games. "You can support customers when it is convenient for you, instead of having to drop everything when they call."

In this chapter, you will learn:

- How online systems can help support customers.
- Why online systems actually reduce support costs.
- Methods for creating a successful support center.
- Tips for increasing registrations for software companies.

Benefits of Online Customer Support

The Internet and commercial online services can help your business build relationships with customers by creating online support centers that answer people's questions. Companies that respond to customer's queries quickly can build loyalty that lasts for a lifetime. Also, happy customers tell potential customers—so do unhappy customers!

By creating a customer support center online, your company can benefit from:

- ***Increased loyalty from customers:*** Consumers who are get technical support quickly will remain happy and might see no reason to switch products.
- ***Reduced returns from customers who experience problems:*** Consumers who can't get support quickly can become frustrated with your product and return it for a refund.

- *Reduced bad word of mouth:* Studies have shown that happy customers tell three friends, while unhappy customers tell eleven! One way to reduce bad word of mouth is to have good customer support that helps dissatisfied customers before they unleash a torrent of ill will.

- *Faster response to customer questions:* Some companies with small support staffs are overburdened and can't respond to customers' questions in a timely manner. By using online support centers, they can answer people's questions faster. With the use of libraries of stored text files and software patches, consumers might be able to find what they need without speaking to a support rep.

- *Lower support costs:* Customers can find information that addresses frequently asked questions. Service reps won't have to return expensive phone calls. Toll-free phone numbers won't be used as much. Questions can be answered in a batch, thus making more efficient use of service reps. Questions can be delegated effectively to people who have the right degree of skill to answer.

- *Customers can help answer other customers' questions:* This will lighten your staff's workload, and it will build camaraderie among consumers.

- *Market research:* Customer complaints about certain features might lead to development of new products or features, thus aiding research and development. Dan Bricklin, who invented the first computer spreadsheet, VisiCalc., handled customer support calls and learned of customers' needs, which led to significant new features in other products.

- *Profit Center:* If your support center generates a significant amount of traffic, your company might actually make money from the arrangement contracted with the commercial online service. Smaller companies probably won't make any money, but larger ones can do well. For information on how to create a forum and negotiate a deal, please refer to Chapter 8.

"There is some residual payback, although it is not major. Maybe a couple hundred bucks a month," says Craig Settles, senior strategist, Successful Marketing Strategists, of Berkeley, California. "However, there is no cash outlay for returning phone calls."

Another way to turn the support center into a profit center is to train the service reps to sell additional products to customers. For example, people might call about a product that has been replaced by a new model. The rep can sell the new model. Reps can also sell service contracts, additional copies of the product for friends or colleagues, other items from the product line, and complementary products from other companies.

The computer industry has embraced this concept, as most major hardware manufacturers and software publishers have forums. In fact, several companies offer support forums on multiple services to ensure that they make their support centers available to as many of their customers as possible. Such companies include Microsoft, Lotus, Borland, Symantec, Compaq, Hewlett-Packard, IBM and Apple. Many smaller companies also offer support centers online

Case Study: Computer Chronicles

Computer Chronicles is a television show that discusses numerous computer products each week to a national audience. The company operates a forum `CompuServe: Go CHRONICLES` as a service to its viewers, not to make money. The forum provides information about the show, its editorial calendar, topics covered and also a bulletin board for people to talk to each other.

"The primary purpose is to provide an avenue of support for our customers and an outlet for them to get the products they want in a cost-effective manner for them and for us," says Stuart Cheifet, executive producer of Computer Chronicles. "They see lots of neat toys and ask, 'How can they get that? What does it do? How much does it cost?' If they miss info on the show, they can find it on the forum."

Viewers called the program before the forum came online. The company devoted a full-time employee to answer people's questions. The forum receives about a hundred calls a week, which are answered at the convenience of a staffer.

"We can answer questions in one sitting, instead of having a person be on call all day to answer," he says. "It saves us one full-time person and a lot of telephone costs. It is a real solution to a problem."

Since online members are a friendly lot, they frequently answer each other's questions, thus saving the staff even more time.

Case Study: Road Scholar Software, Inc.

Road Scholar Software, Inc., of Houston, is a leading publisher of digital maps, screen savers and entertainment software. With a large customer base, the company found its two-person support staff overwhelmed with support calls for its products, City Streets for Windows and Razzle Dazzle, the 3-D Screen Saver.

"The problem was the constraints of telephone and fax. Technical support is labor-intensive and expensive," says Jim Nichols, product manager. This led to issues with consumer satisfaction. "The average support call might run 25–30 minutes, and response time can suffer when calls stack up. At peak periods, sometimes 80 customers were awaiting callbacks. It could take several days to help customers.

"Furthermore, support is expensive because nearly all the support calls are callbacks, which the company must pay for."

Road Scholar prides itself on maintaining close contacts with its consumers, and so the delays were unacceptable to the company, as well as irritating to users.

The company first set up a fax response system. It created 45 topics for all its products that consumers could select from a menu. Topics ranged from installation to screen displays. They were written in a friendly, readable format with such titles as "My screen is distorted. What should I do?" Answers ranged in length from half a page to three pages. The material featured troubleshooting tips or step-by-step-instructions—the same material that support personnel were telling people on the phone. Instead, customers could get the answers without waiting for a human to call them, and the company could save manpower as well. And they could get the information well after business hours. "This echoes what we tell them on telephone tech support," says Nichols.

Based on this success, the company decided to expand its customer support to its customers who are members of CompuServe to complement its support center.

"The idea was to get on CompuServe's PC Vendor Forum to improve support and increase accessibility on the part of users to enable them to get answers quicker to their questions," Nichols says. "The goal with the online services was to take that fax response system and put it out there online to make it more effective. CompuServe members can read the questions and answers online or download the files and read them offline `CompuServe: Go RoadScholar`. They can get help without talking to a person."

Dealing with the online services was painless.

"It was easy. They have people who handle the vendor forums. They are very accessible and responsible. The process itself is straightforward," says Nichols. "There is a little bit of paperwork, but not much. We had to write a company overview and some explanatory material for the online version, but the help sheets remained the same."

CompuServe also wants its vendors to publicize and promote the forum by listing information in manuals and by providing brochures or postcards in the product packages. With CompuServe providing the templates for the material, all Road Scholar needs to do is fill in the blanks. "It is the logical thing to do," says Nichols. "Having a forum and promoting it enhances the value of your product."

Getting online—from initial inquiries with CompuServe, to writing the material, to posting it online and going live—took less than one month. Road Scholar is not paying for the service, although all contract terms vary from company to company. For a full discussion of factors that affect negotiating online space on the commercial online services, see Chapter 8.

The project has been a success.

"This has helped our staff by allowing them to handle the exceptional calls that aren't covered by the printed topics. It helps customers get support in the middle of the night without waiting for a support technician. It is more cost-effective for us as it frees up manpower who can concentrate on new problems and difficult situations."

Road Scholar saves money by not having to return support phone calls.

"It dramatically reduces telephone bills," says Nichols.

The company plans to expand the services offered in its support forum to include posting bug fixes, which consumers can download. Road Scholar also will post demonstration versions of new products, which can be downloaded. An ordering mechanism will be included so that people can buy products.

"We've been able to reduce our support costs while improving customer service," says Nichols. "What could be better than that?"

Case Study: Inset Systems

A customer support center not only helps customers find answers to problems, it can help the company make better products. Inset Systems, of Brookfield, Connecticut, is the publisher of the Hijaak software program, which allows computer users to capture screen images and convert them to any picture file format. The company runs a forum on CompuServe `CompuServe: Go Inset.`

"We use it for market research," says Maurice Hamoy, vice president of communications for Inset Systems `maurice@inset.mhs.compuserve.com, 203-740-2400`. "We ask people for their suggestions and feedback to make future versions better."

Hamoy includes his business card with every new product and asks people to tell him what features they would like to see in new versions.

"About nine of every ten people respond with e-mail. I get about ten people a day e-mailing me with suggestions," he says. "They are very comfortable with e-mail. It encourages communications. People never used to call."

The suggestions have been invaluable, he says. "You'd pay people good money for this kind of feedback."

Practical Considerations for Creating an Online Support Center

While many aspects of establishing a customer support center are outside the realm of this book, there are several questions that online marketers should address in creating a plan to create an online customer support center:

- *Online services:* Which online service should be used? Many hardware and software companies have customer support centers on each major online service because their customers use only one service. Plan to do the same. This might add to your costs, but you will guarantee a wider area of coverage for your customers and create more opportunities for positive interactions between the consumer and the company. Associations and companies that are not in the computer business might limit their online participation to one major system. This choice can be based on which online service offers them the best terms, or which service is currently used by most of its members.

- *Manpower:* The support center will need to be staffed by competent professionals who not only know the ins and outs of the product but can build rapport with people online. This is important as people who call support centers are frequently angry and frustrated because they cannot get the product to work properly. Consequently, their messages might be caustic. Support staffers must be able to deal with the situation by diffusing the anger, solving the problem and building bridges to positive communications with the consumer. The company cannot afford to have one angry customer tell his experiences to thousands of people online!

- *Content:* Online libraries can store a great deal of technical information. Having consumers find this information by themselves can help the company save a great deal of time and expense. This can be accomplished by carefully organizing the information by the appropriate classifications. For example, a software company can have these file folders: product, installation, usage, printing, upgrade, common errors, error codes explained, how do I accomplish task x? and many others. Material can be cross-referenced. The material should be hyperlinked so that consumers can jump from one area to another with ease.

- *Cost:* The budget for an online support center will vary by company. While planning the budget, don't think of it as a drain on expenses. Instead, think of it as a way to save money by unburdening other forms of support—telephone, mail and fax. Also, think of the benefit in positive customer relations. Finally, create ways to turn the support center into a profit center by encouraging messages that create sales opportunities for new product versions, complementary products and long-term support and training contracts for large companies.

Strategies to Provide Customer Support

Many tools exist to help online marketers support their customers. This section will discuss popular strategies.

Strategy: Use E-mail and E-mail Boxes to Help Customers

Benefit: Provide fast response to customers at a low cost to the company.

Discussion: Most people on online systems have access to e-mail and use it. Unlike other tools, like file downloads, there is virtually no barrier to learning how to use e-mail, nor is there any hesitancy in using it. Because companies require e-mail usage to communicate with one another, this tool is nearly universally used by online consumers.

To help support customers, companies should promote the use of e-mail as the preferred way of communicating with the company. In this model, the customer sends a note to the support department, where the support representative fields the query promptly and courteously. The company benefits from decreased support costs and the customer benefits by fast response time. The e-mail addresses can be listed in manuals, fliers and advertisements or can be spoken aloud on the telephone messaging device.

To use online services to their potential, consider this scenario. Create multiple e-mailboxes that deal with separate products (i.e., `printers@yourcompany.com`, `computers@yourcompany.com`.). Consumers send e-mail to the mailbox of their choice, where the expert can field the question. This removes a step in the sorting process. For instance, if every e-mail note went to `support@yourcompany.com`, a secretary would have to read each message and send it to the proper technician.

Strategy: Create Mailbots to Respond to Common Questions

Benefit: Reduce or eliminate personnel costs in handling certain inquiries; customers receive answers faster.

Discussion: Many consumer questions are identical. Support personnel spend a great deal of time repeating the same information. By creating e-mail files of these questions and hooking them in to a mailbot companies can help people find and receive information faster.

For example, if a company publicized a list of topics, consumers could send e-mail to `printers@company.com` and receive data, almost immediately.

Although the Internet can provide mailbot service, the commercial online services do not. However, operators can manually send e-mail files to consumers.

Strategy: Create FAQs

Benefit: Reduce or eliminate personnel costs in handling certain inquiries; customers receive answers faster.

Discussion: The problem and benefits are similar those in the preceding discussion. Posting FAQs—files containing frequently asked questions and their answer—to your companies forum, Web home page or other archiving service enables consumers to find the information they need without drawing on your company's personnel resources.

Action: Interview support personnel for information. Write the FAQ.

Strategy: Keep Track of New Questions

Benefit: Creates new material for FAQs; alerts company to new problems.

Discussion: Questions that aren't answered in these files can be handled individually. The file can then be updated with these new pieces of information. This makes the best use of the support representative's time. Also, by learning of new problems, companies can uncover bugs in the product, flaws in the instructions or the need for new features and products to make the existing merchandise more useful.

Strategy: Use File Libraries and Archives for Software Downloads

Benefit: Solve customers' problems without incurring expensive production and shipping charges.

Discussion: Product upgrades, software patches and bug fixes can be stored in file libraries as well. Consumers can download these files at their convenience. Since the company is not manufacturing the new version on a disk and mailing it to hundreds of thousands of customers, it can save a considerable amount of money.

Strategy: Create Training Tapes

Benefit: Consumers become better educated about your company's products without burdening staffers.

Discussion: Companies can create self-running computer programs that teach people how to use their products more effectively. As they become more conversant with the program, they will depend less on calling for technical support, thus saving money for your company.

Strategy: Create a Mailing List of Customers

Benefit: Quick distribution of important announcements.

Discussion: Mailing lists can be created to send notices to registered users about program updates and bug fixes, as well as special notices about sales and upcoming products. For netiquette, ask people if they want to be on the list.

Increasing Registration

When someone buys your product, you don't know who he or she is. This is bad, because today's customers can become customers for life, as they buy product upgrades and other products in the family. Capturing their names is vitally important as a source of recurring revenue. Gathering names and information can also help marketing efforts, as the research staffs can plot sales patterns across the country and also gather demographic information and other points of interest to marketing staffs, such as reason to buy and who influenced the buying decision.

Unfortunately for manufacturers and software publishers, most people don't register their products. Software publishers might have a better chance to capture the names of their customers if they use electronic registration cards.

"Most of your customers don't register for good reason. You don't make it easy enough for them. End users view the registration process as important but inconvenient," says John Hussey, president of Husdawg Enterprises of San Francisco (415) 241-9214. "An electronic registration program is a registration screen generated by your application during the installation process. The electronic registration process involves capturing user information (name, address, etc.) and sending it via modem, fax, mail, disk or phone."

This process gathers more names than other methods because it is convenient, it offers the customer more registration opportunities and it works within the application (Fig. 13-1).

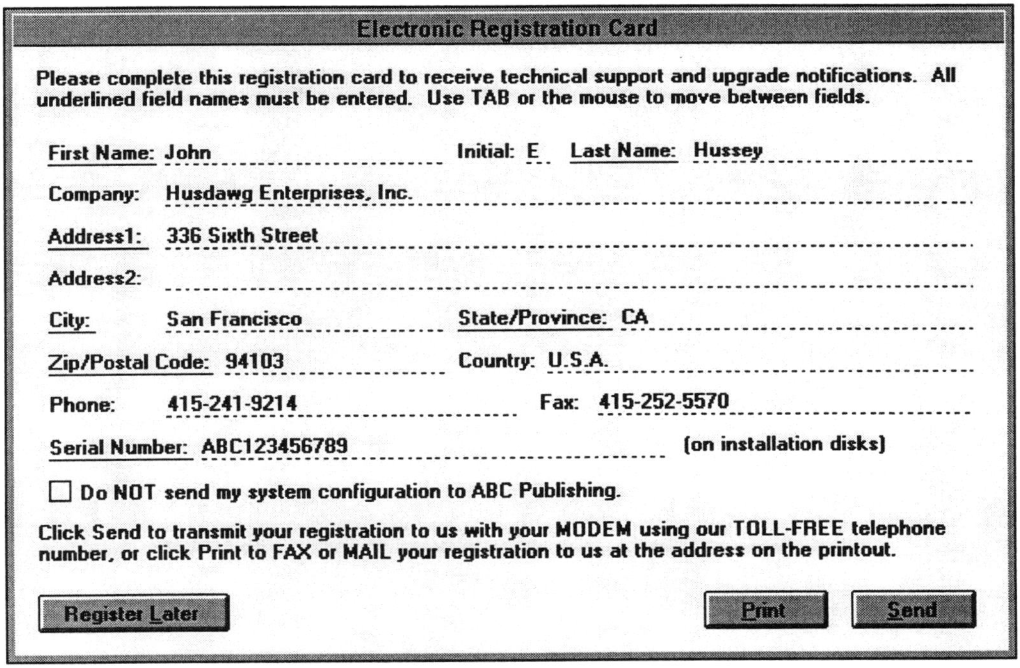

Electronic Registration Card

Please complete this registration card to receive technical support and upgrade notifications. All underlined field names must be entered. Use TAB or the mouse to move between fields.

First Name: John Initial: E Last Name: Hussey

Company: Husdawg Enterprises, Inc.

Address1: 336 Sixth Street

Address2:

City: San Francisco State/Province: CA

Zip/Postal Code: 94103 Country: U.S.A.

Phone: 415-241-9214 Fax: 415-252-5570

Serial Number: ABC123456789 (on installation disks)

☐ Do NOT send my system configuration to ABC Publishing.

Click Send to transmit your registration to us with your MODEM using our TOLL-FREE telephone number, or click Print to FAX or MAIL your registration to us at the address on the printout.

Register Later Print Send

Figure 13-1. Electronic registration helps companies keep track of customers .
(© Husdawg Enterprises)

"Electronic registration becomes part of the installation process," Hussey says. "Your customers want to install their new software correctly by following all of the necessary steps in the process. Thus electronic registration becomes a necessary step. Standard registration cards don't work as well because customers have only one chance to see the card—when they open the box. But they are more concerned with running the program."

A report by Soft-letter found that program-generated forms seem to perform significantly better than in-box registration cards, by a 60% to 38% differential.

Companies using this system include WordPerfect, Broderbund, Maxis, Intuit, Delrina, Peachtreee and Spectrum Holobyte.

The electronic registration program can also be used to create a survey about how customers like using the product, an electronic suggestion box, an electronic catalog to sell additional products and a way to transfer files between customer and company.

There hasn't been any negative reaction, Hussey says.

"Even companies that are forcing their customers to register are getting little or no negative reactions. All of the accounting industry is moving to forced registration programs. And now other consumer and home-based business products are starting to use forced registration with good results. Just make it easy for the user to register, be as unobtrusive as possible and you should not have any problems.

"If you want to maximize your registration card response, electronic registration is the most effective way to go," says Hussey. "When you've made it fast, easy and convenient for customers to register, you may have just found the goose that laid the golden egg."

Summary

Making the sale is the beginning, not the end, of the relationship for a long-term customer. To keep the customer happy, every effort should be made to ensure that questions are answered quickly and courteously. An upset customer can tell an online audience of thousands about his misfortune faster than you can ever hope to repair the damage. By following the strategies in this chapter, you can help build bridges to your customers that can last forever.

CHAPTER 14

The Future

The commercialization of the Internet and commercial online services is creating excitement on a par with the introduction of the IBM PC and the Macintosh. The mass media is covering these developments closely as a major news story. While some of what is reported is hyped way out of proportion, this book tries to put in perspective an industry that makes giant changes on a weekly basis. This final chapter will take an educated guess at the future of marketing on the Internet and commercial online services.

In this chapter, you will learn:

- Where business stands today with online marketing
- Emerging trends.
- Ethics and privacy.

A Market in Flux

Marketing on the Internet and commercial online services is a study in transition. While many of the rules of traditional marketing have been thrown out the door by futurists, these models have not been completely replaced by standards. In fact, the Internet and commercial online services are a perfect example of an immature market. Confusion reigns as prices and pricing models are in flux.

The entire advertising industry is struggling to cope with the new paradigm of online marketing. No one is sure how to charge for advertising. Nor can agencies predict the return on investment. They can't even agree on how to repurpose ads for the new media.

One point is certain: To be successful tomorrow, companies will have to experiment today. It is like training for a marathon. You don't go out and run 26 miles the first day. Instead you loosen up, work out and train. Eventually you learn what works and what doesn't. Ultimately, you cross the finish line. However, this would not have happened if you hadn't taken the first step. The same is true of companies that sit on the sidelines and watch others pass by.

Nevertheless many success stories emerge—from marketers who are embracing new tools and techniques and pushing the envelope of interactive communications with consumers. Yet the static ads of yesterday and the text-based shopping messages are still seen to work by companies that rely on traditional formats. If it ain't broke, they ain't gonna fix it.

That thinking might work in the short term but, as methods are found to work, and the public's expectations get higher and higher, these ostriches must be willing to lift their head from the sand or risk extinction.

The bottom line is that the Internet and commercial online services are in their infancy. The market is immature, as are the pricing models, tools, competitors and marketing paradigms. This means there are many opportunities for companies to come into the market and win sizable market share, as well as provide jobs for a new breed of consultant who understands the online community.

Trends

Marketing paradigms and business models for the Internet and commercial online services change rapidly. Here are some key trends to look for in online publishing. Many of these ideas are adapted from comments made by Michael Kolowich, president of AT&T Interchange Online Network.

1. From individual documents to compound documents.

Individual documents contain text. You read it. You close it. You are done. Compound documents integrate text, pictures and video for a richer online experience.

2. From isolated items to universal linking.

Individual documents exist in their own space. They are linear. They don't take you to related files. Universal linking creates dynamic documents that help readers by taking them to items of interest, whether it be an ad, a product review by a reporter, company documents or a discussion on a forum.

3. From general interest services to special interest services.

Two generations ago, magazines that published to broad audiences, like *Saturday Evening Post*, *Look*, *Collier's* and *Life,* led the field. Today, special interest publications reach out to targeted markets, such as skiers, boaters, amateur photographers and brides. The commercial online services began as broad-based information services, and many will continue as such. But, increasingly, special interest online services will become more prevalent as the online services market grows. Interchange, for example, offers a publishing platform to specialized publishers seeking niche markets.

4. From subscription-only pricing to advertiser and sponsor subsidies.

Advertising works better in special-interest information services than in general interest information services. When online services can deliver the right readers, advertisers will have opportunities to reach highly targeted markets at a reasonable price.

5. From Internet vs. the commercial online services to Internet via the commercial online services.

The Internet's vast libraries of data, information-rich newsgroups and mailing lists present a fabulous resource for commercial online services. The commercial online services are building bridges to the Internet so subscribers can send mail, read files and explore the World Wide Web.

6. From publishing as rocket science to publishing for everyone.

The Internet's tools, low-cost structure and large audience provide the means for any literate person to create an online magazine. While compelling content and viable editorial services remain key considerations for success, financial and technical barriers to entry have fallen dramatically.

7. From CD-ROM vs. online services to CD-ROM integrated with online services.

The slow delivery of information is the Achille's heel of the online world. This will change as CD-ROMs that store advertisements and content tie into online services. Advertisers will be able to deliver messages to audiences that will have the option of playing the ads.

A Call to Action

To create a true paradigm shift in the way people buy products and services, online marketers must be willing to test the limits of the tools of the new media. These times can be great fun for the creative minds that explore uncharted territory to satisfy consumers' desires. But, first, they must do the little things right, like putting e-mail addresses on all written communications and ads.

A Call for Better Tools

While there are many tools available today, some sophisticated and easy—to—use, and some difficult to use, more work needs to be developed to create an easy way for consumers to find information and communicate their orders to the company. Time and time again, consumers have shown the computer industry that hard-to-use products will not be used. Online services are meeting the problem by developing graphical user interfaces that are much easier to use then previous-generation interfaces. The Internet's World Wide Web could very well be the killer application that offers ease of use and a model for other systems to follow. However, the tools needed to find information and to telnet, ftp and use Gopher are far from easy and syntaxes are difficult to type and hard to remember?

Why is it that you can rent a car in any city in the country, get into a rental car that you've never seen before and drive away without looking at an instruction manual? You can pretty much figure out how to turn on the radio and find a decent station within seconds. That's because manufacturers of those products truly understand consumers and have created products that are easy to use.

Computer technology companies are only fooling themselves if they think that today's tools offer true ease of use for the average consumer. They can argue all they want to with me on this point, but the massive amount of time and expense needed to staff support centers is the only point I need to diffuse the argument.

A Call to Integrity

Because consumers must actively choose to read online advertisements and visit online stores instead of passively having messages presented to them, the online marketer depends on its good name to maintain positive relations with consumers. Nothing can violate this trust faster than abusing the privilege of creating relationships with consumers. Therefore, online marketers should strive to do well by doing good, by maintaining the highest levels of ethical standards, by acting to provide service to consumers at a fair price and by protecting customers' rights to privacy. Only then can companies earn the trust needed to make relationships work online.

Conclusion

The goal of this book was to provide marketers from all types of companies, from general consumer goods to entertainment to services to high-technology, with an overview of the Internet and commercial online services so they can see what opportunities and roadblocks exist. This volume tried to downplay the hype of the published reports about online services and separate fantasy from reality. The primer introduced readers to new concepts and mindsets in marketing and offered commentary by leading marketers and examples of cutting edge marketing creating (ads, home pages, forums and media relations). The text also provided step-by-step instructions for creating online presences—technically, financially and editorially—and getting the most marketing value from them. If we have reinforced your decision to go online—or given you points to think about as you decide if online is for your company—then we hope you think the book has been successful.

Appendix

Contacting the Commercial Online Services

CompuServe
5000 Arlington Centre Boulevard
Columbus, OH 43220
614-457-8600
800-848-8199

Prodigy Service Company
445 Hamilton Avenue
White Plains, NY 10601
800-776-3449

America Online
8619 Westwood Center Drive
Vienna, VA 22182-2285
703-448-8700
800-827-6364

Genie
401 North Washington
Rockville, MD 20850
800-638-9636

Delphi Internet Services
1030 Massachusetts Avenue
Cambridge, MA 02138
800-695-4005
askdelphi@delphi.com

AT&T Interchange Online Network
25 First Street
Cambridge, MA 02141
617-252-5000

Microsoft Network
One Microsoft Way
Redmond, WA 98052-6399
206-882-8080

eWorld
Apple Computer Inc.
20525 Mariani Avenue
Cupertino, CA 95014
408-996-1010

Further Reading

Advertising Age
965 E. Jefferson Avenue
Detroit, MI 48207-9966
1-800-678-9595

Boardwatch
1-800-933-6038
subscriptions@boardwatch.com
http://www.boardwatch.com

Interactive Age
P.O. Box 1194
Skokie, IL 60076-8194
708-647-6834

Interactive Week
100 Quentin Roosevelt Boulevard
Garden City, New York 11530
516-229-3700

Computer Industry Almanac
225 Allen Way
Incline Village, NV 89451-9608
800-377-6810

Internet Business Journal
613-565-0982
mstrange@fonorola.net

Internet World
P.O. Box 713
Mt. Morris, IL 61054
800-573-3062
815-734-1261
iwsubs@kable.com

Marketing Computers
1515 Broadway
New York, NY 10036
800-722-6658

NetGuide
600 Community Drive
Manhasset, NY 11030
800-829-0421
904-445-4662 ext. 420
netsubs@cmp.com
http://www.techweb.cmp.com/net

Online Marketing Update
657 Doral Drive
Danville, CA 94526-6206
510-831-0900
update@janalpr.com
76004.1046@compuserve.com
CompuServe 76004,1046
http://www.janal-communications.com/janal.html

Internet Beginner Books

Internet Guide for New Users, by Daniel Dern (Random House).
The Internet for Dummies, by John Levine & Carol Baroudi (IDG Books).
Windows Internet Tour Guide, by Michael Fraase (Ventanna Press).
The Whole Internet User's Guide, by Ed Krol (O'Reilly and Associates).
The Internet Yellow Pages, by Harley Hahn and Rick Strout (McGraw Hill).
Navigating the Internet, by Mark Gibbs and Richard Smith (SAMS Publishing).

For a list of Internet books, send e-mail to:
`mail-server@rtfm.mit.edu`
with the message
`send usenet/news.answers/internet-services/book-list`

Web Browsers and Internet Software

Air Mosaic
Spry Inc.
`800-777-9638, ext. 26`
`206-447-0300`
`info@spry.com`

Enhanced Mosaic
Spyglass, Inc.
`708-505-1010`
`info@spyglass.com`
`http://www.spyglass.com`

Internet Chameleon
Netmanage
`408-973-7171`
`sales@netmanage.com`
`http://www.netmanage.com`

NCSA Mosaic
National Center for Supercomputing Applications
217-244-0072
orders@ncsa.uiuc.edu
ftp.ncsa.uiuc.edu

Netcruiser
NETCOM On-Line Communications Services
800-353-6600
408-983-5970
info@netcom.com

Netscape Navigator
Netscape Communications Corp.
800-638-7483
415-254-1900
info@mcom.com

Prodigy Service Company
800-776-3449
914-448-8000
webmaster@wwww.astranet.com

Project Normandy
Quarterdeck Office Systems
310-314-3222
info@qdeck.com
http://www.qdeck.com

Web Explorer
IBM Corp.
800-342-6672
914-765-1900
http://www.ibm.com

Glossary

Baud: The speed at which modems transfer data. The speed is listed in BPS or bits per second.

Download: Retrieve files from a computer.

FAQ (Frequently Asked Questions): A file that contains questions and answers about specific topics.

Flame: Abusive hate mail.

FTP: File Transfer Protocol: retrieve files from the Internet

HTML: Hypertext Mark-up Language: The standard format for documents on the World Wide Web.

Hypertext: A system where documents scattered across many sites are directly linked.

Hypermedia: A system where documents, pictures, sound, movie and animation files scattered across many sites are directly linked.

ISDN (Integrated Services Digital Network): Technology that makes it possible to move multiple digital signals through a single, conventional phone wire.

Leased line: A permanently installed telephone line connecting a LAN to an Internet Service Provider.

Lurking: Reading messages in a forum or newgroups without adding comments.

Modem: A device that connects a computer to a phone line and enables users to transmit data between computers.

Mosaic: A software program that allows users to browse the World Wide Web.

Netiquette: The etiquette of Internet.

Newbies: Newcomers to the Internet.

Service Provider: A company that provides connections to the Internet.

Signature or **.sig**: A personalized address at the bottom of a message often containing contact information and a short commercial description.

SLIP and **PPP (Serial Line Internet Protocol** and **Point-to-Point Protocol)**: Two common types of connections that allow your computer to communicate with the Internet.

Smileys and emoticons: Typographical versions of faces that display emotions in text messages.

Spam: Posting or mailing unwanted material to many recipients. A flagrant violation of Netiquette.

TCP/IP   (Transmission   Control   Protocol/Internet   Protocol): The standardized sets of computer guidelines that allow different machines to talk to each other on the Internet.

Sysop (SYStem Operator): The person who administers a forum. Same as Webmaster.

Upload: Send a file from your computer to another.

URL (Uniform Resource Locator): A type of address that points to a specific document or site on the World Wide Web.

Usenet: A collection of discussion areas (bulletin boards) known as newsgroups on the Internet.

WAIS (Wide Area Information System): A system that allows users to search by keyword through the full text contained on many databases.

World Wide Web (WWW or W3 or The Web): A hypertext and hypermedia system that enables users to find information about companies.

Index

posting messages to
newsgroups about, 182
printing address in
advertisements, 182
printing address on company
materials, 182
publicizing of, 177–83
reaching, 131–32
registering address in a
Directory, 177–81
for small businesses, 133
speed and, 136–37
user interface of, 173
Hosts, renting space from, 192
HoTMetaL, 187
Houston Chronicle, 183
HTMARCOM, 114, 240–41,
246–48
HTML (Hypertext Markup
Language), 185, 186–89
codes, 188–89
HTML Assistant, 187
http (hypertext transfer protocol),
131

Index, home page, 174
IndustryNET, 155–62
Industry Report, 155
Industry standards, 105
INET-MARKETING, 113
InfoPlace, 148–50
Information, 87
access and retrieval of, 38
easy access to, 175
persuasion vs., 28–29
resources for online, 90–105
Information providers, 195, 197,
209–11
examples of, 211–13

negotiating, 215–24
range of, 214–15
who should be, 213–14
Inset Systems, 339–40
Integrated marketing, 23, 132,
275–76
Intellectual property rights, x
Intelligent agents, 102–3
Intelligent Market Analytics, 40
Interactivity, 22, 23, 26–28, 30,
34, 37, 121, 139, 269–72
the Web and, 129–30
Interchange, 96
Interfaces
for forums, 218
for home pages, 173
Internet, 14–15, 47–53. *See also*
USENET newsgroups; World
Wide Web
behavioral norms of, x–xi
classified advertising, 263–64
commercial transaction
processing on, ix
connecting to, 190–95
consumer market, 12
customer's attitudes toward
marketing on, 53
demographics of, 49–50
digital audit trails and, 126
Domain Name System, 192
ease of use with, 39, 47
educational and
entertainment of, x
Finger, 249–50
history of, vii–x, 48
information resources, 95–96,
100, 102, 104, 105
mailing address formats, 249
mailing lists, 113–14, 115–